Boom Town

The Early History of Tomahawk, Wisconsin

1886-1924

by Robin L. Comeau

Copyright © 2013 by Robin L. Comeau

All rights reserved. No part of this publication may be reproduced, stored in a retrieval system, or transmitted, in any form or by any means, electronic, mechanical, photocopying, recording, or otherwise, without the written prior permission of the author.

Printed in the United States of America

Boom Town/Comeau- 2nd Edition

ISBN: 978-0615784939

1. Boom Town- Nonfiction 2. Tomahawk, Wisconsin 3. Social History
4. History 5. No Frills Buffalo
1. Title

For more information please visit nofrillsbuffalo.com
No Frills Buffalo
119 Dorchester Road
Buffalo, NY 14213

Boom Town
Early History of Tomahawk, Wisconsin
1886-1924

Including biographical information on early settlers,
prominent citizens
and ordinary folks

By Robin L. Comeau

No Frills
<<<>>>
Buffalo
Buffalo, NY

In commemoration of the platting of the city of
Tomahawk, Wisconsin –survey recorded June 1, 1887

A portion of the proceeds from the sale of this book
will go directly to the Tomahawk Historical Society

Cover photo – Early postal card of Tomahawk
(Courtesy of the Tomahawk Historical Society

CONTENTS

Introduction	6
Early History	7
Sawmills	30
City Incorporation	33
In the News	39
Public Utilities	53
Postal Service	55
Spreading the News	56
Library	59
Fire and Police Departments	60
Scenic City Areas	61
Churches	62
Clubs, Societies and Organizations	74
Business and Industry	79
Banks	90
Schools	94
Lodging	98
City Directories	102
Military	128
Pioneers	131
Biographies	134
Index to Biographies	290

INTRODUCTION

A little more than 120 years ago, men carved out a city among the pines of northern Wisconsin at the juncture of the Somo, Tomahawk and Wisconsin Rivers. Founded on the vision of one man, William H. Bradley, a millionaire lumberman from Maine, the city of Tomahawk literally 'sprang up over night.' Bill, as he was called by his associates, along with the other members of his company - the Tomahawk Land and Boom, funded many if not most of the first building projects in the city; built a railroad, school and church and established a bank. In laying out the city, he provided for its needs well into the future. Through his foresight Tomahawk has a heritage of unusually wide streets, beautifully parked areas and boulevards, and a wide-open welcoming business thoroughfare.

Today, businesses are still flourishing, pines are still standing, and the population of the city has increased threefold. We honor the vision of Mr. Bradley by preserving the history of this wonderful city for generations to come

The early history of Lincoln County has been well documented in an expansive text compiled by George O. Jones and others, which was published in 1924. The following information pertaining to the city of Tomahawk has been extracted from that source: "History of Lincoln, Oneida and Vilas Counties Wisconsin.

Additional information, from other sources, has also been included to add interest and for completeness.

Tomahawk, a thriving city in the northern part of Lincoln County, is reached by the Chicago, Milwaukee & St. Paul and the Marinette, Tomahawk & Western railways, and by State Highways Nos. 10 and 63. It is a manufacturing center of considerable importance and a prominent lumbering point. Situated in Townships 34 and 35 North, Range 6 East, its population in 1920 was 2801. The story of the development of most cities begins with a tiny cluster of rude pioneer huts; the passing years begins a slow, sometimes scarcely perceptible growth to this embryonic metropolis; finally a railroad extension, or a waterpower development, or the discovery of mineral resources, lend impetus to the process of growth. The site is officially laid out; a village or city charter is obtained; other railroad and manufacturing interests turn their attention to this scene of new activity, and so the city comes into being.

The history of Tomahawk, however, deviates from this picture. The stage of her existence as a lethargic, slowly developing hamlet was so curtailed as scarcely to have existed at all, and a full-fledged, bustling city sprang into being almost over night. The locality was a practically uninhabited wilderness previous to 1886, in which year Bradley's Tomahawk Land and Boom Co. began operations here. In the spring of 1887, this company laid out the site of the city of Tomahawk; the survey of the place, made under the direction of Thomas M. Doyle, was recorded on June 1, 1887, and the first lots were offered for sale at auction in Milwaukee on June 25th of the same year. The announcement of a new town in the making was made public in one of the early newspapers (Lincoln County Advocate) published at Merrill, Wisconsin.

THE NEW TOWN: When the greater portion of the spring drive passes, the dam will be completed and the sorting works and boom put in during the summer. The dam will be 1,500 feet in length and the approaches completed by the time the ice goes out. The river channel is 280 feet wide. The railroad will be there by September 1, when a move will be made toward building sawmills. The new town will be platted in May or June   ----Lincoln County Advocate, March 31, 1887

PLATTED AT LAST: The Tomahawk Land & Boom Company have platted about one hundred acres of land at the Forks. The name of the new town is Tomahawk. The plat is on file at the register's office. -----Lincoln County Advocate, June 11, 1887

TOMAHAWK: One half of the lots in the new town of Tomahawk will be offered for sale at the Milwaukee office from June 22 to 25, and the other half at the First National bank in this city, June 27 and 28 and at Tomahawk June 29 and 30.
   ----Lincoln County Advocate, June 18, 1887

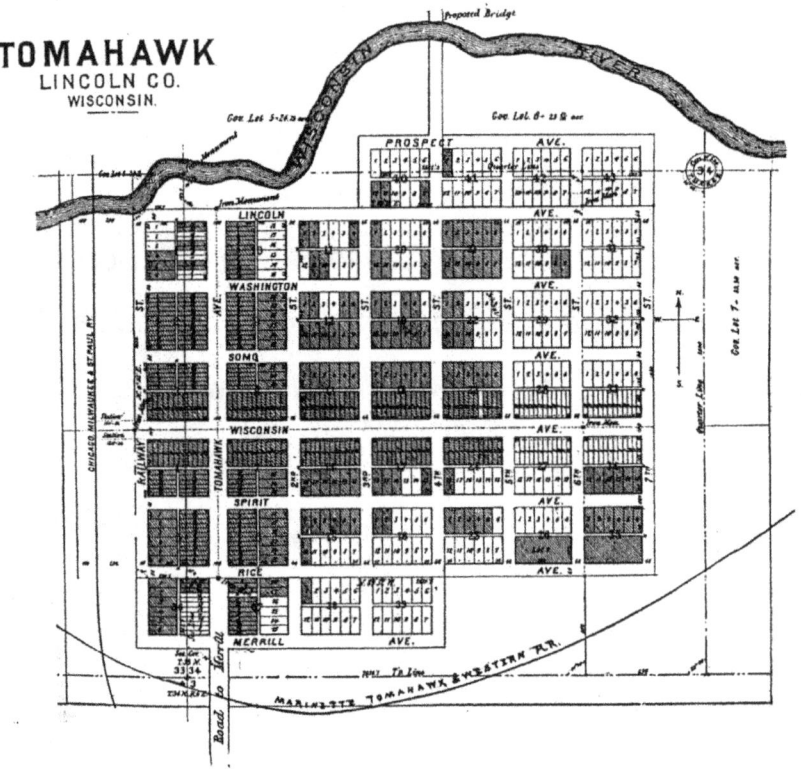

LOTS FOR SALE:

These lots in the new city of Tomahawk were offered for sale. Prices were $100 to $200. Note that the route south of town was designated "Road to Merrill" and that a Fourth Street bridge over the Wisconsin River was "proposed".

Scene on the road between Merrill and Tomahawk
(Courtesy of McMillian Memorial Library Digitization Project
Art Work of the Wisconsin River Valley: 1901.)

CITY IN THE WOODS: The [Milwaukee] State Journal tells its readers all about "the city in the woods," as follows: Most readers will want to know where Tomahawk is. It is not on the maps of the state. It is not to be found in the Official Post office guide. There is no railway within twenty-five miles of there. The telegraph station is as far away. The blazed highway to Tomahawk, through the sand and over the pine needles, is not yet graced with telephone poles. The average resident of Wisconsin, setting out to walk to Tomahawk, would not know to what point of the compass to point his toes. And yet Tomahawk is booming. It is not an ordinary boom, wither. It is the biggest boom of the season. Nobody down here where people live, ever heard of Tomahawk before. Yet the dispatches inform us that great stores are contracted for, that two railroads are being extended to the place, that visions of a junction and certain car shops are held up by boomers—in short, that Tomahawk is the coming city. The boomers are kind enough to locate it for us, in their screaming dispatches. It is a clearing in the woods, an opening in the heart of the great pinery, 25 miles due north of Merrill, the great jumping-off place; it is on the Wisconsin River, away up where the logs come from- where the raging Tomahawk river comes cutting and scalping its way through the hardpan, eagerly scampering to join the waters of the 'old Wiscons' previous to their break neck plunge down the cliff-confined falls of the Grandfather Bull. The St. Paul is to extend its line from Merrill to Tomahawk; the Minneapolis, Sault Ste. Marie & Atlantic has Tomahawk 'on the list' of projected stations. In fact, northern Wisconsin is 'pointing with pride' to the remarkable career of Tomahawk, and there is a mad scamper among settlers for the honor of building the first house in the future metropolis of the upper Wisconsin.

----Lincoln County Advocate, July 16, 1887

Just as the newspapers predicted – on September 15, 1887, the tracks of the Wisconsin Valley Division of the Chicago Milwaukee & St. Paul railroad, then in the process of extension from Merrill to Minocqua, reached Tomahawk, and the first train came in over these rails on October 8, 1887. Sawmills and other industries flourished and the census of 1890, just four years after settlement began, found Tomahawk with a population of 1,816.

The sole mark of civilization previous to 1886 was a tavern or station kept by Germaine Bouchard, which was located on the north side of the Wisconsin River and the West side of the Tomahawk, where the Tomahawk and Somo rivers flowed into the Wisconsin. Bouchard had kept this station since 1858, also operating a ferry here, and the locality was variously known as the Forks and Bouchard's. He continued to conduct the station until 1888 when his land was inundated by back water from the dam which was being constructed two miles below;

THE BRADLEY DAM: The building of the dam at the improvements will cause the Wisconsin River to raise several feet as far up the stream as Bouchard's –three miles from the works.   ----Lincoln County Advocate, June 11, 1887

Land, Log and Lumber Co., which consisted of O. P. Pillsbury, D. M. Benjamin, the Bradley brothers – William, Edward and James, the Kelly brothers of Chicago, Lovejoy of Janesville, and T. D. Stimson of Chicago. William H. Bradley was the first president of the Tomahawk Land and Boom Co.; it is thought that construction of the dam was first suggested by O. P. Pillsbury.

The site of the station is now a small island just north of the west end of Rodgers Island, where the Rodgers mill was located, the island being a part of the city's park system.

The completion of the final treaty with the Chippewa Indians to relocate to their reservations at Odanah and Lac du Flambeau in 1886, the Tomahawk Land and Boom Co. began construction of camps two miles south of the present city as a preliminary to building their dam there. Fifty-one per cent of the stock in this company was owned by the Chicago Milwaukee & St. Paul Railroad Co. and the balance by the Land, Log and Lumber Co., which consisted of O.P. Pillsbury,

D. M. Benjamin, the Bradley brothers (William, Edward and James), Kelly brothers of Chicago, Lovejoy of Janesville, and T. D. Stimson of Chicago. William H. Bradley was the first president of the Tomahawk Land & Boom Co.; it is thought that construction of the dam was first suggested by O. P. Pillsbury.

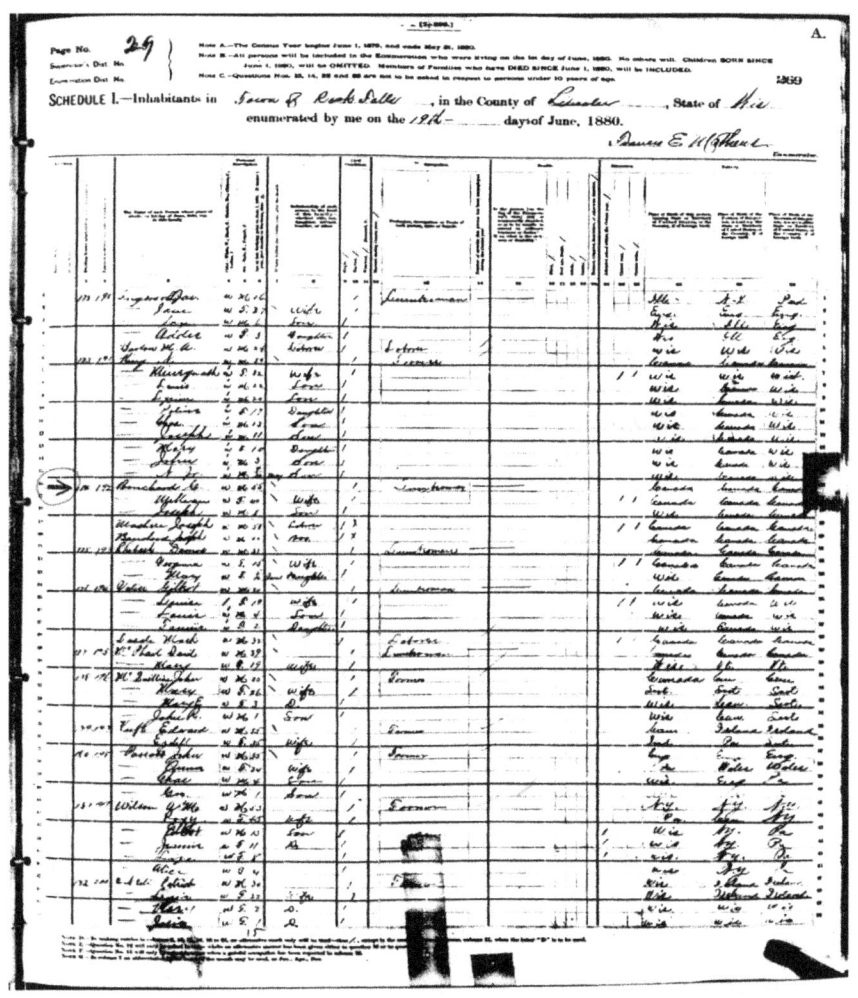

1880 Federal Census of the United States; Town of Rock Falls, Lincoln County, Wisconsin. (Arrow points to entry of Germaine Bouchard residing with his wife and son).

TOMAHAWK LAKE NEWS: A special train, yesterday, came up the line with railway officials, who went into the Tomahawk country: We understand that the parties who came up from Milwaukee, yesterday, are on their way to Tomahawk lake to see about erecting saw mills and manufacturing lumber the coming year at that point. This recalls a circumstance that may not be generally known. The Land, Log & Lumber Co. was the original owner of the plant at the mouth of the Tomahawk, and last November sold 51 percent, interest in it to the St. Paul Railroad Company, and the Tomahawk Land and Boom Company was then organized. The former owns 49 percent, of the stock in the boom company and is also the owner of about one thousand million feet of timber accessible to the improvements at Tomahawk and at Tomahawk Lake. The probability is that saw mills will be constructed at Tomahawk Lake the coming winter.

----Lincoln County Advocate, May 16, 1887

Actual work on the dam began in the winter of 1886, and it was completed in the winter of 1888-89; built for the purpose of forming a lake wherein the logs could be sorted before being manufactured into lumber, and where they could be sorted – logs for the different mills farther down the river being separated from those that were to remain. George Gans was superintendent of the construction work on the dam, and Angus Buie had charge of the sorting works which were established in 1889 and which employed a crew of 100 or more men during the summer session.

TOMAHAWK TRAFFIC COMPANY: The way they rush things at Tomahawk reminds one of the growth of a mushroom. The Tomahawk Traffic Company organized, hauled the lumber from Merrill, built a store building 20 x 40 and had it stocked in full running order within two weeks. John C. Clarke, who has been for some time in the southern states, has returned to his first love—the pines of Wisconsin—and assumed the position of general manager of the above company.
        ---Lincoln County Advocate, June 25, 1887

The first building to be erected on the site of the present city was put up by Angus Buie in October 1887; it was constructed of logs. The first frame building was a residence at 115 West Rice Avenue, built by C. C. Lincoln in July of 1887 and which was still standing.

C.C. Lincoln, the Merrill carpenter, commenced to build, had a chance to sell out, accepted the offer and made some money out of the operation.

----Lincoln County Advocate, July 16, 1887

TOMAHAWK NEWS: C.C. Lincoln, who recently sold his lot and partially erected building made $300 instead of $200, taking as part payment a span of horses. He purchased another lot, paying $175 therefor and already has lumber on the ground for a building 20 x 40, two stories in height. The size of the lot is 50 x 142. He moved his family up from this city [Merrill], Wednesday.

----Lincoln County Advocate, July 23, 1887

The store building erected by John Oelhafen, Sr., in 1887 was the first building of this nature to make its appearance in the newly begun settlement; it is still standing at 117 West Wisconsin Avenue and now houses a general store conducted by William Oelhafen, a son of its builder. It is recalled by those present at the time when the roof of this building was being shingled, that four deer ran down the street on which it fronts.

TOMAHAWK NEWS: John Oelhafen, of Wausau, is building a hardware store up there. He bought six lots, paying over $2,000 for them, and a few days ago sold one for $720, the party buying it intending to put up a building at once. These lots all face Wisconsin Street. Mr. Oelhafen's hardware store will be 24 x 60, with twelve-foot posts. The frame is now up. There are twelve buildings started and lumber on the ground for more. Builders are putting up shells to be completed when the railroad gets there. It is said that the ground is so level that it will require but little excavation or filling, and the grade is probably where it always will be.

J. Theilman has two teams on the road between Merrill and Tomahawk delivering meat to the extension builders. They consume between four and five thousand pounds every week.

Mr. John Landry has sold and contracted about twenty lots at south Tomahawk, and several parties have already put up buildings on the land. The owners do not ask as big prices as were paid for lots at the Great Tomahawk, and the C., M. & Sat. Paul railroad will pass about one and a half miles to the north of it, but the ground is suitable for building purposes, and it will certainly be a good trading point. In time, it is *probable that several mills will be erected there, and that it will become a prosperous town.*

There are two boarding tents – one 32 x 70 and the other 19 x 32. Board and lodging is four dollars per week. Tomahawk people say to Merrill tenderfeet, "Don't come up here expecting to stay overnight. If you do you will have to sleep on a board."

----Lincoln County Advocate, July 23, 1887

There are now about forty-five buildings in the course of erection, and on an average of a load of lumber daily passes this corner of Rice and Railway streets, mostly from Merrill, but some from the company's mill.

----Lincoln County Advocate, August 6, 1887

TOMAHAWK NEWS: The Day Bros. are pushing their hotel as rapidly as possible. The house is located in the corner of Railroad and Wisconsin streets. They will probably be ready for the public in forty days.

----Lincoln County Advocate, August 6, 1887

The Tomahawk Bridge.

The resolution of P. Samphier, member of the county board from Rock Falls appropriating $3,200 to apply toward the building of a bridge across the Wisconsin, at Tomahawk was voted down. While a majority of the county board seem to be willing to make an appropriation for the bridge, the impression, seems to be that the bridge they desire to build is more expensive than necessary. The large amount of tax already levied, about $37,000, will be a heavy burden to the tax payers, and the members of the county board who feel like holding things in check should be commended. Tomahawk needs a bridge, and should have it; but isn't a $6,400 bridge a little high?

The Lincoln County Advocate reported in November 1888 that the Lincoln County Board voted against appropriating $3,200.00 toward the building of a bridge across the Wisconsin at Tomahawk. The board felt that $6,400.00 to complete the bridge was too much.

Early Stores

Oelhafen's Pioneer General Store, left background, was one of Tomahawk's first stores. It was built by John Oelhafen Sr. in 1887. To the right are the Mitchell Variety Store and the Mitchell Hotel. The truck, equipped with chains, was from the City Cash Market. Photo submitted by Evelyn Petersen of Tomahawk.

1907 Street Scene

Tomahawk had a dirt street and wooden sidewalks in this 1907 photo. At the right is Webster's Pharmacy, with a sign proclaiming "Drugs, Books, Stationery, Toilet Articles, Sporting Goods, Paints, Oils and Brushes, Prescriptions Gratefully Prepared."

The Tomahawk Leader, Special Supplement, July 2, 1986

Newborg Shoe Store—1900

The City Shoe Store had a sign out front that advertised "Shoes of All Kinds, First Class Repairing, City Shoe Store," in about 1900. The store was founded by G.O. Newborg and was operated by Oscar Newborg for many years. The building now is Friends and Fashions Store. Photo submitted by Norman Newborg.

The Tomahawk Leader, Special Supplement, July 2, 1986

The first hotel was the Somo House, the next, the Windsor, was built by Pat and Mike Day in September 1887

The Windsor House, owned and run by Day Bros., and built by Dexter Bros., was opened to the public on September 5, with Chas. Wilson at the desk.
    ----Lincoln County Advocate, September 24, 1887

STAGE TO TOMAHAWK: Louis Hildebrand runs a daily stage to Tomahawk. It leaves Merrill at 1 pm and will be driven through to Tomahawk the same afternoon if parties desire; otherwise a stop overnight will be made at Grandmother. In the event of driving through, the same day, passengers arrive at their destination at 9 pm. Fare, $1.50.
    ---- Lincoln County Advocate, August 20, 1887

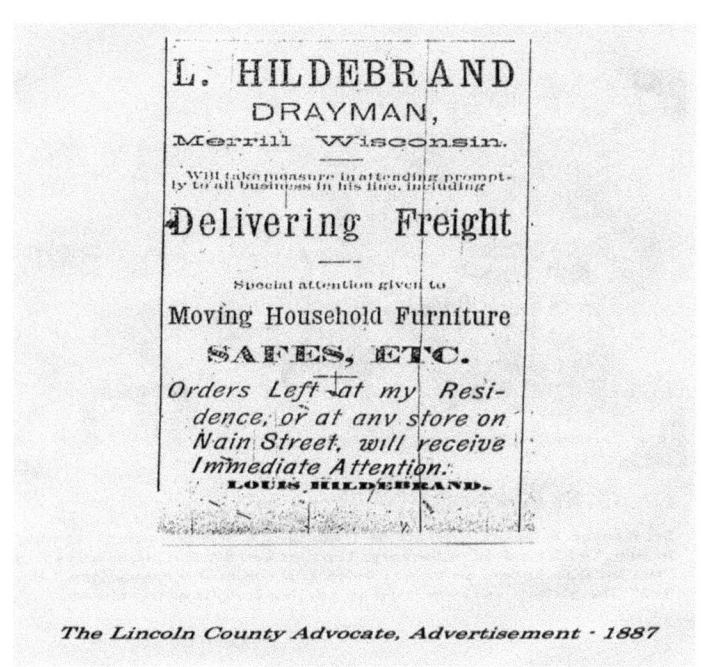

The Lincoln County Advocate, Advertisement - 1887

Dr. J.D. Cutter, who still is actively engaged in the practice of his profession here, came on December 19, 1886, and was doctor and timekeeper at the dam. He was a passenger on the first stage operated by Louis Hildebrand that ran between Merrill and the Wisconsin River dam site. The same stage eventually traveled to Tomahawk, once that city was established.

Other doctors followed Cutter's arrival – Jay Johnston, George R. Baker and later J. W. Bird, Poutre and Lamb. The first hospital was constructed in 1894 after the Sisters of Sorrowful Mother started taking patients in a two-story home one year earlier that soon became too small.

Dr. G.R. Baker

Dr. George R. Baker was one of Tomahawk's first physicians, coming here in July, 1900. He died in January, 1961, at age 87. The photo is identified as "the Dr. G.R. Bakers on an excursion trip while at a convention," in about 1907. The picture was submitted by Adeline E. Holtz of Tomahawk.

The Tomahawk Leader; Special Supplement, July 2, 1986

Sacred Heart had a rough start early on, but was able to grow thanks to the site and a $12,000 donation made later by the Bradley Company. The hospital was ...

able to turn a profit by selling tickets to lumberjacks.

Small Building

Their first "hospital" was a small two-story building located, according to some early settlers, at Fourth Street and Wisconsin Avenue. The place proved to be too poorly suited for the purpose, however, and after a few months of cold and privation the sisters accepted the opportunity to rent Mrs. E.J. Roller's residence at 127 Spirit Avenue and Sixth Street.

On a cold winter day, the sisters' two patients were transferred by means of a bobsled to this second "hospital." The early records of the hospital show that nine patients were admitted between Dec. 2, 1893, and Jan. 12, 1894.

During the winter of 1893-94, Fr. Joch drew the plans for a new hospital. After a conference with William H. Bradley, a prominent Tomahawk businessman who owned much of the land in and around town, it was agreed that the site for the hospital should occupy a plot of ground directly north of the newly erected church and parsonage.

The site was donated by Bradley.

Home Was Hospital

Tickets were bought chiefly by the lumberjacks who had no home in the vicinity. In time of illness their home was the hospital.

In the memoirs of Sister M. Dionysia, now deceased, it is related that one such lumberjack bought a ticket regularly every year. Whether he was sick or not, he always came to the hospital and said, "I must visit my home at least once a year."

The early sisters testified that the lumberjacks, men of many nations — Russians, Poles, Swedes, Germans, Irish, French — were good men, respectful and obliging toward the sisters.

At the hospital the men would help along with the work when they were able, sawing and splitting wood, painting around the house and helping in barn and garden.

During the first 14 years of its history, Sacred Heart Hospital prospered and accomplished much good. In 1908, an addition increased the length of the building by 60 feet and raised the capacity to about 32 beds.

Difficult Years

The first seven years were difficult ones for Sacred Heart Hospital. The income was insufficient and consequently the sisters had to use every means to enable them to keep the institution open. They begged for worn out sheets and pillow slips so they could pull the threads apart and use the lint instead of purchasing cotton batting, which was then somewhat expensive and difficult to obtain.

From the woods directly in back of the hospital, the sisters gathered firewood and so reduced their fuel expense. For a short time they were even forced to beg alms and to travel from one logging camp to another to sell hospital tickets to the lumbermen.

After 1900, several good ticket agents employed by the sisters helped to bring in more patients and more income.

The ticket agents were assigned to a certain territory where they went from camp to camp selling tickets at $5 and later at $7.50. The ticket entitled the holder to admission and to medical and surgical treatment in the hospital at any time during one year from the date of the ticket, for such length of time within the year as the attending physician judged necessary for the patient suffering from injury or sickness.

The Tomahawk Leader, Special Supplement, July 2, 1986

One of the first lawyers was A. H. Woodworth. A local boy, Patrick T. Stone, passed the State Bar Exam before graduating from Marquette University in 1912, and went on to be a lawyer and judge. He brought great pride to Tomahawk when he was selected as the first federal judge appointed by President Roosevelt for the Western District Court of Wisconsin in 1933, and stayed for over twenty years on the bench. Among other prominent pioneers may be mentioned Dr. J. R. Dodd, dentist, Alexander Rodgers, John Woodlock, M. C. Hyman, Frank A. Larsen, Robert C. Theilman, A. B. Crane, and William H. Bradley, just to name a few. Mr. Bradley, often referred to as the "father of Tomahawk", as previously described was a leading figure in the founding of the city, and much of the subsequent progress was brought about through his activities and benefactions.

Tomahawk, rather Thomas Hawk (verified by the author through primary source documents) was born at the dam April 30, 1887. Thomas, son of Mr. and Mrs. Angus Buie, was the first white child to be born here and was presented with a lot at the corner of Sixth Street and Washington Avenue because of that fact. He is now married and lives at Detroit, Michigan; Angus Buie, his father, died March 2, 1907. It is also important to note that in addition to building the first homestead in Tomahawk as was mentioned earlier, Angus also constructed the first post office in 1887 and was elected as the City's first mayor from 1891-92.

Mattie Lewerenz, daughter of Mr. and Mrs. William Lewerenz, was the first child to be born in what is now the city proper. Her father, who is now engaged in farming near the city, at that time held a contract for building the side tracks and a mile of the main line for the Chicago, Milwaukee & St. Paul, and she was born in a tent on the west side of the railroad tracks, just south of West Spirit Avenue in August of 1887. She is now living in Washington, D. C.

However, the *Lincoln County Advocate* has the first-born honors bestowed on another young lady:

HONOR TO THE FIRST LADY: Born to Mr/Mrs Duncan McMillan, Saturday, September 24, a daughter. This is the first girl born in Tomahawk and she has been the recipient of many presents.

       ----Lincoln County Advocate, October 8, 1887

The city's early life was founded on the lumber industry, and the coming of the railroad almost simultaneously with the beginning of the settlement brought about the rapid growth previously referred to. New sawmills appeared in rapid succession to swell the tide of the city's prosperity. Many being destroyed by fire nearly as quickly as they were built.

SAWMILLS

The first sawmill was built by King and Weymouth of Winneconne, Wisconsin in the spring of 1888. This mill was subsequently sold to the Bradley interests and was known as Mill No. 1. It was next owned by the Rice River Lumber Co., and from this concern it passed to the Somo Lumber Co., who operated it for a time and then sold it to the John Oelhafen Lumber Co. It was acquired from the last named company by its present owners, the Raymond Lumber Co., in 1923. It is located west of the Marinette, Tomahawk & Western tracks and north of Bradley Park, across the bay.

The next sawmill to be erected was put up by the Tomahawk Lumber Co. in the winter of 1888-89, making its first cut in the spring of 1889. This was known as Bradley Mill No. 2, W. H. Bradley being the moving spirit of the Tomahawk Lumber Co. It was situated on the Wisconsin River west of the Chicago, Milwaukee & St. Paul tracks. It burned down in 1897 or 1898 and the new mill with which it was replaced was also destroyed by fire. The mill now standing on this site was moved from Woodboro, Wisconsin by the Bradley interests, who operated it for several years and then sold it to its present owners, the Mohr Lumber Co.

The Crane mill was moved here from Gagen, Wisconsin in the winter of 1889-90 and started making lumber in the spring of 1890. It was owned under the name of Crane Bros., by Timothy and Abner B. Crane, who had come to Wisconsin originally from the state of Maine. This mill was located across the river, north of the present city pumping station, and was sold and moved out of town in 1904, having finished sawing the timber from the Crane Bros.' holdings here.

What was known as No. 3 Mill was built by the Farmers' Lumber Co. in 1890 and was owned and operated by Robert Hall and George R. Gray of Muskegon until its ownership was combined with that of the Bradley and Rodgers mills. It was located across the Wisconsin River north of Tomahawk Avenue, and was destroyed by fire in 1893.

The Rodgers Mill, or No. 4, was moved here from Muskegon in 1889 and was located west of the railroad tracks on the west end of what is now known as Rodgers or Foss's Island. It burned in 1903 or 1904.

There were several other mills of more or less brief duration. Alexander Rodgers erected a shingle mill across the river just north of Mill No. 2 in 1890. This mill was dismantled after one or two seasons of operation. The Bradley Company built a large box factory in 1890, located just west of the intersection of the Marinette, Tomahawk &

Western tracks with the street that runs to Rodgers Island and the No. 1 Mill. This factory burned down in 1893 or 1894. At a later date W. H. Foss had a box factory on the east end of Rodgers Island; the plant was built in 1908 and destroyed by fire in 1913.

The Bay Mill, which burned in 1903, was built by W. H. Bradley at the location still known as Bay Mills, west of the city of tomahawk. A settlement grew up about the mill, and previous to the fire, which destroyed the plant, a post office was located there.

At the heyday of the lumber industry here the annual cut at Tomahawk ran from 60,000,000 to 75,000,000 feet of lumber with about 25,000,000 shingles. Another industry, which has played a prominent part in the city's history, both early and recent, is the manufacture of pulp and paper. This industry will be discussed at length later in this book.

CITY INCORPORATION

Incorporation as a city was carried out in 1891. Angus Buie was the first mayor, and the first aldermen were as follows:

J. C. Gilman – First Ward

T. Twoomey – First Ward

M. C. Hyman – Second Ward

Richard Dawson – Second Ward

Felix Marcouillier – Third ward

John Knauff – Third ward

Joseph Chevrier – Fourth Ward

Frank Liberty – Fourth Ward

A. J. Olson was the first city clerk, being followed a short time later by John Shirk, then editor of the "Tomahawk" newspaper. A. H. Woodworth was the first city attorney; James O; Connell was the first chief of police, with William Dumont as night watchman; L. L. Edmonds was the first city treasurer, and John Tobin the first assessor; the last named resigned a short time after taking office and was followed by A. Allen. The first city hall is now a residence owned by H. L. Hildebrand; after it was discontinued as a headquarters of city government it was moved to a different site and served for some time as a school building, after which it was moved to its present site. The present city hall was built in 1900 on the site originally occupied by the first city hall.

FIRST CITY COUNCIL — Here is Tomahawk's first governing body. Members were Angus Buie, mayor, and Aldermen Richard Dawson, J. C. Gilman, J. Chevrier, F. Marcouiller, F. Liberty, John Knauf and T. Toomey.

The Tomahawk Leader, Special Supplement July 2, 1986

City Hall

Built in 1900, Tomahawk's City Hall nearly ended its official duties in a Christmas Day fire in 1948. The blaze destroyed the third-floor library and roof, with damage estimated at $50,000. There was a move to build a new hall, but the City Council voted to repair. The photo at bottom is a 1909 postal card.

The Tomahawk Leader, Special Supplement, July 2, 1986

KNOW ALL MEN BY THESE PRESENTS:-

That at a regular meeting of the common council of the City of Tomahawk, of the County of Lincoln and State of Wisconsin, held at the council chamber in the city of Tomahawk aforesaid, on the first Monday of December, being the second day of December, 1895, an ordinance for the adoption of the general charter laws of this state in place of the existing charter of said City was offered as follows:-

"The Common Council of the City of Tomahawk do hereby enact and "ordain as follows:-
" Section 1. Chapter 326 of the laws of 1889, as amended by "Chapter 312 of the laws of 1893 of Wisconsin, is hereby adopted as a "City Charter by the City of Tomahawk, in lieu of Chapter 58 of the "laws of 1891.
" Section 2. The class in which the City of Tomahawk shall be, "shall be determined by the last census taken by the state of Wisconsin.
" Section 3. This ordinance shall take effect and be in force from "and after its passage and publication."

That notice was thereupon duly given by the Common Council of the said City of Tomahawk that the above and foregoing ordinance would be considered by said Council at its regular meeting to be held in its council chamber on the third day of February, 1896, at 7:30 P.M., by the publication of said proposed ordinance together with a notice f the time when the same would be considered by said Common Council once, on the twenty-fourth day of January, in "The Tomahawk Blade", the same being the official newspaper of said city.

That said ordinance was laid over at least thirty days before final action was taken thereon.

That final action on said ordinance was taken at said regular meeting held on said third day of February, 1896, at the time and place aforesaid. That at said meeting of said Common Council last

Ordinance to adopt the general charter laws of Wisconsin to replace the existing charter of the city. Adopted by the Tomahawk City Council December 2, 1895 mentioned a full attendance of the members of said Common Council was had, and due proof having been made and filed with the Clerk of said City of Tomahawk, of the publication of said proposed ordinance and notice of the time when action would be taken thereon, the said ordinance was thereupon adopted by a vote of more than three-fourths of the members of said Common Council, there being but one dissenting vote.

NOW, THEREFORE, By virtue of the facts above recited, which facts all appear of record in the office of the Secretary of State, --

THESE LETTERS PATENT certify that the following territory described in Chapter 58 of the laws of 1891, towit:- All that district of country included in Section Number Two (2), Three (3) and Four (4) in Township Number Thirty-four (34) North, Range Number Six (6) East, Sections Number Twenty-six (26), Twenty-seven (27), Twenty-eight (28), Thirty-three (33), Thirty-four (34) and Thirty-five (35) in Township Number Thirty-five (35) North, of Range Number Six (6) East, of the Fourth (4) principal meridian, of the County of Lincoln and State of Wisconsin, constitutes the boundaries of said City of Tomahawk.

That said territory above described constitutes a body corporate and politic, by the name of the City of Tomahawk, and shall be governed by the General Charter laws of this State, as set forth in Chapter 326 of the General Laws of this State for the year 1889, together with all amendments thereto by the legislature of this State, applicable to the class of cities in which said City of Tomahawk falls, as determined by the last census taken by the State of Wisconsin.

In Testimony Whereof, I have hereunto set my hand and caused the Great Seal of the State to be hereto affixed. Done at the Capitol in

Ordinance to adopt the general charter laws of Wisconsin to replace the existing charter of the city. Adopted by the Tomahawk City Council December 2, 1895.

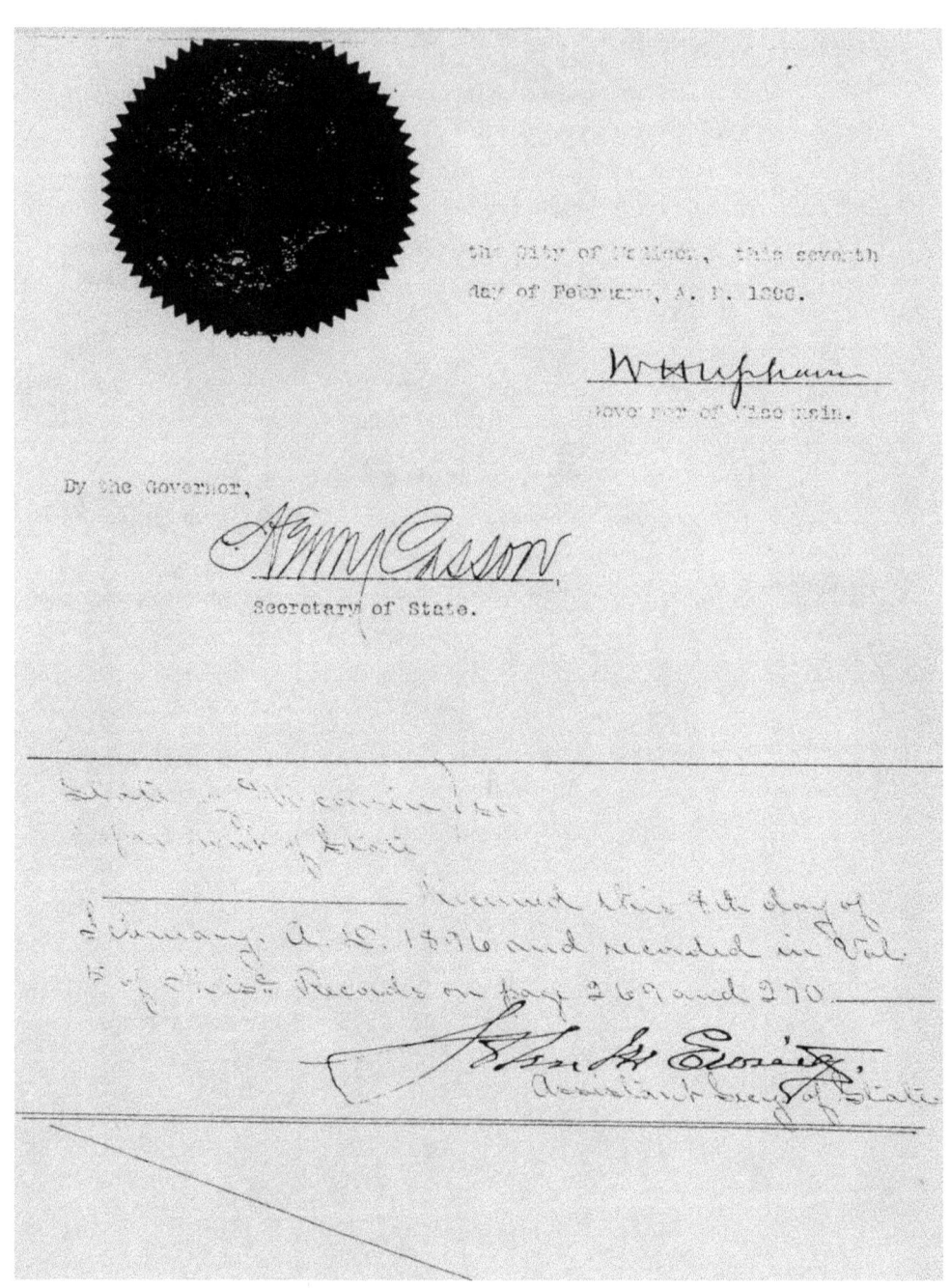

Ordinance to adopt the general charter laws of Wisconsin to replace the existing charter of the city. Adopted by the Tomahawk City Council December 2, 1895.

IN THE NEWS

Advertisements from the newspapers of 1896 show the following concerns then in existence: James O'Leary, attorney; A. J. Olsen, real estate, insurance, hardware and agency for American Express Co.,; C. E. Macomber, druggist; W. L. Marshall, real estate and insurance; Robert Daigle proprietor – Tomahawk Livery Stable; W. H. and J. W. Bradley, bankers – The Bank of Tomahawk; J. H. Soli, groceries; J. W. Bird, physician; N. Emerson, timber and farming lands; L. Kabat, cigar manufacturer; C. Ostrander, carpenter and contractor; John P. Hughes, attorney; R. J. Stinzi, harness and saddlery; Theilman Bros., meats; Howard Burrington, fruits and confectionery; Albert Hauer, dealer in lumber; Nick Bros., furniture and undertaking; William Bohn, merchant tailor; Everson Bros., hardware; John Oelhafen proprietor – Pioneer Store; E. W. Whitson & Co., groceries, feed and etc., Howen & Fleming, dry goods; Piper Bros., meats; Tomahawk Pulp & Paper Co.; Charles A. Ayer, bakery; C. A. Seidle, taxidermist; Earl Lincoln, barber; L. D. Goodnough, barber; and Abram Gennett, barber.

TOMAHAWK BUSINESS DIRECTORY.

HAY, STRAW, FEED.

In this line I bid defiance to competition. If you are needing anything in this line I want to see you without fail.

I have taken the agency for the sale of selected hay, straw and feed from a party in Dane County and can furnish you the best articles in the market at the most reasonable prices.

J. C. GILMAN,
TOMAHAWK,
WISCONSIN.

TO SWAP HORSES

In the middle of the stream is not considered good judgment, neither is it good for an advertiser to change his medium in the midst of his advertising. Yet it is better to change than to drown. Right here is where good advertising calls on good judgment; for to choose a poor newspaper is poor judgment. Like a bad account the quicker it is closed the less the loss. He that learns without such costly mistakes and strikes the best newspaper first, avoids the change that kills and scores the quickest and greatest success.

THE TOMAHAWK

Is not the original and only best, but it is the best in Lincoln county, the best and the greatest in all that great section of our state north of Oshkosh and south of Ashland.

1500 CIRCULATION

Is the exact average circulation of THE TOMAHAWK for the past two years and it is fully equal to the combined circulation of any other two Lincoln county papers. There's luck in advertising if you strike the right newspaper. Isn't it better to start in with the best first?

W. H. & J. W. BRADLEY,

BANKERS

TOMAHAWK,
WISCONSIN.

JOHN P. HUGHES

Attorney at Law.

Office over Smith & Parker's

BOHN
THE FASHIONABLE
TOMAHAWK TAILOR.
Prices Reasonable.
SATISFACTION GUARANTEED.
WISCONSIN AVENUE

J. W. BIRD
M. D.
PHYSICIAN
—AND—
SURGEON,
Office in Hyman Block.
Night calls at Office.

A. J. OLSON

—DEALER IN—

HARDWARE,
Stoves and Tinware.

JOHN BARCLAY,
—THE—
MERCHANT TAILOR
FALL
AND
WINTER
SUITINGS
FITS OUR SPECIALTY
TOMAHAWK, WISCONSIN.

J. H. RAMSEY,
D. D. S.
RESIDENT DENTIST
BEST WORK :-: LOWEST PRICE.
WIS. AVE.
TOMAHAWK

W. A. FOSTER,
General Insurance Agent.,
Fire
Life
Accident.

R. C. THIELMAN
FRESH,
SALT,
AND
SMOKED
MEATS
FISH AND GAME

FRED Miller Brewing Co.
Brewers and Bottlers of
—SUPERIOR—
MILWAUKEE BEER
AND PORTER
L. L. EDMONDS, Agt.

C. E. MACOMBER
DRUGS,
MEDICINES,
PERFUMES
PRESCRIPTIONS ACCURATELY COMPOUNDED.

LAKESIDE HOTEL
Special Rates to Theatrical Companies.

Tomahawk Leader 1896

TOMAHAWK CORRESPONDENCE.

Richard Dawson will build on lot 2 block 18. W. J. Moore, contractor.

Engineers are now surveying a forty acre addition to Tomahawk.

Geo. Baxter, of Tomah, is building a dwelling house, 18x26, on Second street.

James McConnell is building a dwelling house on Second street. Building, 24x24.

Pat Day's family arrived from Ashland last Thursday and are now quartered at the Windsor house.

Jack Clarke has his store on Railroad street nearly completed. The second floor will be used for a hall.

K. Benson is building on Washington avenue and Third street. Building to be 18x40, two stories high.

Mr. Tobin, the milkman, had his ponies hitched to a huge milk can this morning delivering milk to all parts of the city.

John Stone has moved into his new store and sells a cider called the O. F. C. Taylor & McBrier. Dexter Bros. built the store.

John Holland has gone to Prentice to meet his family. Geo. Luts will have charge of the culinary department during his absence.

Messrs. Day, Wilson, Anthony, Dexter, Doyle, Holland and Cochran were seen at church. They are all members of the choir, Mr. Day being the leader.

The Windsor House, owned and run by Day Bros., and built by Dexter Bros., was opened to the public on Sept. 5, with Chas. Wilson at the desk.

Richard Scott has completed his store on Fourth and Somo streets. It is the only store or house of any kind that is plastered as yet, say nothing of his brick chimney which is the first and only one in Tomahawk.

TOMAHAWK, Aug. 10.—We had quite a storm here on the 8th. It blew part of the Tomahawk House down. The proprietor, George Winchester Corkscrew, stood like a hero with his shoulder at the helm until the storm was over. The tent of Leverns, the railroad contractor, blew down as flat as a pancake, but no lives lost. Deacon Doyle's house was found trying to go east.

The hotel of Anthony Holland stood the racket all right. All the boarders of the Tomahawk house had to come over to get dried out.

John Stone's building will be completed the first of next week.

Day Bros. will have a very fine hotel when completed.

S. B. Roberts is opening a large grocery store on Tomahawk avenue.

Gilman & Rice have a large saloon corner Wisconsin avenue and Railroad street, where the thirsty can get anything they want.

Hotel arrivals at Tomahawk House: Chas. Wilson, Boston; C. C. Lyons, New York; Frank Hadden, Memphis; Ole Glonesson, John Johnson, Ole Margarine, Limerick.

Hotel Anthony: R. R. Scott, England; James Day, Ashland; S. B. Roberts; N. Champigne, Merrill; J. D. Becker, Garry Denberg, C. M. McDonald, D. A. McDonald, Dave Bailey, Angus McDonald, Frank Whitenall, J. C. Burns, William Dehl, Burt Barlow, La Crosse. HAWK.

The Lincoln County Advocate reported weekly on the progress of the young, booming town of Tomahawk.

(Various clippings from 1887 are shown here as well as on the following pages.)

The Tomahawk Blade, in speaking of the number of children in the place and the necessity of a school house says: We do not want our children to grow up in ignorance and develop into a town board." This must have brought the town of Rock Falls to its senses as they have passed a resolution to build a schoolhouse, at a cost of $1,000.

One of the stations above Tomahawk has been named Flanigan in honor of the jolly material agent in the Merrill yard.

Jo Pommerville came to Tomahawk Thursday, to put up the shelving in the store building of Heineman Bros. A complete stock of goods have been ordered and will probably arrive by the middle of next week.

As Tomahawk builds up and the lots disappear from the company's plat another scheme presents itself. Two additions, one on the northeast and the other on the southwest corner of the town are to be platted, each to contain six blocks.

Messrs. Isbell & House have contracts for two store buildings in Tomahawk. Corwith Bros. & Hall are to have a building 24x60, in which a business similar to the one conducted by Corwith Bros. in Merrill will be engaged in. The other building is to be 20x40 and is owned by Milwaukee parties. Both are to be two stories and substantial buildings.

A meeting was held at the Windsor house, Tuesday evening, for the purpose of organizing, to get a school established here. J. C. Clark was unanimous choice for chairman. A committee of five was appointed to confer with the town board of Rock Falls, and a committee of three to look over the boundry lines of the proposed new town of Bradley.

Tomahawk.

Our police force will be dressed in uniform next week.

The Tomahawk dam will be completed by January 1, 1888.

Hansen & Colleran, of Merrill, have opened a branch store in this city.

Mr. Marks, of Milwaukee, was in the city looking for a site upon which to build a brewery, for the Miller Brewing company of Milwaukee.

Hilderbrand the drayman is the maddest man in town. He was to take a party of eight to Bradley and to receive $8 therefor. He blew in a shiner on them and they all walked.

Geo. Gibson, Merrill's chief of police took dinner at the Windsor, Wednesday. He went to his logging camp the same day.

SATURDAY, SEPTEMBER 10, 1887.

Railroad Notes.

The steam whistle was heard in Tomahawk, for the first time on Thursday of this week. The track laying is finished to that point and now the work of leveling up will be pushed as rapidly as possible. A gravel or sand pit has been opened on the north side of Prairie river. Men are here, ready to commence work on the permanent bridge across the Wisconsin river at Tomahawk.

While the train was passing C. C. Munos's, at Chat. some one tossed a bundle, containing the wardrobe of one of the men, to a gentleman whose name we are unable to learn. He made the catch; but an ax in the bundle cut his hand severely. The wound was dressed by a Merrill surgeon.

George Gans, of Tomahawk Dam, came down on the new railway. That is to say, he boarded the train and rode down.

The C. M. & St. P. R'y will commence hauling freight to Tomahawk, next Tuesday, Then the new city will begin to grow in earnest.

Tomahawk.

About sixty passengers went up the line on the first train; among them several St. Paul officials. A large delegation met them at the Tomahawk depot.

A Few Will Stay.

Under the heading "New Residents," the Tomahawk Blade says:

Three families numbering fifteen souls moved to Tomahawk last week, from Merrill. The rest of the town will probably not arrive before next week.

After reading the above an ADVOCATE man started out to see if he could find any one who was entirely decided that he would not move to Tomahawk at once. We found one man besides the postmaster who had never given the matter any serious thought; and we are of the opinion that as our city election comes so soon we may be able to induce enough to stay here so that we can fill the city offices. It is no use Jed, Merrill will be a city of many thousand souls when Tomahawk lives only in the mind of the "Oldest inhabitant."

Tomahawk.

A number of the papers throughout the state have upon different occasions printed articles regarding the new town of Tomahawk that might cause some people to believe that it was a very hard town. One item says: "Tomahawk has 13 buildings, 7 saloons, two houses of ill-repute and two stores." Now this is not giving it to the world in its true light. In company with a Mr. Wetzler, of Milwaukee, and C. S. Howard, of Mauston, the editor of this paper drove from Merrill to Tomahawk last Tuesday. We reached this future lumber metropolis at 7 p. m., and it took but a casual glance to satisfy us that that they were a peaceable, sober and industrious people. Abstemious in their habits, drinking only when thirsty and rarely eating except when driven to it by hunger. In this, the sole remaining quarter section of paradise, the crops grow without cultivation. Even in the cool chilly days of September we discovered strawberry vines twining themselves around the lamp posts, and violets and roses growing between the street car tracks. Nature is indeed kind. So

SPECIAL FROM TOMAHAWK.

Tomahawk, Aug. 29.—Mr. Edward Roller has bought lot 5 in block 4 and will at once erect a store 24x50, with basement. The building will be veneered and used as a flour and feed store.

Mr. T. Trudall has sold his building to Conroy & Martin, of Michigan. Consideration, $1,000. Mr. Trudall had just got the frame of the house up when the sale was made. Mr. T. bought more lots that afternoon and will build at once.

Jack Clark is building a store on Railroad street 40x60. Wholesale and retail groceries.

Marquardt Bros. have began building a store on Tomahawk avenue. It will be ready for occupancy about Sept. 20, with a full line of groceries and dry goods.

The citizens of this place got out a petition to the town board for a patrolman. Wm. Black was their choice for the office. He will also attend to lighting the street lamps. As he stands 6 feet 7½ inches he will dispense with the usual ladder.

Mr. Rader, of Wausau, will at once erect a large ice house for this winter. He will also build a large store house for beer.

Mr. Chas. Helke, of Wausau, was looking over Tomahawk and while here bought three lots in block 7, where he will build at once. Mr. H. owns a large wholesale and retail furniture store, which business he will engage in here.

John Laverence who took the contract to grade the streets, has the brushing all finished. John has done good work so far, and if the grading looks like his clearing, the streets will be a credit to the city. John Kelly is foreman. Give John a small mountain of sand and forty teams and he will show you how they used to move mountains before the war.

END OF DIVISION.

Machine Shops and Round House for Tomahawk.

NEW DEPOT BEING ERECTED.

The New Boom Across the Wisconsin Completed—Telegraph Line Nearly Up. Progress of the Work on the Extension—Notes.

Thursday morning the editors of this paper jumped onto a flat car and took a ride to Tomahawk. The track is fine as far as the ballasters have gone, then it resembles the crooked back of a camel. Telegraph poles are set all the way and wire strung to within a few miles of the town. That which was a wilderness, en route, a few months ago, has driven the first stake of civilization and the thought naturally arises that Lincoln county is elbowing her way through the vast throng toward the rostrum.

There were twenty-three cars in the train, loaded with timbers for the new depot at Tomahawk—spikes, rails, ties, material for builders, workmen and people going up to see the sights.

A level territory meets the eye, with buildings in all stages of erection. The foundation for the depot is going in—the building to be 102 feet in length by thirty in width—larger than the regulation size. A mammoth well is being dug and an excavation being made for the foundation for the tank. West of the track will be the machine shops and round house of the company, for it has been decided to make Tomahawk one end of the division. It would seem that the new town is to be the pet of the St. Paul company, for indications show that they are bound to make a town of it—prejudicial reports to the contrary notwithstanding.

The Windsor House, by Day Bros., furnishes a good meal. About one hundred took dinner there Thursday. Prices moderate and editors treated in a royal manner.

TOMAHAWK, Oct. 3.—The gravel train came in with buildings of all descriptions on wheels and about 150 souls on board. They have side-tracked here for two weeks.

Charles Helke has his lumber on his lot to build a temporary store 20x40, to be used this winter for business and next spring he will move the building on the back part of the lot and erect a brick structure for his undertaking business 25x75, double store, two stories high. Mr. H. is the right man in the wrong place, for we never die here.

We are going to have a school house before we have a policeman or a jail. We suppose jails and policemen are necessary evils, but the schools we must have. The laws of Wisconsin are compulsory. The board have done right and they will ever be backed by the citizens of Tomahawk.

Our hotels are all crowded. If some good hotel men would come here and build good houses it would be a great accommodation to the traveling public, as the few hotels, although first-class in every respect, cannot accommodate all.

Matt Malady, of Wausau, is now building a hotel on the corner of Second and Somo. The building will have twenty-four rooms, exclusive of the culinary department. There are eighteen carpenters at work and the building will be up in about a month.

The Anthony & Holland house had forty-five for breakfast, Sunday morning. Holland John is head chicken picker. Mr. Anthony just returned from Merrill. He rode down on the train but came back afoot, inspecting ties, all on account of some misunderstanding with the "con."

The Helke furniture store furnished Matt Malady his hotel furniture. Mr. Lincoln also bought of him. James Doyle purchased his hotel furniture of the same dealer. Mr. Helke is a cabinet maker from the old school.

Robert Harriett and J. F. Woodock are erecting a butcher shop, dwellings and barns for W. M. Leverance. The dwelling house on Fifth street is a credit to Tomahawk. Mr. Leverance will spare neither time or money on his new home.

Ed Evanson, of Iola, is business manager for T. Thompson (from same place), the leading grocer of Tomahawk. Mr. Thompson has opened his store on Tomahawk avenue and from all appearances is taking the lead.

The present excitement seems to be the pancake fever. It is not at all fatal, as those affected with it are the most robust and healthy, but they cannot avoid giving the sign when they have the cake fever.

Capt. Geo. Page talks of organizing a Grand Army post at this place. The captain knows his business now as well as when at Vicksburg, where balls were as thick as politicians at La Crosse.

Ernest Anthony is devoting his sparetime to the evils of being a member of the culinary department. He, I think, has a touch of the pancake fever.

John Stone is putting the finishing touches on his house. John is doing a good business. Pete Seibel is John's head compounder.

John Kelly, foreman for Leverance, has to grade two miles for the railroad company on the west side of Railroad street.

Lant Rice lost a revolver. If the finder will leave same at Tomahawk house he can have——contents, and no questions asked.

The various contractors for the Boom company have their brushing finished and the company are now raising a head of water.

Stephen Howard, of Mauston, has opened his sample room with David Cass as head mixer.

Mr. Bigelow has his family here and they are living in his new house on Rice street.

Alderman Gilman, who keeps the corner grocery on Railroad street, has been in Merrill the past week.

The bridge-builders have one span of the Howe truss completed and will finish the left span by Saturday.

L. Beauregard, Wilkins and Patzer will be here Oct. 10 to fish and hunt.

Pete Sibell, of Oshkosh, is now mixing mint juleps for John Stone.

Who was with you, Pete, when the lights went out?

For hair, lime or mortar, apply to P. Day.—HAWK.

Tomahawk, Wisconsin, Saturday, March 16, 1895.

GONE UP IN SMOKE.

Fitzgerald, Fingerhut and Newborg Closed Out by Fire.

GREATEST FIRE IN TOMAHAWK.

The Fire Fiend Visits Our City and Wipes Out a Portion of the Business District.—Loss Heavy, Partly Covered by Insurance.—Absence of Wind Prevents a More Serious Conflagration.

The fire company was called out at eleven o'clock Thursday night by a fire in the Stewart building on Wisconsin avenue occupied by Paul Fingerhut as a merchant tailoring establishment. The fire had gained complete control of the building before the alarm was turned in rendering it utterly impossible for the fireman to check its ravages. It rapidly consumed the building and took in two adjoining buildings occupied by Fitzgerald Bros. as a grocery and G. O. Newborg as a boot and shoe store. It was by the most determined efforts that the building of E. W. Whitson & Co. was saved from destruction. Buildings across the street were in imminent danger of being lapped up by the fiery fiend. Johnson Bros. hotel at one time being on fire. The plate glass windows in Piper & Tipson's market and Fairfield's dry goods store were badly cracked by the heat as were also the windows in Ayer's tobacco store.

The loss falls the heaviest on G. O. Newborg who had but fifteen hundred dollars on building and stock. Mr. Newborg saved but very little of his stock of which he carried a large line. He is an industrious hard working mechanic and made his money all by hard work and he has the sympathy of the entire community in his sad misfortune.

Fingerhut carried a stock of furnishing goods and clothes upon which he carried an insurance of five thousand dollars. Owing to the headway that had been gained by the fire before the alarm was turned in it was impossible to save any of the stock. He had about nine hundred dollars worth of suits ready for delivery which were destroyed.

Fitzgerald Bro's. who occupied the store on the east succeeded in saving a greater portion of their stock. They carried an insurance of $1200 on the building and $1800 on the stock.

Early panoramic views, shown here and on the previous page of Wisconsin and Tomahawk Avenues showing the railroad depot, Mitchell Hotel, Bradley Bank, the Standard Mercantile and others. *The Tomahawk Leader, Special Supplement, July 2, 1986.*

FIRST WARD

Allard, David -Allard, Moses -Abbat, N. -Aloy, Fred -Andrrewson, Ole -Able, Geo., Andrewson, Ole -Andrews, Irvin -Baker, Geo. -Berry, F.N. -Braustred, John Buckley, Pat Baker, D.W. -Baley, John -Butcher, J.H. -Bauer, Aug. -Bell, Jas. -Bunders, Wm. Bey, Aug. -Berquest, Aug. -Chadwick, Joe -Carilue, John -Clark, O.F. -Coyle, Wm. Chisty, Alx. -Cutcher, Ando -Duchene, Joe -Donaldson, John -Doll, Peter -Doxtater, F.L. Dawson, Richard -Donaldson, Wm. -Dood, J.R. -Deming, C. -Eaglekrout, J.N. Eppley, R.D. -Elson, John R. -Flaherty, James -Flanagan, Pat -Froehlich, John -Fry, John Fredrickson, Chris -Ford, Charlie -Fogerty, J.L. -Fisk, James -Faulk, Herman - Foley, John -Flaherty, Mike -Flaherty, Wm. -Flannagan, Patrick -Goodman, R. Goodman, Bert -Grady, James -Gretzmacher, Henry -Gunderson, Erick -Gunderson, Ole Gensman, Tony -Hitchcock, D.A. -Harris, Sam -Hein, H.J. -Hein, Peter - Harrington, Frank -Hanson, C.C. -Hanson, H.P. -Haen, John -Hanson, Simon Herman, Aug. -Hatland, Andrew -Herman, Frank -Halverson, E. -Hanisch, Ernest Jeannot, Wm. -Jeannott, W.E. -Jauvin, Peter -Johnson, J.E. -Johnson, B.P. - Johnson, Wm. -Jugerman, Aug. -Jeannot, Edward -Kendrick, A.P. -Dutchers, John Kutchers, Frank -Kraft, Carl -Koist, Herman -Kelly, John -Kreuger, Arthur -LaTulippt, L. LaRusch, Nels -Ladd, Geo. -Larson, Lars -Lutz, H.L. -Martz, L.W. -Miller, Herman Marauit, Phillip -Mrcure, Joe -Miller, John -Manecke, Aug. -Marrion, Ed -Mitchell, Wm. McCollie, John -McCutcheon, David -Mass, Geo. -Murphy, Alex. -Morancy, Louis McCormick, Robert -Manthy, A.W. -Manthy, Gustave -Ninman, Ed -Naven, John Nick, Mat -Oelhafen, John -Oelhafen, Wm. -Ostrander, C. -Ogran, Andrew - Peterson, Andrew -Poutre, Joe -Pride, A.M. -Parsons, S.D. -Poutre, Chas. -Perant, Joseph Roberts, Harry -Rich, Wm. -Richardson, Geo. -Roe, Alford -Ryan, chas - Rammell, Anton -Ratziew, R. -Rice. W.T. -Sister, A. -Shultz, H.F. -Sayers, Tom Seymour, N. -Seth, James -Stenerson, Tom -Sorrenson, Able -Smith, W.T. -Sodke, Chas. Sweeny, Martin -Sayers, James -Solberg, John -Sullivan, Ben -Shirk, W.M. -Stutz, Mat Sister, Geo. -Tigum, Hans -Twoomey, T. -Tully, John -Travis, John -Vincent, R. Welty, O.K. -Woodburty, Milo -Wilson, J.F. -Watson, James -Webster, Alex. - Warner, C. -Zastrow, Aug. -Zuberg, Peter

List of Registered Voters – Tomahawk First Ward
The Tomahawk, March 12, 1898

SECOND WARD

Anderson, Erick -Buteau, Ferdinand J. -Bohn, Charles F. -Boudreau, Jerry -Bowen, George -Bird, J.W. -Boudreau, William -Brayback, Fred -Bohn, William -Burrington, Howard -Barbian, John -Beard, Mike -Bruno, George -Burnett, F. -Buchanan, Albert -Baker, David -Cutter, John D. -Chave, Thomas T. -Clark, Charles -Caldwell, Peter -Cheverier, Peter -Clapper, George -Clark, Joseph T. -Carlson, Chas. -Dubois, Peter -Bubois, Joseph -Dubois, Sevell -Daigel, Robert -Dumars, August -Dregen, William -Delthue, Gust. -Eldridge, James -Emerick, John -Enberg, Nels -Fournier, Colin -Fitzgerald, James A. -Foley, Thomas -Fountaine, Alex. -Fuller, Henry L. -Garland, Fred S. -Gagnon, David -Goodnough, L.D. -Goff, R.N. -Gun, Robert -Gostofson, Oscar -Hauer, Albert -Hyman, M.C. -Hickey, James -Hathaway, John -Howen, Andrew -Houlehan, Edward -Henenkowsky, Aug. -Hanson, Hans -Jarvis, Ezra -Johnson, John -Johnson, Nels -Johnson, Andrew -Kreutz, Reinhart -Knoblach, N.S. -Knutson, Albert -Kottkoe, Robert -Lauthley, Clifford -Laabs, Julius -Larson, Frank A. -Luchinske, Benjamin -McCarthy, Jerry -McCarthy, Richard -McCarthy, Henry -McCarthy, Garret -McCarthy, Thomas -Meunier, J.N. -McBride, James -McBride, Frank -Miller, W.H. -Murphy, John -McMahon, Robert -McCabe, Thomas -Myre, Elzear -McDonald, William -Marshek, Frank -McGraw, John -Olson, Anton J. -Obev, Gust -Olson, Benjamin -Olson, Gust. -Peterson, Charles -Reich, Herman -Ristow, Gottlieb -Ruldie, Mike Sr. -Ruldie, Mike Jr. -Riebel, John -Roux, Z. -Soll, John H. -Schmitz, Mike -Seymour, Joe -Samphier, P. -Smith, Abram -Swanson, Swan -Swanson, Nels -Sondburg, Olls -Searl, Edward -Shores, John -Sargent, J.H. -Schelbe, William -Seipt, Alexander -Turgeon, Peter -Tulley, Patrick -Taylor, Henry J. -Thielman, Robert -Thielman, Louis -Thieme, Adolph -Wiskow, Charles -Wiskow, Henry -Wolke, John -Walquist, Erick -Woodworth, A.H. -Williams, Geo. G. -Wissing, Fred

List of Registered Voters – Tomahawk Second Ward
The Tomahawk, March 12, 1898

THIRD WARD

Allord, Peter -Burhanan, Chas. -Bebeau, Enos -Boucher, Edward -Bolsvert, Jas. -Bouchard, Able -Bohn, Gust. -Binger, Wm. H. -Boudreau, Amos -Bartz, Herman -Bouchard, Octave -Bunday, Fred -Bernley, Joseph -Bally, J. -Bell, Joe -Buchanan, Jas. A. Cotie, Louis -Coniff, matt -Conant, T.A. -Coon, Matt -Caron, Hector -Caroll, Jas. -Coyle, Wm. -Chapell, Wm. -Drever, W.m. -Deering, martin -Baigle, Peter -Danleis, D. O. -Doon, Jas. -Doland, Wm. -Doth, Thomas -Dunemaker, Michael -Ducare, T. -Eibel, Wm. -Evenson, Edward -Edmonds, L.L. -Elden, John -Frank, Frank Fuller, H.L. -Foster, Geo. -Foraker, Reese -Fitzgerald, Morris -Fountain, Joe -Gagne, Tule -Gahan, Benj. -Gesell, Chas. A. -Gould, Frank -Gillett, Geo. H. Garritt, Frank -Getsell, Wenzell -Hokanson, A.D. -Hemenway, H.H. -Hodes, SamÕl Heath, D.P. -Hechendorf, Albert -Hanson, C.J. -Hold, Archey -Herts, Jacob -Iverson, Andrew -Johnson, Andrew -Johnson, Chas. -Johnson, Julius -Jocques, Ed. -Johnson, John -Johnson, Alfred -Kaphaen, Wm. -Kahat, Leanard -Koth, Ben F. Kellsher, Frank -Kath, Louis -Kunze, Fred -Kluss, Theodore -Knox, Henry -Little, G.M. Leroux, Joe -Londo, Orvill -LaTondre, John -LeMay, Everest -LeBoeuf, Noal -LaTondre, Paul -Lee, John -Langlois, Archey -LaTulippi, Geo. -Lerene, Peter -Merritt, Sherman A. -Menrau, Fred -Macomber, C.E. -Marcoullier, Phillipp -Marcoullier, Felix -McDonald, A.R. -May, Thomas -Meyer, Henry -Marshall, W.L. -Mayo, Frank -Murphy, John -Macomber, Calrence -Moore, Wm. -Madjer, Louis -Marie, Michael -McWithey, Seth -Markus, Geo. -Murray, Felix -Murray, Eli Marceau, Fred -Newborg, Geo. O. -Nooman, Michael -Nick, Jacob -Nelson, R.C. OÕLeary, Jas. -Osterbrink, E.F. -Oelhafen, John W. -Oelhafen, Andrew -Olson, Albert Piper, Wm. R. -Piper, George -Piper, Geo. H. -Rodgers, Hugh -Reiley, Michael Robarge, Thomas -Robarge, Alex. -Ruelle, Peter -Schultz, Edward -Searl, E.E. Stelter, Christ. -Squires, Hiram -Seidel, Chas A. -Stintzi, R.F. -Stark, F.G. -Smith, C.M. Scott, Richard -Theiler, Martin -Thomas, Chas. -VanGalder, H.R. -Violett, Frank -Violett, Geo. -Violett, Joseph -West, Julius W. -Worl, Gust -Waffler, John -Webater, J.C. Whitson, E.W. -Weingard, Antone -Wipperfurth, W. -Wooley, Henry

List of Registered Voters – Tomahawk Third Ward
The Tomahawk, March 12, 1898

FOURTH WARD

Anoth, Ralph -Allie, Joe -Ash, L.P. -Allord, Geo. -Atchernon, H.A. -Anderson, Chas. -Anderson, Noah -Burritt, Ronland -Burritt, R. G. -Burritt, H. -Bucke, Martin -Burgess, John -Burg, Ole -Blackwood, John -Bunda, Pete -Beabeau, John -Bouranssan, Dolph -Bulie, Angus -Brossenoult, John -Burrington, C.W. -Barney, Wm. -Blanett, John -Buchanan, L.R. -Bishop, Mike -Bates, Hugh -Bishop, C.E. -Buchanan, Chas. -Bilevan, Joe -Belmore, Dennis -Braustead, John -Calluwett, Fred -Costigan, James -Chas, John -Choulnard, Archie -Couey, Fred -Cardinal, John -Cardinal, N. -Cyr, Joe -Clotier, Dolf -Conkrite, K. -Couryver, F. -Clark, D.A. -Crane, Frank -Carmichael, J.D. -Como, Peter -Carlson, Chas. -Charbeno, Marcell -Como, Alex. -Conkrite, H.S. -Cheverier, Joe -Derosso, Frank -Doon, Henry -Boye, Wm. -Dubey, Guess -Dickeus, R.S. -Ducett, James -Dubey, Henry -Ductee, H. -Ducett, Dan -Dewing, Clifton -Doe, Oliver -Edwards, W.M. -Erickson, Hans -Eveland, A.W. -Emerson, Norman -Eckerland, Charles -Ehmann, W.N. -Eckland, John -Erickson, Martin -Erickson, Andrew -Eno, Richard -Foss, W.G. -Fetherston, Wm. -Fryer, Rodger -Fryer, P.J. -Fetherston, John -Foster, W.A. -Flynn, Frank -Flynn, John -Fryer, Fred -Globensky, Alphous -Gaudette, C. -Gray, G.R. -Hall, B.E. -Bevert, Eli -Hilt, Nick -Hedlof, John -Hoogsteel, Chas. -Hilt, Mike -Hanson, Fred -Henderson, Henry -Iottee, Louis -Iottee, -Johnson, H.A. -Johnson, Rasmus -Jones, D.A. -Jordan, B. -Kopplin, R.L. -Kelley, James -LaBlanc, Peter -LaFond, Alex. -Lambert, Leo -Linquest, Andrew -Lavigne, Peter -Larson, Benj. -Lockhart, H. -Levis, Jos -Lavigne, Guy -Levis, Geo. -Loftus, John -Lambert, Paul -Lambert, Felix -McDermott, W.H. -McCutcheon, Alex. -McIntyre, M.M. -McGee, Wm. -McCabe, Mike -Menore, Mike -Monde, Louis -Moe, hans -Mercure, Geo. -Martell, Geo. -Moran, Geo. -Martinson, C. -MacNeill, S.M. -McWithy, Fred -McWithey, Seth -Menzie, T.T. -Nick, Mat. -Nostrom, A. -Nass, E.A. -OŌConnell, James -Olson, Henry -Olegard, Over -Olson, John -Olson, Nelse -Olegard, Olf -Partridge, P.M. -Pelloqua, Felix -Pool, thomas -Pelliter, Joe -Pontre, J.E. -Peltier, W.M. -Parker, Paul -Russell, R.F. -Roy, Frank -Robinson, James -Rice, J.E. -Raymond, Joe -Sheean, John -Strong, G.D. -Scheffener, John -Sarchet, M.M. -Sutliff, A.E. -Scott, Dave -Stoneburg, Chas. -Schelk, Robt. -Scheffener, Frank -Suvoy, Jos. -Stone, Pat -Smith, G.W. -Smith, Ed -Swanson, Carl -Saeger, Victor -Shea, Mike -Thorson, Olf -Tierney, Chas. -Tonguey, math. -Thom, Adam -Turgeon, T. -Turson, Oscar -Thrall, B.H. -Trombley, Joe -Veitch, Wm. -Vankirk, James -Venne, J.A. -Venne, H.A. -Walker, John -Whitney, W.C. -Wiley, John -Wiley, Iza -Wolworth, Steve -Watson, Peter

List of Registered Voters – Tomahawk Fourth Ward
The Tomahawk, March 12, 1898

To supplement the general account of the early history of the city in the preceding paragraphs, mention will now be made of various industrial developments, existing at the present time (1924), including public utilities, banks, schools, churches, manufacturing and other interests.

PUBLIC UTILITIES

The plant of the waterworks was installed in 1891, the city council having resolved at a meeting held June 11th of that year to bond the city for $16,000 for this purpose. There are now between five and six miles of water mains, and 54 fire hydrants. The standpipe system is used, the reservoir having a capacity of 60,000 gallons. A straight pressure system is substituted for this, however, when the water in the three wells forming the source of supply is low. There are two pumps, one with a capacity of 1,500 gallons per minute and the other of 1,000 gallons per minute; two boilers of 60/60 horsepower furnish steam for the operation of these pumps. The plant is run on a 24-hour schedule, with J. August Bauer as chief engineer and Gustav D. Engleman as superintendent.

Electric power and telephone service is furnished by Wisconsin Valley Electric Co. The original concern in this field here was the Electric Light and Water Co., which carried on operations from March 28, 1890, to February 7, 1896. A new charter was secured by the Bradley interests on the latter date, under the name of the Electric, Water and Telephone Co., with a capital stock of $15,000.

The power plant of this concern was located in the yards of the Tomahawk Lumber Co. On February 28, 1912, the Tomahawk Light, Telephone and Improvement Co. was formed with a capital of $50,000, and took over the interests of its predecessor. The original officers of the new concern were R. B. Tweedy, president and treasurer and E. G. McNaughton, assistant secretary. Later in the same year Andrew Oelhafen and Victor Extrom purchased the stock of this company and it was operated under their ownership until 1918, when Mr. Oelhafen purchased the entire capital stock. Under the organization then effected the officers became: Andrew Oelhafen, president and treasurer; John Walter Oelhafen, manager; and Arthur R. Oelhafen, secretary. Control passed from this concern to the present owners on July 21, 1922. M. R. Frederickson is the present local manager. Power is obtained from a dam which was built at Tomahawk Rapids, about one mile north of the Tomahawk River, in 1893.

POSTAL SERVICE

The United States Government started issuing postage stamps in 1847, and in Tomahawk's early years, the mail was delivered by stage coach from Merrill. The original post office, before the coming of the railroad, was located at the dam then being built below the present city.

NEWS FROM TOMAHAWK: They want a post office up there and the usual number of aspirants to be postmaster just now feel very friendly toward Mr. Cleveland.
        ----Lincoln County Advocate, July 16, 1887

After the railroad came through and was able to bring mail, Angus Buie constructed a post office building and Frank A. Larsen became Tomahawk's first postmaster, receiving his appointment September 28, 1887.

PERTAINING TO TOMAHAWK: F. A. Larsen has been appointed postmaster. He is a merchant at that place.
        ---Lincoln County Advocate, October 8, 1887

This office was first located on block 23, lot 8 and was moved in August 1888 to lot 2, block 7, where it remained until the building on this site was destroyed by fire. The office was next quartered where H. H. Roehrborn's tire repair shop is now, the building being then owned by Kate Clark; after about two years there, the office was moved back to lot 2, block 7, on Wisconsin Avenue adjoining the new bank building, and from here it was moved to its present location in 1919.

It is an office of the second class, and employs three clerks and an assistant postmaster, in addition to the postmaster and carriers. Two rural routes and three star routes are operated, the latter routes running to Spirit Falls, Harrison and Bradley respectively. There are three city carriers and two rural carriers; H. L. Brooks has been postmaster since October 1922.

SPREADING THE NEWS

An excellent weekly newspaper, the Tomahawk Leader, is published by Osborne Bros.; the paper has a subscription list of about 1,000, and three job presses operated in conjunction. It was established in 1896, the first issue appearing on Saturday, July 4th of that year. Charles Deming, previously of Columbia County, was its first publisher, with W.

M. Shirk as editor. The day of publication was changed from Thursday to Saturday with the fourth issue. The paper changed hands in the winter of 1897-98, H. D. Bliefernicht becoming publisher and editor. Ownership passed from him to Ware & Lee with the issue of May 6, 1904. Robert G. Lee purchased his partner's interests about 1910 and operated the paper alone from that time until 1915, when he sold out to Russell & Dozer. The following year Mr. Russell acquired sole ownership, and it was operated by him until January of 1917, when Robert G. Lee again became the owner, with L. W. Osborne as manager. The present owners, L. W. and L. M. Osborne, took over the paper on December 1st of the same year. They built a 24 foot addition to the building housing their plant at 24 S. Second Street in 1923, giving the building a total depth of 78 feet with a frontage of 22 feet, and they have met with very good success in conducting the paper. September 17, 1913, the Leader was consolidated with the Tomahawk, which was established in 1886 by W. H. Bradley and was conducted in June of 1887 by W. M. Shirk & Son and was published by them until the end of 1894, when P. W. Swift took it over. Mr. Swift published the Tomahawk during 1895, from 1896 to October of 1903 it was conducted by the Tomahawk Publishing Co., who then sold it to W. D. Lambert; the latter conducted it up to the time of its purchase by Robert G. Lee, then publisher of the Leader, who consolidated it with the latter paper. Besides these two papers one other, the Tomahawk Blade, has been published here; it was established about 1888 and was published by Jed W. Coon until 1895 or 1896.

J. W. Coon has just moved his Blade printing outfit in and John Shirk is erecting a building for the Tomahawk, another paper. Everything is on the rush to get a warm shelter for winter.

----Lincoln County Advocate, September 24, 1887

Paper Described Tomahawk

The first issue of the Tomahawk Blade, first newspaper to be published in Tomahawk, gave an account of the new settlement. Volume I, Number 1 was published on Sept. 8, 1887. It said:

"The Chicago, Milwaukee and St. Paul Railway will have its extension completed to Tomahawk by Saturday night. Regular trains will commence coming into Tomahawk within two weeks.

"Tomahawk is now very rapidly settling up. Seven-hundred people are already on the ground and at least 200 buildings have been completed, while as many more are in the process of construction. A good hotel opened yesterday.

"There are over 100 carloads of building material consigned to Tomahawk, waiting shipment from Merrill. This will commence to be forwarded next week. Up to the present time building material and all supplies have had to be hauled and packed 30 miles.

"H.C. Payne, who was interested in founding the town, predicts that there will be 2,000 people housed at Tomahawk before the snow flies.

"Next week the Blade will contain a writeup of the town and its businessmen. It is impossible to do so in this issue."

The Tomahawk Leader, Special Supplement, July 2, 1986

LIBRARY

A good public library is maintained, receiving its financial support from the city. It was established during the summer of 1909, the movement to this end having been set on foot by the women's clubs of the city. It has occupied the same quarters since the beginning, on the second floor of the city hall building. Control is by a board of seven trustees appointed by the mayor; the present (1924) membership of the board is as follows; Mrs. H. S. Olson, president; V. E. Labbe, secretary; Frederick Elk, Mrs. H. L. Wakefield, L. M. Osborne, R. T. Reinholdt, and Mrs. E. P. Werner. Esther Venne* is librarian and Esther Bloomquist assistant librarian. At the close of the year 1922 there were 6,847 volumes shelved, the registration was 2,095, and a circulation of 13,253. The only predecessors of this institution were the various traveling libraries which were established from time to time, probably the earliest of these was that founded by W. H. Bradley in 1897.

*Esther Venne started with the Tomahawk Library as an assistant in 1916, became the librarian in 1919, and remained until she retired in 1966 after nearly 50 years of service.

FIRE DEPARTMENT

There is a volunteer fire department of unusual efficiency, composed of 22 members. It was established at an early period in the city's history, with Robert McGregor as the first chief. Robert Theilman was the second to serve in the capacity of chief, and he was followed by M.A. Stutz; after Mr. Stutz, Louis Theilman filled the office, to be followed in 1907 by Leo Martz, the present chief. A Republic motor driven fire truck was added to the equipment in 1919, making the apparatus fully commensurate with the city's needs. A yearly salary of $125 attaches to the office of chief, while the other members of the department receive $90 annually.

POLICE DEPARTMENT

Tomahawk's first Police Department was established in 1891 with James O'Connell as Chief of Police.

SCENIC CITY AREAS

The spirit of city pride and love of beauty which prevail here are well illustrated in the beautiful park system that has been built up, making the city well qualified to serve in its position as the gateway to the wonderful scenery of Northern Wisconsin. Bradley Park, a tract of 105 acres of natural park land immediately adjoining the city on the west, was acquired from the Bradley company in 1910 at a cost of $10,000; the timber alone on this property today has a value far in excess of that sum. This picturesque park was thrown open to tourists in the summer of 1922, one camp site being located in the midst of the splendid timber and another on Mirror Lake; besides these a camp site was maintained on the Wisconsin River, near the Fourth Street bridge and just off of State Highway No. 10. Besides Bradley Park the city owns frontage on both sides of the Wisconsin River for a distance of approximately two and a half miles northeasterly.

The present Fourth Street bridge over the Wisconsin River was built during the summer of 1922 at a cost of approximately $60,000; it is a steel girder bridge with concrete foundation, having a driveway of 26 feet in width and a sidewalk 6 feet wide; the total length of the structure is 450 feet.

(Courtesy of the Tomahawk Historical Society.)

CHURCHES

The religious needs of the city are well cared for. Church services have been held since settlement first began here, and today (1924) there are organizations representing eight different religious denominations. The First Congregational Church was the earliest to effect formal organization, this step being taken at a meeting held November 22, 1887. Rev. Dr. Grassie of Madison, representing the Congregational denomination, presided over the meeting and it was through his efforts that the organization was brought about. First services were held in a room over what was then Hyman's saloon, where the Robert C. Theilman meat market and offices are now located. The congregation was incorporated on April 10, 1888, and then began the erection of a church edifice in the same year, located on the present site of Washington Avenue and Fifth Street. This building was remodeled and enlarged during 1920, with over $11,000 being expended in carrying out this project. It is now one of the best arranged church plans of its size in the state. Besides supply pastors, the following have served in the pulpit: Rev. George M. Heckendorn, now deceased, who remained about one year; Re. W. D. Stevens, also deceased who served six months; Rev. W. M. Ellis, now principal of the Christian Endeavor Academy, Endeavor, Wisconsin, whose services here extended over a period of three years; Rev. A. Thompson, now deceased, who also served for three years; Rev. J. C. Ablett, who was here about one year; Rev. J. Jones who was ordained here and served about one year; Rev. Samuel MacNeill, now living at Wauwautosa, who served about three years; Rev. Grant V. Clark, now at Ladysmith, Wisconsin, who was married here and was also ordained in this church, his services continuing for four years; Rev. F. W. Heberlein, now superintendent for the Western District of Congregational Churches at Ashland, Wisconsin, served here for six years; Rev. W. Bosard, now of Oklahoma, who was here for one year; Rev. T. W. Barber, who served here for two years and is now living at Anoka, Minnesota; and the present pastor, Rev. R. G. Heddon, whose ministry here began November 1, 1919. The first death among the members of the congregation was that of Mrs. Angus Buie, and the first baptism that of Tomahawk Buie. Among the charter members and early workers may be mentioned the following: Mr/Mrs H. A. Johnson, who are still residing in the city, as vitally interested in the work as ever; Mr/Mrs C. W. Burrington, Mr. Burrington, now deceased, having been during his residence here in partnership in the lumber business with H. A. Atcheson; Mr/Mrs H. P. Hatch, both of whom are now deceased; Mr/Mrs T. T. Clave, of whom Mr. Clave is now deceased and Mrs. Clave is residing at Pasco, Washington; Mr/Mrs F. G. Stark, of whom Mrs. Stark is now deceased and Mr. Stark is living in Rochester, New York; Dr. J. W. Coon, of Stevens Point; Mr/Mrs Angus Buie; Mrs. Louise Norse, now of California; and Mrs. John Durkee.

St. Paul Evangelical Lutheran Church had its beginning in services held here by the Lutheran pastors Rev. W. Bergholz of Naugart and Rev. J. Dejung, Sr., of Rhinelander, starting at a time when only a very few houses had been erected in the city. April 6, 1886, the congregation was formally organized under the leadership of Rev. W. Bergholz, five other Lutherans, as follows, being active in the work of the organization; William Lewerenz, W. Bohn, Louis Gerke, Robert Tillman and R. Krenz. The new congregation was at once affiliated with the Joint Synod of Wisconsin and Other States, and on April 13, 1886, it was incorporated under the laws of the state. The first services were held in the homes of members, but within a few years after organization a church edifice was erected at the corner of Sixth Street and Somo Avenue. Pastors from neighboring churches, particularly Rev. J. Dejung of Rhinelander, served the congregation until 1897, when the first resident pastor, Rev. C. Voges, now of Mindoro, was called. Rev. Voges served until 1901 and was followedby Rev. G. Voss, now of Plainfield, Illinois, who remained until 1906; Rev. Leo Kirst, now of Beaver Dam, Wisconsin, was the next to fill the pulpit, and he was succeeded in 1911 by Professor E. Kowalke, now president of Northwestern College, Watertown, Wisconsin; Rev. A. P. Sitz, now of Rib Lake, Wisconsin, came in 1912 and remained until 1918. In the latter year Rev. M. Glaeser, the present pastor, took the charge. Though having had a resident pastor since 1897, the congregation was not sufficiently strong in finances to erect a parsonage until 1902, when a building of this nature was put up near the church at Sixth Street and Somo Avenue. The original church was not large enough to meet the needs of the growing congregation, and it was decided in 1903 to begin gathering funds for a new building. In 1904 the Baptist congregation offered for sale their church property, located at the corner of Wisconsin Avenue and Fourth Street, and this church, with its fine location in the heart of the city, was purchased by St. Paul Lutheran congregation in the same year for an amount less than the erection of a new building would have required. In 1914 the congregation provided for the future by buying an extra lot next to the church. In 1920 the Ladies' Aid Society and the Luther League financed the excavation of a basement under the church, the installation of a modern heating system, a kitchen, and an assembly room for the meetings of these societies. In the same year, through the untiring efforts of one of the young women of the congregation, a large bell was purchased and dedicated. On February 26, 1923, the last debt of the congregation was paid by the Ladies' Aid Society; this society has done most praiseworthy work from the beginning and much of the financial prosperity of the church is due to them. The present officers of the society are: Mrs. R. Manthey, president; Mrs. E. Whitmore, vice president; Mrs. August Krueger, treasurer; and Mrs. J. Boheim, secretary. Two members of the congregation, Mr. Herman Bartz and Mr. Leo Martz, have served as elders for between 15 and 20 years. The first marriages solemnized in the church were those of Ed Jaques and Anna Crass, May 12, 1895, and John Scheffner and Minna Lewerenz, July 2, 1896; the first baptism was that of Jessie Anna Kopplin, born April 12, 1889, daughter of Mr/Mrs Robert Kopplin, and baptized October 26, 1890; the first confirmation class was that of June 6, 1892, the members being Maria Lager and Robert Schuelke; the first funeral services were those held for August Bude on October 16, 1893. The Sunday School in connection with the church has a membership of 87, with 11 teachers. Church services are held in English and German every Sunday, and the pastor also conducts services at Tripoli, Highland Flats, and in various country school houses. The present officers of the church are: Herman Bartz, president; Leo Martz, treasurer; William Berger, secretary; and William Kleinfeld, Allen Spencer, A. H. Bahr, trustees.

The Methodist Episcopal Church here was established in 1889 by the Appleton district of the Wisconsin Conference. The present building, at the corner of Third Street and Somo Avenue, was erected in 1891. The first pastor, Rev. O. H.

Berry, left December 30, 1889, and the following ministers have since filled the pulpit: Rev. J. A. Powers, January 1890 – October 1891; Rev. H. L. Williams, October1, 1891 – August 8, 1892; Marcus Deland, October 27, 1892 – April 2, 1893; John T. Strettou, April 1893 – September 19, 1893; Robert S. Ingraham, September 25, 1893 – September 30, 1894; Charles J. R. Bulley, September 30, 1894 – October 1896; W. W. Edmondson, October 1896 – October 1897; William Clark, October 1897 – October 2, 1899; Thomas W. Sprowls, October 2, 1899 – October 3, 1900; John Milton Judy, October 8, 1900 – October 15, 1901; Andrew A. Bennett, October 15, 1901 – September 16, 1903; W. J. Ward, September 16, 1903 – 1904; Robert McKim, September 18, 1904 – September 17, 1905; J. U. Woodward, September 25, 1905 – September 26, 1906; Oliver Saylor, September 26, 1906 – August 31, 1907; Irving H. Lewis, September 1907 - September 1917; Vernon C. Switzer; T. W. North; Herbert F. Heilig, January 1919 – September 1919; Ira W. Ellis, September 1919 – September 1920; George W. Verity, January 1921 – September 1921; and L. E. Jones, the present pastor, who came October 30, 1901. Rev. Switzer, mentioned in this list, gave up his life in the service of his country during the World War. Among the members of the congregation at its first services may be mentioned the following: Mrs. W. D. Stewart, Mrs. Mary Goodman, Miss Elizabeth Wiley, Mrs. C. C. Lincoln, and Mrs. Angeline Harrington. The congregation now number about 100 members; the Sunday School has an enrollment of 130, with nine teachers; there is an active Epworth League with a membership of about 25, a Junior League of 55 members, and a Ladies' Aid Society having 40 members. A Boy Scout troop, which was organized by Rev. Jones, the present pastor, in March of 1922, is also in active existence and has 22 members.

St. Mary's Catholic Church of Tomahawk had its beginning in a mission known as St. Mary's Congregation, attended from 1888 to November of 1889 by the Rev. Father July, then resident priest of the Rhinelander parish. Services were held at stated intervals in the frame building now used by the Foresters as a meeting place, which was erected in 1888. On May 23, 1892 at a ceremony presided over by the Right Rev. S. G. Messmer of Green Bay, the cornerstone of the present church edifice on Seventh Street was laid, the site for this building and for the hospital in connection having been donated by William H. Bradley on the sole condition that "suitable and substantial buildings be erected thereon." The church, built of brick, is 50 X 115 feet in dimensions and has a height from floor to ceiling of 32 feet; substantial and artistic furnishings and decorations were installed, and here the congregation now has a beautiful and commodious home. A parsonage 36 X 40 feet in dimensions with an 18 X 22 foot addition was built just north of the church the same year; conservative estimate places the value of the church property today (1924) at $70,000. The building up of this fine property was brought about largely through the untiring efforts of the Rev. Father Hoogstoel, and this great work he accomplished while severely handicapped by ill health. Father Hoogstoel was born in Flanders, Belgium, December 1, 1856, and pursued his studies for the priesthood there, taking courses in philosophy at the College of St. Troud and theology at the American College in Louvain. He came to the United States in 1884, arriving at Green Bay, Wisconsin, in November of that year, and his first mission was at Stiles, Wisconsin. Through his work at Stiles a parsonage was erected and the church building enlarged and furnished throughout. Later he built the Church of St. Charles at Maple Valley, Wisconsin, St. John's Church at Gillett, Wisconsin, and the Church of St. John the Baptist at Coleman, Wisconsin; besides serving at these places he conducted missions at Beaver, Ellis Junction and Pembine. Father Hoogstoel is now chaplain of Mercy Hospital at Milwaukee. His first period of service at

Tomahawk was from 1890 to 1894.; Rev. Father P.S. Dognault then served until 1895, when Father Hoogstoel returned, this time remaining until 1900. Rev. Charles Caron was the priest from that time until 1904, being followed by Rev. J. Looze, who served the congregation from January to October of 1904; Rev. Father George Pesch was then here until 1912; Rev. Van Helden was the next priest; he served for five years, and his place was taken by Rev. Father Siboth, who was here from 1917 until Father Habraken came in 1919. The latter remained until October 5, 1923, when he was succeeded by the priest pastor, Rev. Father Smits. The congregation now numbers 350 families, and the following societies are represented, all having good memberships: The Alter Society; Catholic Knights of Wisconsin; League of the Sacred Heart; Catholic Order of Foresters; St. Joseph's Union; Confraternity of the Holy Face; and the Young Ladies' Sodality. St. Mary's School, operated in conjunction with the church, and was founded in 1916 under the administration of Rev. A. J. Hadden as priest. The present two-story brick veneered building, with five school rooms, was erected at that time, at a cost of $10,000, and school was opened in September of 1916 with 205 pupils. Five teachers from the Teaching Sisters of the Sorrowful Mother organization at

Marshfield are employed, and eight grades are taught; the average attendance is 250.

    St. Barnabas Episcopal Church had its beginning about 1890, Archdeacon Jenner conducted the first services here. The church edifice was erected in 1892, funds for the purpose of the site and for much of the work of construction being furnished personally by Bishop C.C. Grafton of the diocese of Fond du Lac. W. H. Bradley was very active in the project and furnished the material for the construction and part of the funds. Following his ideas a church very large in proportion to the needs of the congregation was erected, having a seating capacity of about 400. The first regular priest was Charles Trask Lewis, who was ordained in St. Barnabas Church and who served the Tomahawk congregation in addition to his church at Merrill. November 4, 1900, Rev. Frederick Waldo Barker took charge of the Merrill and Tomahawk congregations, resigning the Tomahawk charge in 1906. Rev. Floyd Keeler was then sent here as the first resident priest, taking charge July 29, 1906; his wife and little girl died here and he resigned his charge November 20, 1906. Following this, services were held occasionally by Father Barker of Merrill until October 13, 1907, when Rev. Henry Gibbs was sent to take the charge. Father Gibbs had been a missionary among the Seminole Indians in the everglades of Florida for some time; in many ways he was unsuited in the charge here and his service was attended by many difficulties. He resigned May 30, 1909. The church was served from Merrill by Fathers Webber, Herman F. Ahrens, and J. Russell Vaughan in turn. The last name resigned the Tomahawk charge in June of 1912, and the church was then vacant until June of the following year, when Rev. Claude Crookston was ordained as resident priest. June 13, 1915, Father Crookston resigned on account of illness, being succeeded by Father A. E. Pflaum, who remained about one year. Father Vaughan then served the church from Merrill again, as did his successors in the Merrill charge, Father Claude B. N. O. Reader and Father Joseph Crookston. The latter, who is now in charge of the Merrill and Tomahawk congregations, is mentioned above as Father Claude Crookston, who served the Tomahawk charge from June 1913 to June 1915. After recovering his health, Father Crookston became a member of the Order of St. Francis, receiving the designation of Father Joseph. He became vicar of the parish in May of 1918.

The Scandanavian Lutheran Church here was organized April 27, 1893, by Christian J. Hansen, Gustave Newborg, Martin Erickson, Erling Ness, Ole Thorsen, Simon Hansen, Nels Robertson, Hans Moe, and Rasmus Johnson. The Church edifice was purchased from the German Evangelical congregation. The following pastors have served here: Rev. Mickelson, Rev. Loftus, Rev. Knudson, Rev. Smartemo, Rev. Madland, Rev. Hougstad, Rev. Helland, and Rev. Horeland.

The Scandanavian Congregational Church was organized July 13, 1922, with the following charter members: Mr/Mrs. Peter Hamrin; Mr/Mrs. John Nelson; Mr/ Mrs. Edvin Johnson; Mr/Mrs. Oscar Selander; Mr/Mrs. Gust Kall; Mr/Mrs. Oscar Nyberg; Mr/Mrs. O. Ehn; Mr/Mrs. John Haugland; and Mrs. Anna Johnson. A church building was erected during the same year, services meanwhile being conducted in the homes of the members. The congregation is served by the Rev. J. Albert Peterson, resident pastor for the church of this denomination at Merrill.

CLUBS, SOCIETIES & ORGANIZATIONS

Among the fraternal organizations of Tomahawk, several date from a very early period in the city's history. The Blue Lodge of the Masonic order, No. 243, celebrated its 30th anniversary during the summer of 1922; this lodge holds regular meetings in the Gesell building and has about 90 members. The Masons are also represented by Forest Chapter of the Order of the Eastern Star. Lodge No. 30 of the Independent Order of Oddfellows is also about 30 years old; its 62 members hold their meetings at Koth's hall; in connection with this organization there is also Rodah Rebekah Lodge, and Lincoln Encampment No. 80, the latter having 42 members and having been organized September 3, 1898. Aerie No. 752 of the Eagles is about 20 years old and has 152 members. There are also active branches of the Knights of Columbus, the Equitable Fraternal Union, the Catholic Foresters, the Maccabees, and the Woodmen of the World. The Knights of Columbus organization is Council No. 2066 and has over 100 members; it was organized about three years ago (1921). The Equitable Fraternal Union has about 130 members here, and the Maccabees have 73.

The Women's Literary Club has been organized for 30 years, and the Tuesday Club, another prominent women's organization, for about seven years. Both of these clubs have been very active in civic work, and many movements which have been of permanent benefit to the city were brought about directly through their efforts.

The Tomahawk Helping Hand Society, an institution for charitable purposes and the greatest of its kind in the county, was established March 9, 1911, at a meeting held at the home of Mrs. James Smith. Mrs. Mabel Oelhafen was active in bringing about the organization, and she was permanently appointed to the office of president by the then charter members. Other appointments made at the first meeting were: Mrs. Hulda Smith, vice president; Mrs. Elizabeth Drever, secretary; Mrs. Katherine Oelhafen, treasurer; and Mrs. Elizabeth Zastrow and Mrs. Carrie Lambert, investigating committee. Incalculable good has been accomplished by the society. Funds are raised by subscription and by means of various enterprises, including bazaars, moving picture entertainments, suppers, dances, etc., and these are expended in philanthropic work of the most helpful kind. As an example of what is being done, the records of the society show that during the first year of existence, from March 9, 1911, to March 9, 1912, 29 needy families were relieved, nine being furnished groceries and fuel; 31 children were clothed; shoes were furnished to 15 children; the services of a physician and nurse were provided in the case of several afflicted families; and a Christmas time 18 full Christmas dinners were sent to families who would otherwise have been deprived of this symbol of the Christmas spirit and Christmas cheer. During the Christmas season of 1921, 31 boxes were sent out, each containing provisions for two meals for a family; 266 sacks of candy, nut and fruit were dispensed, bringing Christmas joy to the hearts of as many children of needy families; and three boxes of clothing and many individual gifts were distributed. The membership of the society has increased, there being as many as 88 members in 1919. The present officers are: Mrs. Mabel Oelhafen, president; Mrs. Elizabeth Drever, first vice president; Mrs. Henry Hildebrand, second vice president; Mrs. Charles Siedel, secretary; and Mrs. A. J. Olson, treasurer. In purpose and accomplishment the Helping Hand Society is one of the institutions that go to make the world a better place to live in, and in its work one sees reflected the ideals of the noblest type of womanhood.

The Tomahawk Commercial Club and the Tomahawk Agricultural Society both had their origin in the Council of Defense, which was organized among the citizens of Tomahawk during the World War. This institution was reorganized at the close of the war as a commercial club, with A. S. Griffith as president, Victor Labbe, secretary, and J. A. Olson, treasurer, and it has continued to exist as such down to the present time, performing all the useful functions of an organization of this nature. The present officers are: F. P. Werner, president; William Bingham, secretary; and A. J. Olson, treasurer. In 1919 the club appointed a committee of three on agriculture, consisting of H. A. Atherson, A. E. Sutliff, and John P. Lee. The purpose of the committee was to further the agricultural interests of the vicinity and thereby aid int eh welfare, growth, and development of Lincoln County. The society was launched in 1919 as a private concern, with John P. Lee as chairman, H. A. Atherson, secretary, and A. E. Sutliff, treasurer. It held fairs at Tomahawk in 1919 and 1920, no admission being charged, and in 1921 it was incorporated under the laws of Wisconsin. Yearly membership dues were fixed at $1.00 and life membership at $10.00. In 1921 it received appropriation of $1,000 from the county, and in 1922 $1,500 was received from this source. The present officers are as follows: H. L. Brooks, president; Ray Atherson, secretary, and Harry Herman, treasurer. The activities of the society extend over the 10 northern townships of Lincoln County, and the work has done much to stimulate scientific agriculture and to promote community spirit. The project has been successful financially and the society now has $3,500 in its treasury.

Tomahawk Branch of the Lincoln County Chapter, American Red Cross, was organized in 1917 under the leadership of Mr. G. R. Baker. The society maintained an office in the city hall during the war period, and invaluable work was accomplished. Though the organization here is still in existence the only branch now active is the home service section, of which Mrs. H. L. Brooks has been chairman from the beginning. Dr. W.I. Macfarlane is chairman of the

Tomahawk unit, Mrs. G. R. Baker, vice chairman; F. P. Werner, treasurer, and Margaret Gesell, secretary.

Bronsted Post No. 93 of the American Legion at tomahawk was established in 1919; it now has 125 members, and meetings are held in the Forester's Hall. William Nick is commander, Dr. A. R. Houns, vice commander; L. W. Osborne, adjunct, and James Kopplin, financial officer.

BUSINESS & INDUSTRY

The paper mill industry was started in Tomahawk in 1890, when Mr. Newton, of Sparta, and A. M. Pride built a pulp mill on the east side of the river at the dam, and in 1895 a paper mill was added to the plant. Mr. Newton subsequently sold his interests to C. B. Pride of Appleton. A second paper mill was built in 1904 and 1905 at the west end of the dam, and is now known as Mill No. 2 of the Tomahawk Pulp and Paper Co. Anson M. Pride, the founder of these mills, died in 1916 and his interests in them were acquired by his brother, Charles B., who continued their operation, together with that of another pulp mill which is located at the King Dam. The latter dam was constructed by the Bradley Company in 1909 or 1910 about three miles east of the city at a place called King's, owing to the fact that a station or tavern was kept there at an early day by a man named King. The old military road running north to Eagle River and Marquette crossed the river by a ford at this point.

The Tomahawk Pulp & Paper Company was a pioneer in the process of paper manufacturing, using large quantities of old newspaper and wood pulp. During the year 1920 another paper mill was built and styled the Pride Pulp and Paper Company but was in no way a part of Tomahawk Pulp & Paper Company. The Tomahawk Pulp & Paper Company, then manufacturing catalog paper could not supply as much paper to their customers as they consumed and required, and the president of the Tomahawk Pulp & Paper Company, C. B. Pride, agreed to establish another independent paper mill, the company to be called the Pride Pulp & Paper Company, and the mill to be large enough to furnish as much paper as the Montgomery Ward & Company consumed. Montgomery Ward & Company, Seaman Paper Company, and Mr. C. B. Pride agreed to furnish the necessary capital for the development of this new company's plant. This plant was all completed and put into operation a short time after the war was concluded. At that time there was not such a great demand for catalog paper and it was decided to sell the interest of the new Pride Pulp & Paper Company to the Mosinee Paper Company, which was done, and the new company is now styled the Tomahawk Kraft Paper Company, and is no way a part of the Tomahawk Pulp & Paper Company institution, each being entirely independent of each other. The Pride Pulp & Paper Company was incorporated for $700,000 but the investment was increased to about $1,300,000. According to the plans of its builders, the plant was ultimately to represent an investment of $3,500,000, and to include three paper machines, sulphite mills and a ground wood pulp mill. In addition, to derive the power to operate these plants, water power developed from Nigger Island and Grandmother Falls on the Wisconsin River will be used. Neither of these water powers was improved, and the company only installed one paper-machine. These added improvements, which were first intended, are now being made by the new company, which when finished, will make a complete well developed paper manufacturing plant, and the same as was first outlined by the officers of the Pride Pulp & Paper Company.

The Tomahawk Shoe Company was founded April 1, 1913, by J. W. Quance. During the early period of operation infants' shoes exclusively were manufactured July 14, 1913, the business was taken over by a stock company and incorporated at $20,000, with R. B. Tweedy as president, J. W. Froelick, vice president and treasurer; F. P. Werner, secretary and assistant treasurer, and E. C. Mcnaughton, assistant secretary. Mr. Quance received 74 shares of stock in the new concern in return for his previous holdings. On October 20, 1914, H. C. Freeman, James W. McHenry, and F. J. Larkin, all of Milwaukee, purchased a controlling interest in the company, Mr. Freeman becoming president, Mr. McHenry, vice president and treasurer; Mrs. McHenry, assistant secretary, and Martha Piske, secretary. Mr. Freeman withdrew on June 21, 1921, and since that time the officers have been as follows: James W. McHenry, president; W. H. McHenry, vice president; R. T. Reinholdt, treasurer; and A. C. McNaughton, secretary. The industry has grown to very large proportions. On March 11, 1918, the capital stock was increased to $75,000, the citizens of Tomahawk subscribing for the amount of the increase; and on December 5, 1922, another $25,000 was added, making the present capitalization $100,000, of which $50,000 is paid-in stock. In July of 1918 a branch factory was established at Merrill, and the cutting and fitting has since been done there, the uppers being sent to Tomahawk for the bottom and finish work. Metallic-fastened dress and work shoes for boys and men are manufactured. About 900 pairs of shoes are turned out each day. When first established here the company employed only 20 persons and the plant was operated on a part-time basis; now 140 people are given steady employment. The plant is equipped with 200 shoe making machines; the building at Tomahawk contains 13,000 square feet of floor space, and the Merrill plant is a three-story brick building 43 x 75 feet in dimensions. Burt Richey is manager of the Merrill branch, while the Tomahawk plant is under the personal supervision of Mr. McHenry. The product is distributed throughout the central states.

The Tomahawk Steel and Iron Works were established as the Tomahawk Iron Works by Alexander Rodgers, of Muskegon, Michigan, in 1888; the plant erected at the time being located in the milling district. W. H. Bradley became associated with Mr. Rogers a short time later, and the business was conducted by Rogers and Bradley in partnership for a number of years. Shortly after the death of Mr. Bradley, the Bradley estate purchased the entire interest in 1904, and later that year ownership passed from them to William Drever. Mr. Drever had been employed by Mr. Rogers in a shop at Muskegon, and when the latter came here and established the plant he brought Mr. Drever with him as an employee; when the Bradley interests acquired the concern Drever was made manager of the plant, and he continued as such until he purchased the business. In the operation of the plant he associated himself with J. H. Knaggs, a boilermaker who had come to Tomahawk from Wausau in 1889. In 1911, however, Mr. Drever purchased Mr. Knaggs interests and a reorganization of the business was effected; incorporation was carried out under the name of the Tomahawk Steel and Iron Works, with William Drever as president and treasurer, R. E. Ashley of Muskegon as vice president, and J. F. Callan of Tomahawk as secretary. Previous to this reorganization the business had been laboring under a handicap and had often undergone a severe struggle for existence; with the new capital made available by the reorganization, however, a healthy growth began at once, and in the years between 1912 and 1920 the business of the concern was doubled and many improvements were made in the plant and equipment. In 1920 Mr. Callan withdrew, and his interest having been purchased by William G. Bauman of Chicago; the present officers of the company are: William Drever, president and treasurer; William G. Bauman, vice president and general manager; and Lenora Larsen, secretary. April 21, 1921, the company's entire plant was destroyed by fire, the loss amounting to $60,000 on the plant and equipment and $25,000 on work under process of construction or repair in the shop. Nothing daunted by this severe misfortune, however, the concern at once began the erection of a new plant; a site was purchased on Somo Avenue, near the

Chicago, Milwaukee & St. Paul tracks, and the present structure was erected; this is a thoroughly modern plant, of steel and cement construction, furnished throughout with the best equipment obtainable; in it anything in the line of iron work, either machinery or boiler construction, can be carried out with complete efficiency and with the highest quality of workmanship. The building has a frontage on Somo Avenue of 100 feet and a depth of 190 feet; a portion of it is two stories high and the balance one story. The business is one of Tomahawk's leading industries, and the plant is widely known as the largest and best equipped in this entire section of the country. Under normal conditions from 35 to 40 men are given employment.

The Mohr Lumber Company operates the mill which was originally established by W. H. Bradley as the Tomahawk Lumber Company. This plant was sold by the Bradley interests to the Tomahawk Veneer and Box Company, and it passed from the hands of this company to its present owners on October 17, 1916. C. F. Mohr of Portage is President of the company, F. E. Burbach, also of Portage, is vice president; D. Danielson, treasurer, and John S. Griffith, secretary and manager. For the past ten years this company has logged and sawed timber from its holdings, and there are still many thousand feet on its tract near Tomahawk. Their product is chiefly hemlock and hardware lumber. The capacity of the mill is 50,000 feet per day; 75 or 80 men are employed in the mill and a like number in the lumber camps operated by the company. The mill is equipped with a single band saw, two resaws, and one surface planer and matcher. The product has a distribution covering the greater portion of the United States.

The Tomahawk Tannery was established by William H. Bradley in 1903, but was soon afterward taken over by its present owners, the Union Tannery Company of New York. The plant was destroyed by fire in 1906, but was rebuilt by its present owners in 1907-08. The building is 64 x 560 feet in dimensions, and the industry is an extensive one; 80 to 120 people are employed here. The product, which is sole leather tanned from cow hides, is sold chiefly in St. Louis and Chicago; the hides are shipped in from points as far as South America. Both electric and steam power is used, and there are six rolling, fleshing, and hairing machines and two riggers.

Tannery Crew

The Union Tannery crew posed for this photo in front of the office in 1922. The tannery, on the Tomahawk River in "Jersey City," burned in 1928.

The Tomahawk Leader, Spec. Suppl. July 2, 1986

The Tomahawk Creamery was established by Godfrey and Sons, who conducted it for a number of years subsequently. A co-operative association of farmers then purchased it and operated it for four years, after which it was taken over by Art Searl. It passed from Mr. Searl to its present owner, Anton Nerli, but it has been built up by him into a first-class plant, and he is operating it along modern lines. During the flush of the season the creamery has as many as 150 patrons and buys nearly 400 gallons of cream per day; in the summer of 1922 the weekly output of butter sometimes ran as high as five or six thousand pounds, and during the winter it was about two thousand pounds. In

1923 facilities for the manufacture of ice cream were added to the other equipment, an expert ice cream maker being brought from the Sessions Ice Cream Manufacturing Company at Fond du Lac to take charge of this branch of the work. The ice cream manufacturing equipment consists of a homogenizer for breaking up the fat and combining it with the solids, a glass-lined holding vat to age the mix, and a hardening room with a capacity of 500 gallons.

The Raymond Lumber Company operates its sawmill erected by King and Weymouth in 1888, the first sawmill to be built in Tomahawk. Mark L. Raymond is the proprietor, and offices are maintained in the Mitchell Hotel. Besides conducting the mill, in which lumber and lath are manufactured, the company buys standing timber and logs it off, supplying logs to the mills at Merrill and other points.

The feed mill conducted by Art Searl and Co. was established by Mr. Searl February 1, 1920. The mill has a capacity of 10 tons daily and grinds all kinds of feed for stock and poultry. A wholesale and retail flour, feed and hay business is conducted in conjunction with the mill. Five men are employed, and delivery service is furnished by means of a three-ton truck.

The Emerich Mercantile Company is conducting a fine store in Tomahawk which is a branch of a similar institution in Merrill. The officers of the company are: J. A. Emerich, of Merrill, president; Emil C. Keipke, of Merrill, vice president; Lyndon B. Emerich, of Merrill, secretary and treasurer; and Erwin R. Emerich, of Tomahawk, manager of the Tomahawk, branch. From the parent store in Merrill, Lyndon B. and Erwin R. Emerich, sons of the president of the company, used to visit Tomahawk and the smaller towns and summer resorts of this section, carrying selected articles of stock in trunks, from which they sold. They enjoyed good trade and from their two or three season's experience became convinced that at Tomahawk a successful business could be established. In keeping with this idea, on February 28, 1921, the company opened a branch store in this city, beginning in a small way in the Mitchell building, which has a corner location. From the very start the venture was successful and the business grew so rapidly that in the spring of 1922 the company decided that larger quarters were necessary. Accordingly they bought a lot on West Wisconsin Avenue and in that year erected a strictly modern store building, one of the best in the city. It has two stories, with a front of 25 feet and a depth of 100 feet. Early in November 1922, the company moved into it and the business has since enjoyed a steady and healthy growth. They carry an up to date stock of dry goods, ladies ready-to-wear, ladies and gents clothing, furnishings, phonographs, records, and many other things, seeking to supply the best of everything for which there is a reasonable demand and to do so at a price that will appeal to the buyer.

Woodworking and sawmill activities was conducted by Robert Gillie in 1910 producing doors, frames and sashes.

BANKS

The Bank of Tomahawk was established as a private institution in 1895 by Charles E. Macomber, who was then engaged in the drug business at 124 West Wisconsin Avenue. The bank was conducted by Mr. Macomber at the same location as his previous business until 1904, in which year it was incorporated under the banking laws of Wisconsin and the present two-story brick building at 201 West Wisconsin Avenue was erected. The first officers were: C. E. Macomber, president; J. A. Fitzgerald, vice president; E. W. Smith, cashier; G. M. Macomber, assistant cashier,; directors, C. E. Macomber, J. A. Fitzgerald, M. L. Fitzgerald, Edward Evenson, S. C. Jones, James Kelly, and Joseph Poutre. The capitalization was at $10,000. The bank has had a most successful career; its present deposits are $400,000, and the accounts of 1,000 depositors are carried. The capital has been raised to $30,000, and the surplus and undivided earnings now amount to $19,500. The bank is the depository for the city's funds and also carries funds of the town, county and state. The present officers are: C. E. Macomber, president; J. A. Fitzgerald, vice president; Edgar Welfley, cashier; Balnor Nelson, assistant cashier. These officers with Edward McDonald, Joseph Poutre, Edw. Evenson, and D. C. Jones, constitute the Board of Directors. Miss Helen Johnson is bookkeeper. The steady, healthy growth which this bank has had during the entire quarter century and more of its existence says much for the soundness of its financial policies.

The Bradley Bank was first established as a private bank by William H. and James W. Bradley when Tomahawk was little more than a clearing in the woods. Business was begun in a small wooden structure at the northeast corner of Tomahawk and Wisconsin Avenues; this was replaced in 1900 by a substantial brick building, and on January 15, 1923 the bank was removed to its present beautiful quarters, which had been erected during 1922 to accommodate the needs of the rapidly growing institution. The change from private ownership to incorporation was carried out in 1903, the capitalization being fixed at $50,000 and the first officers being as follows: J. W. Bradley, president; R. B. Tweedy, vice president; and J. W. Froelich, cashier. This arrangement continued until 1912, when the Bradley interests were acquired by local capital and reorganization was effected with J. W. Froelich, as president, C. H. Grundy, vice president, F. P. Werner, cashier, and Katherine Veitch, assistant cashier. In 1917 Mr. Froelich resigned and moved to California, owing to ill health, and subsequently until 1921 the personnel was as follows: C. H. Grundy, president; F. P. Werner, vice president; Katherine Veitch, cashier; and J. L. Eckstrum was then made cashier, with P.M Smith as assistant cashier. No further changes have been made in the personnel; the present board of directors consists of W. E. Brooks, Dr. J. D. Cutter, C. B. Pride, John Oelhafen, and V. E. Labbe, and the capitalization is now $60,000, the change in the latter having been made in 1922. The resources have increased from $300,000 in 1903 to nearly $1,000,000 at the present time, and the institution has enjoyed a steady and thoroughly satisfactory growth in all the branches of its activity. The present home of the bank is one of the most finely constructed and beautiful buildings in this section of the country. It is located at the corner of Tomahawk and Wisconsin Avenues, directly across the latter thoroughfare from the previous quarters, and is constructed of tapestry brick with Bedford stone trimmings. It is single story with basement, and has a frontage of 50 feet and a depth on Tomahawk Avenue of 66 feet. The interior is beautifully decorated and finished, the counters of mahogany finish. The steel equipment is of the best and most modern, York safe and lock equipment being used. There are three vaults, one used as a repository by the bank, one containing safety deposit boxes for the accommodation of the patrons, and one for the safe keeping of the books and records of the institution. In the basement a large and commodious room has been finished and furnished as an audience room for the use of agricultural organizations and for other public gatherings. The architectural design of the entire structure is excellent in every detail, and the building commands the full admiration of the beholder.

Bank of Tomahawk Building (1904).
201 W. Wisconsin Avenue, Tomahawk, Wisconsin.
Photo and reproduction June 30, 2002; ©Lynn Scheller.

(Courtesy of the Tomahawk Historical Society.)

SCHOOLS

The excellence of the school system is particularly noteworthy. Attention was directed to this important feature at a very early date in the city's history, a school house being erected at the corner of Washington Avenue and Fifth Street in the spring of 1888; school was opened in this building with Miss Maud Tyner as the first teacher. The building is still standing and is now being used as a kindergarten. Larger quarters were soon required to meet the needs of the rapidly growing city, and the Whittier school at the east end of Wisconsin Avenue was built, opening its doors in the fall of 1894. High school subjects were taught in the new school, and in 1896 it was made an accredited high school through the efforts of its principal, Julian West. The first commencement exercises were held on Friday evening, June 4, 1897; there were seven in the first graduating class as follows: Alta Olson, now Mrs. F. P. Werner of Tomahawk; Violet E. McMurphy, now Mrs. J. H. Floyd, also of Tomahawk; Anna Oelhafen, who is now Mrs. Siems of Wausau; Mary Marshall, deceased; Margaret Mcbride, who is now in New York City and is a prominent vocalist; Louis Bohn, an official of a large Western railroad; and Lester Clark, who is very prominent in newspaper work in Portland, Oregon. Under the first city charter, the school board, consisting of a superintendent and four members, one member from each ward, was elected at the spring elections. The first school board consisted of the following: Dr. J. D. Cutter, superintendent; Henry R. Bradley, member from first ward;

Frank A. Larsen, member from second ward; William L. Marshall, member from third ward; and Adam Thrim, member from fourth ward. John O'Connell, now of Washington D. C., was principal at the time the city schools were organized; following his resignation W. H. Crowley, now a civil engineer living in Denver, was elected, and under his management for three years the schools attained a high standing. Dr. Cutter was subsequently superintendent for four years, and he was followed by Oscar M. Smith. After the Whittier, the Longfellow, also called "Swamp School" was the next to be opened on Merrill Avenue. It was turned into a vocational school after WWII when it became too crowded. One or two other buildings were used at various times to relieve congestion, one of these being an old store building which stood across the street from the Whittier school. The present high school building "Washington School" was erected in 1907 and cares for the sixth and seventh grades in addition to the four years of high school work. It is a large and thoroughly modern brick structure, one of the finest school buildings in the county, and brings Tomahawk's educational facilities to a point of development of which she can well be proud. Frederick Elk is the present superintendent. During the school year of 1922-23 there were 210 students enrolled in the high school and approximately 500 in the grades; 10 high school teachers and 14 grade school teachers were employed. Washington School was destroyed by fire in 1978. The decision to consolidate and close the rural schools occurred over time, which moved all the children to one central location. The most recent Tomahawk School complex was constructed on Kings Road, first as a high school in 1958, with subsequent additions, junior high and elementary added over the years.

Whittier was first high school.

Washington School, built in 1909, burned in 1978.

The Tomahawk Leader, Special Supplement, July 2, 1986

LODGING

In the early days of Tomahawk, the Somo and Windsor House existed. By 1893, W. H. Bradley had erected the Mitchell Hotel named after his friend from Milwaukee, Alexander Mitchell. This 142 foot structure had three floors that housed 72 bedrooms and suites, an elegant lobby with winding staircase, six fireplaces, reception and reading rooms, dining rooms, a saloon, bowling alley, barbershop, parlors, bandstand and spectator area. Its guests enjoyed all of the latest conveniences including transportation from the railroad, electricity, running water, a sewage system, fire protection, the first telephone operations, and heat supplied by the same steam plant servicing the Irving Hotel, Standard Mercantile, Bradley Bank, Northern Hardware, and a steam laundry, all of which were owned by Mr. Bradley. Both the Mitchell and Irving were operated under Tomahawk Hotel Co. In 1929, the beautiful Mitchell Hotel landmark went up in flames, spreading so quickly that nothing could be saved. Tobin Hotel on Railway Street became popular after the Mitchell burned. It was operated by John and Mary Tobin, then later by William and Christina Hemminger.

Looking Back—About 1890

It took plenty of scaffolding to construct Tomahawk's famous Mitchell Hotel. It was built about 1890 by W.H. Bradley at a cost of about $85,000. It was not entirely completed for five years. The hotel burned in March, 1929, in the city's most famous fire. Construction photo courtesy Tomahawk Public Library. Fire photo submitted by Mel Farrand of Tomahawk.

Mitchell Hotel was Tomahawk showplace.

The Tomahawk Leader, Special Supplement, July 2, 1986

(Courtesy of the Tomahawk Historical Society)

ARRIVALS AT THE MITCHELL.

Chas. Inman, Merrill; E. H. Beardsley, Chicago; Walt. McNall, St. Louis; F. Garrison, Centralia; T. E. Nash, Nekossa; Paul Filzen, Osceola; B. Godkin, Bay City; A. Allen, Portage; H. E. Salsich, Hartland; John O'Day, H. H. Foster, J. Lander, Merrill; Frank E. Case, Fond du Lac; W. H. Nickey, Milwaukee; Wm. B. Rose, Chicago; Fred Borngesser, Minneapolis; W. J. Ennis, L. Spangenberg, Milwaukee; W. W. Kings, Frankfort, Ind.; A. G. Cook, McKenna; D. A. Root, Indiana; Louis Freid, John Daly, A. H. Stange, Merrill; T. N. Ferris, Cleveland; C. J. DeJean, La Crosse; W. E. Weatherby, C. E. Reese, Chicago; Louis Glasser, Milwaukee; Mrs. F. M. Allen, Chicago; H. W. Rice, Duluth; G. Young, Merrill; E. J. Miller, Oshkosh; Wm. Latta, Evenston; W. H. Williams, R. J. Code, F. D. Irish, Milwaukee; J. H. Battin, Wausau; M. Hunter, Milwaukee; A. A. Brooks, Eau Claire; T. C. Keith, Chicago; J. E. Harrod, New York; Julius Block, Buffalo, N. Y.; T. E. Keefe, Chicago; J. E. Harrod, Yonken, N. Y.; W. W. Smith, Sparta; Will Smith, Milwaukee; R. P. Manson, Jr., A. N. Secord, Wausau; W. H. Miller, Duluth; S. R. Boyar, Milwaukee; T. R. Lacy, Geo. J. Stevens, Minneapolis; A. N. Montgomery, Grand Rapids, Mich.; D. J. Shea, Sam Dunn, Merrill; R. R. Minturn, Tomah; Thos. J. Anketell, Merrill.

Last Sunday's Dinner Bill at the Mitchell.

Caviar on Toast

Cream of Chicken   English Mutton Broth

Celery

Fried Whitefish, Tartare Sauce

Olives   Chow Chow   Pickles

Boiled Ham, Tomato Sauce

Roast Beef, Drip Gravy

Roast Turkey, Oyster Stuffing

Roast Breast of Lamb, Browned Potatoes

Mashed Potatoes   Boiled Potatoes

Sweet Bread Patties

Fricassee of Chicken

Apple Dumplings { Hard Sauce / Wine Sauce }

Stewed Corn

Green Peas   Stewed Carrots

Lemon Sherbet

Assorted Cake   Confect   Lady Fingers

Apple Pie   Raspberry Pie

Coffee Jelly, Vanilla Cream

Oranges   Apples   Bananas

Mixed Nuts

American and Brick Cheese   Jersey Toast

Tea   Coffee   Milk

Fresh Butter Milk

A list of recent arrivals at the Mitchell, as well as dinner menus were routinely published in *The Tomahawk.* c. 1904

CITY DIRECTORIES

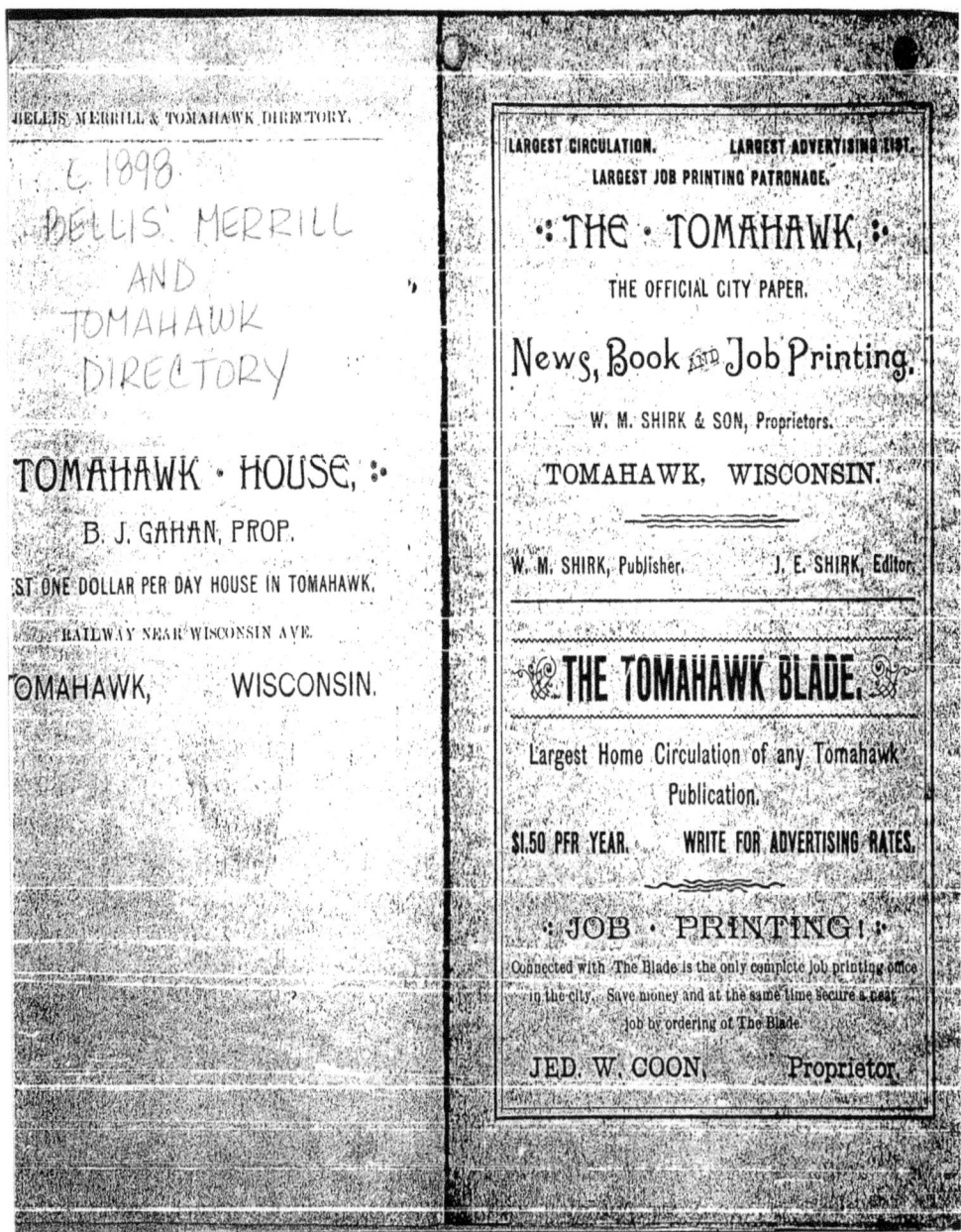

Bellis' Merrill and Tomahawk City Directory c. 1898

BANKS.

W. H. & J. W. BRADLEY BANK.—Incorporated 1890, capital, $50,000. W. H. Bradley, president; John Oelhafen, vice-president; George G. Williams, cashier; n e cor Tomahawk and Wisconsin ave.

CHURCHES.

BAPTIST.

FIRST BAPTIST CHURCH.—Stewarts Hall. Rev. L. P. Russell, pastor. Sunday services, 10:30 A. M. and 7:30 P. M.; Sunday school, 12 M. Weekly meeting, 7:30 P. M.

CONGREGATIONAL.

CONGREGATIONAL.—Fifth cor Washington ave. Rev. W. M. Ellis, pastor; Sunday services, 10:30 A. M. and 7:30 P. M.; Sunday school 12 M.

GERMAN EVANGELICAL.

GERMAN EVANGELICAL CHRIST'S.—Washington ave cor Third. Rev. E. Ortmann, pastor, Sunday services, 10:30 A. M. and 7:30 P. M.; Sunday school, 12 M.

GERMAN LUTHERAN.

GERMAN LUTHERAN.—Third cor Washington.

METHODIST EPISCOPAL.

METHODIST EPISCOPAL.—Somo ave cor Third. Rev. H. L. Williams, pastor. Sunday services, 10:30 A. M. and 7:30 P. M.; Sunday school 12 M.

ROMAN CATHOLIC.

ST. MARY'S.—Rev. Chas. Hoogsteel, pastor; Fifth nr Spirit. Sunday services, 9:30 A. M.; Vespers, 3:30; Sunday school, 2 P. M.; Rev. C. Hoogsteel, superintendent.

INCORPORATED COMPANIES.

FARMERS LUMBER CO.—Incorporated 1890; capital, $50,000; W. H. Bradley, president and treasurer; J. W. Bradley, vice-president; H. R. Bradley, secretary.

TOMAHAWK HOTEL CO.—Incorporated, 1890; capital, $25,000; W. H. Bradley, president and treasurer; H. R. Bradley, secretary.

TOMAHAWK LUMBER CO.—Incorporated 1887; capital, $600,000; W. H. Bradley, president; Hamilton E. Salsich, vice-president; Henry R. Bradley, treasurer; Frank G. Stark, secretary.

TOMAHAWK REAL ESTATE AND INVESTMENT CO.—Incorporated, Jan. 1891; capital, $5,000. A. J. Olson, president; H. A. Atcherson, vice-president; F. A. Larson, secretary; C. W. Burrington, treasurer.

UNITED STATES LUMBER CO.—W. H. Bradley, president and treasurer; Josh Stark, vice-president; H. R. Bradley, secretary. Capital, $350,000, organized 1889.

NEWSPAPERS.

THE TOMAHAWK.—Tomahawk ave. Established, 1887. W. M. Shirk & Son, pubr's and propr's. Democrat. Subscription, $1.50 a year.

THE TOMAHAWK BLADE.—Jed W. Coon, editor and proprietor. Established 1887. Republican. Weekly. Terms, $1.50 per year.

BAPTIST.

BAPTIST CHURCH.—L. P. Russell, pastor. Services at Stewarts Hall. Sunday 10:30 A. M. and 7:30 P. M. Sunday school 12 M. Y. P. S. C. E. Baptist's Union 6:30 P. M. Week day meetings Thursday 7:30 P. M.

OPERA HOUSES.

MCBRIDES HALL.—James McBride, propr. Seating capacity 500. Stage, etc.

POSTOFFICE.

Wisconsin nr Tomahawk ave. F. A. Larson, postmaster. Mail daily. Office hours: 8 A. M. to 8 P. M.

PUBLIC LIBRARIES.

TOMAHAWK LIBRARY ASSOCIATION.—Wisconsin ave. Opens, evenings only, 7:00 P. M. to 10:00 P. M. W. F. Daubenberger, president; Miss Rube Brown, secretary; George G. Williams, treasurer. Directors: G. G. Williams, W. F. Daubenberger, Dr. J. D. Cutter, F. G. Stark, H. R. Bradley, Milo Woodberry, A. M. Pride, Mrs. W. L. Marshall, Miss Rube Brown.

RAILROADS.

CHICAGO MILWAUKEE & ST PAUL RAILWAY.—Depot foot of Wisconsin ave.

WISCONSIN AND CHIPPEWA RAILWAY CO.—W. H. Bradley, president; H. R. Bradley, vice-president; F. G. Stark, secretary and treasurer; W. E. Jeannot, superintendent. Organized 1891, capital $100,000.

SCHOOL BOARD.

SCHOOL BOARD.—N. P. Hatch, president; John Laudry, vice-president; J. W. Coon, M. D., secretary; H. P. Hatch, John Landry, Frank Delonay, O. B. Jourdan, P. O'Neill and W. B. Gilsdorf, directors.

SCHOOLS—PUBLIC.

TOMAHAWK GERMAN SCHOOL.—W. H. Crowley, principal; Miss Annie Vandercook, Miss Rube M. Brower.

TOMAHAWK PRIMARY SCHOOL.—Miss Gertrude Wood and Lulu Dwyer, Miss Vennie Searls, Miss Lois O. Quimby.

SOCIETIES.

A. F. AND A. M.

TOMAHAWK LODGE No. 243.—Meets first and third Saturday of each month at Winegards Hall.—A. Jolson, W. M.; E. W. Whitson, S. W.; Geo. McClellan, J. W.; P. Samphier, secretary.

C. K. OF W.

CATHOLIC KNIGHTS OF WIS.—Tomahawk Branch, meets first of each month. John Maloney, president; R. J. Dawson, secretary; James Kelly, treasurer.

I. O. O. F.

TOMAHAWK LODGE No. 155, I. O. O. F.—Meets every Thursday evening, at Winegard's Hall, J. P. Williams, Noble Grand; R. Koplin, recording secretary.

MISCELLANEOUS.

LADIES' AID SOCIETY OF CONGREGATIONAL CHURCH.—Meets every second Thursday of each month at different houses. Mrs. W. L. Marshall, president; Mrs. W. M. Ellis, secretary; Mrs. J. W. Coon, treasurer.

WISCONSIN HUMANE SOCIETY, TOMAHAWK BRANCH.—Organized 1890; A. H. Woodsworth, president; F. G. Stark, secretary and treasurer; Miss Rube Brower, ass't secretary.

Y. P. S. C. E. OF CONGREGATIONAL CHURCH.—Conducted by the young people of the church. Meets Sunday evenings, 6:45 at church.

Y. P. S. C. E. OF METHODIST EPISCOPAL CHURCH.—Conducted by the young people of the church.

STAGE LINE.

From Tomahawk to Harrison daily, Sundays excepted. A. Boquette, propr.

BELLIS' BUSINESS · DIRECTORY
OF THE
BUSINESS AND PROFESSIONAL MEN
OF MERRILL AND TOMAHAWK.

ABSTRACTS OF TITLE.

Merrill Law, Loan & Real Estate Ass'n, Mill cor Main,   Merrill

AGENTS—COLLECTION.

ALLEN H. R., 310 w Main,	W Merrill
ANDERSON J. P., 303 w Main,	W Merrill
BUMP E. L., 914 Main,	Merrill
CURTIS CURTIS & REID, 1012 Main,	Merrill
FLEET & PORTER, 916 Main,	Merrill
HELMS A. A., 1014 Main,	Merrill
HETZEL H. C., Main cor Poplar,	Merrill
HOYT S. M., Main cor Poplar,	Merrill
WOODBURY MILO, Wisconsin ave nr Second,	Tomahawk
WOODWORTH A. H.,	Tomahawk

AGENTS—INSURANCE.

ALLEN H. R., 310 w Main,	W Merrill
BABCOCK J. R. & CO., 904 Main	Merrill
Bruce J. W., 702 Third,	Merrill
Coon James, 901 Main,	Merrill
MARSHALL W. L., Wisconsin ave nr Tomahawk,	Tomahawk
Werden F. O., Wisconsin ave nr Second,	Tomahawk

AGENTS—LOAN.

ALLEN H. R., 310 w Main,	W Merrill
CURTIS, CURTIS & REID, 1012 Main.	Merrill
FLEET & PORTER, 916 Main,	Merrill
HEINEMANN SIGMOND, Heinemann's new block,	Merrill
HETZEL H. C., Main cor Poplar,	Merrill
WOODBURY MILO,	Tomahawk
WOODWORTH A. H.,	Tomahawk

AGENTS—PENSION.

ALLEN H. R., 310 w Main,	W Merrill

Bellis' Merrill and Tomahawk City Directory c. 1898

ARTISTS MATERIALS.

KALTENBORN R. V., Poplar bet Main and First,	Merrill
STEWART W. D., 315 w Main	W Merrill

BAKERS.

Ballsurmider W., Grand ave,	W Merrill
BOLTZ G. M., 808 First,	Merrill
BOYER MARY MRS., 1005 Main,	Merrill
Meunier J. N., Wisconsin ave nr Railway,	Tomahawk
Walters G., 401 w Main,	W. Merrill

BARBERS.

Empey A. E., w Main cor Prospect,	W Merrill
Empey A. O., 1031 Main,	Merrill
Goodnough L. D.,	Tomahawk
Hellman Ed., 904 Main,	Merrill
King A. C., 1003 Main,	Merrill
Langsdorf Fred, Grand ave cor Genesee,	W Merrill
Lincoln E., Wisconsin ave nr Tomahawk ave,	Tomahawk

BILLIARDS AND POOL.

Brassard Wm., Mill cor First,	Merrill
Ebert O., 905 Grand ave,	W Merrill
LANGE ERNST, Grand ave nr Prospect,	W Merrill
Smith W. G., Second opp C. M. & St. P. Ry. depot,	Merrill

BLACKSMITHS AND WAGON MAKERS.

Broderson & Donner, First, 6th w,	W Merrill
CHRISTY T., Grand ave nr Liberty,	W Merrill
Fleishfresser A., Grand ave cor Genesee,	W Merrill
KOEHLER G. F., Centre ave cor River,	Merrill
Larson Martin, Centre ave cor River,	Merrill
Zamzow Chas. A., Main nr Stuyvesant,	Merrill
Zochert W. R.,	Tomahawk

BOOKSELLERS AND STATIONERS.

CONNERS WILLIAM M., 906 and 919 Main,	Merrill
Felker Gus. A., 402 w Main,	W Merrill
Hillyer L. H., 303 w Main,	W Merrill
Larson F. A.,	Tomahawk
Macomber C. E., Wisconsin ave,	Tomahawk
NORWAY C. A. & CO., 914 Main,	Merrill
Rice J. C., Grand ave cor Prospect,	W Merrill

BOOT AND SHOE DEALERS.

Frank S., 318 w Main	W Merrill
Gerhard C., 812 First	Merrill
Kingsley R. C., 1310 Main,	Merrill
LA CHANCE L. & CO., 1111 Main,	Merrill
Livingston Mentle Co.,	Merrill
Newburg G. O., Wisconsin ave,	Tomahawk
O'ROURK & LEARY, 319 w Main,	W. Merrill
Shafer F. N., 1016 Main,	Merrill
Sukow A., Grand ave,	W Merrill
Runge A. J., 309 Grand ave,	W Merrill
RUNGE FRED J., 1313 Main,	Merrill
WEINFELD & WOLFF, Heluemanns new block,	Merrill
Wertheimer & Son, 908 Main,	Merrill

BOOT AND SHOE MAKERS.

Gaiten J., mill nr First,	Merrill
Lanctot P., 812 First,	Merrill
McCutcheon W. H.,	Tomahawk
Runge A. J., 309 Grand ave,	W Merrill
RUNGE FRED J., 1313 Main,	Merrill
Willett A.,	Tomahawk

BOX MANUFACTURERS.

TOMAHAWK LUMBER CO.,	Tomahawk

BREWERS AND MALSTERS.

RUDER GEO. BREWING CO., River cor Nast	Merrill
RUDER GEO. BREWING CO.,	Tomahawk

BUILDERS HARDWARE.

EVENSON BROS.,	Tomahawk
FEHLAND H. R. & CO., 1212 Main,	Merrill
Montgomery F. M., 309 w Main,	W Merrill
OLSON A. J.,	Tomahawk

CIGAR MANUFACTURERS.

AYERS C. A.,	Tomahawk
Bolotzerkowski M., Grand ave,	W Merrill
Neubauer C., 1312 Main,	Merrill
SCHOENERARG H., Mill opp Lincoln House,	Merrill

CIGARS AND TOBACCO.

Allen E. R., Grand ave nr Prospect,	W Merrill
CONNERS W. M., 906-910 Main,	Merrill
Foote C., Wisconsin ave nr Second,	Tomahawk
Foster P., 307 w Main,	W Merrill
Hyman Bros., Main nr Mill,	Merrill
LANGE BROS., Grand ave nr Ellis Court,	W Merrill
SCHOENEBERG H., Mill opp Lincoln House,	Merrill

CLOTHING.

Frank S., 318 w Main,	W Merrill
HOWEN & FLEMING,	Tomahawk
La Chance L. & Co., 1111 Main,	Merrill
LIVINGSTON MERCHANTILE CO., Main nr Poplar,	Merrill
Nissenbaum J.,	Tomahawk
O'Rourk & Leary, 319 w Main,	W Merrill
Shafer P. X., 1016 Main,	Merrill
Stein A. M., 920 Main,	Merrill
WEINFELD & WOLFF, Heinemann new block,	Merrill

CONFECTIONERS.

Allen Mrs., 315 Grand ave,	W Merrill
Allen F. R., Grand ave nr Prospect ave,	W Merrill
Ballshmider W., Grand ave,	W Merrill
BOLTZ G., 808 First,	Merrill
BOYER MARY R. MRS., 1005 Main,	Merrill
CONNERS W. M., 906 and 919 Main,	Merrill
Dufrane S., Grand ave nr the bridge,	W Merrill
Foster Perry, 309 w Main,	W Merrill
Fuller H. M. Mrs., Park nr Main,	Merrill
Merryfield F., Main nr First, 6th w,	W Merrill
O'Neil A. L., 908 Main,	Merrill
Protteau George, First cor Polk,	Merrill
Rice J. C., Grand ave cor Prospect,	W Merrill
Walker William, 504 w Main,	W Merrill
Walters G., 101 w Main,	W Merrill

CONTRACTORS AND BUILDERS.

Barber A. H., Division cor Alley,	W Merrill
Clark F. H., Seventh nr Spruce,	Merrill
DeVall T., Centre ave cor First,	Merrill
Duteau Pires 209 Cottage,	W Merrill
Heekman H., 800 Cotter, 6th w,	W Merrill
House E. H., 811 Main,	Merrill
VanRuedin J., River nr Fifth,	Merrill

CROCKERY.

Collie C. J., Grand ave nr Prospect ave	W Merrill
HOWEN & FLEMING,	Tomahawk
Kingsley R. G., 1319 Main,	Merrill
PUARIEAU T., 420 w Main,	W Merrill
Wiley R. A. & Co., 910 Main,	Merrill
WILSON & LICKEL, 317 w Main,	W Merrill
Zastrow F. J., 303 w Main,	W Merrill

DENTISTS.

Barber C. C., 914 Main, up stairs,	Merrill
Burger B. E., Main cor Mill,	Merrill
Ramsey J. H.,	Tomahawk
VAN NOSTRAND W. S., Main cor Court,	Merrill

DRAYMEN.

Sweet Geo. W., 1206 Main,	Merrill
Sweet John, Cleveland nr Fifth,	Merrill
West L., Prospect nr Main,	W Merrill

DRESSMAKERS.

Chamberlain L. Mrs., 508 Eighth,	Merrill
Halverson E. Miss, 409 w Main,	W Merrill
White M. Miss,	Tomahawk

DRUGGISTS.

Felker Gus. A., 402 w Main,	W Merrill
Heath D. P.,	Tomahawk
Hillyer F. H., 303 w Main,	W Merrill
King E. S., 1014 Main,	Merrill
Macomber C. E.,	Tomahawk
NORWAY C. A., 914 Main,	Merrill
Wakelin E. S., Main cor Court,	Merrill

DRY GOODS.

Angebeck J. C., First cor Main, 6th w,	W Merrill
Frank S., 318 w Main,	W Merrill
HOWEN & FLEMING,	Tomahawk
Kingsley R. G., 1317 Main,	Merrill
LA CHANCE L. & CO., 1109 and 1111 Main,	Merrill
LIVINGSTON MERCHANTILE CO., Main nr Poplar,	Merrill
Olchafen J.,	Tomahawk
O'Rourk & Leary, 319 w Main,	W Merrill

FANCY AND TOILET ARTICLES.

Felker Gus. A., 402 w Main,	W Merrill
Hillyer F. H., 303 w Main,	W Merrill
King E. S., 1014 Main,	Merrill
Nourse L. C. Mrs.,	Tomahawk
Roller E.,	Tomahawk
Wakelin E. S., Main cor Court,	Merrill

FLOURING MILLS.

Lincoln County Flour Mill, south side,	Merrill

Bellis' Merrill and Tomahawk City Directory c. 1898

FLOUR AND FEED.

Brodersen J., Water nr First, 6th w,	W Merrill
Jaeger A. & Co., 1014 Main,	Merrill
LA CHANCE & CO., 1111 Main,	Merrill
PUARIEA U. J., 420 w Main,	W Merrill
WILSON & LICKEL, 317 w Main,	W Merrill
Zastrow E. F., 303 Grand ave,	W Merrill

FURNITURE.

Clark K. E., Mrs., Wisconsin ave nr Second,	Tomahawk
Grace W. W. & Co., Park cor Main,	Merrill
HANKWITZ F., 110 Prospect,	W Merrill
LITTLEJOHN H., 815-817 Main,	Merrill

GENERAL MERCHANDISE.

BYINGTON O. E., 918 Main,	Merrill
Goodman S.,	Tomahawk
HOWEN & FLEMING,	Tomahawk
LA CHANCE L. & CO., 1111 Main,	Merrill
Lambert J. E. & Co., 1217 Main,	Merrill
LIVINGSTON MERCHANTILE CO., Main,	Merrill
Oelhafen John,	Tomahawk
Roller E.,	Tomahawk
Thune Adam,	Tomahawk
Whitson E. W. & Co.,	Tomahawk

GENTS FURNISHING GOODS.

Frank S., 318 w Main,	W Merrill
Nissenbaum J.,	Tomahawk
O'Rourk & Leary, 310 w Main,	W Merrill
Stein A. M., 920 Main,	Merrill

GROCERS.

Barker B. H., 6th w,	W Merrill
Collie B. J., Grand ave nr Prospect,	W Merrill
Foote C.,	Tomahawk
Gerzon & Korth, Mill nr Main,	Merrill
HOWEN & FLEMING,	Tomahawk
Jaeger A. & Co., 1014 Main,	Merrill
Kingsley R. G., 1317 Main,	Merrill
LA CHANCE L. & CO., 1111 Main,	Merrill
Oelhafen J.,	Tomahawk
O'Neill A. L., 608 Main,	Merrill
Marcouille Phillip,	Tomahawk
PUARIEA U. J., 420 w Main,	W Merrill

Roller E.,	Tomahawk
Rothlisberg J., Main nr Second, 6th w,	W Merrill
Soli J. H.,	Tomahawk
Whitson E. W. & Co.,	Tomahawk
Wiley R. A. & Co., 916 Main,	Merrill
WILSON & LICKEL, 317 w Main,	W Merrill
Zastrow E. F., 303 Grand ave,	W Merrill
Zipp Bros., 710 Second,	Merrill

HARDWARE AND CUTLERY.

FEHLAND H. R. & CO., Main cor Park,	Merrill
Luedke L., Centre ave nr Main,	Merrill
Montgomery F. M., 309 w Main,	W Merrill
OLSON A. J.,	Tomahawk
WEISS HARDWARE CO., Willard Block,	Merrill
Wenzel G. & Co., 314 Grand,	W Merrill

HARNESSMAKERS.

Davidson J. H., 415 w Main,	W Merrill
Kimball B. R. & Co., 1204 Main,	Merrill
RUNGE F. J., 1315 Main,	Merrill
Stinzi R. J.,	Tomahawk

HATS AND CAPS.

HOWEN & FLEMING,	Tomahawk
Kingsley R. G., 1317 Main,	Merrill
LA CHANCE L. & CO., 1111 Main,	Merrill
Shafer F. N., 1016 Main,	Merrill
WEINFELD & WOLFF, Heinimann's new block,	Merrill

HOTELS.

City House, First cor Scott, (rates $1.00 per day)	Merrill
Harrison House, (rates $1.00 per day),	Tomahawk
Hollis House, 1304 Main, (rates $1.00 per day),	Merrill
IRVING (THE), (rates $2.00 per day),	Tomahawk
Kollock House,	Merrill
LAKESIDE HOTEL, (rates $2.00 per day)	Tomahawk
LINCOLN HOUSE, Mill cor Main, (rates $2.00 per day),	Merrill
Minneapolis House,	Tomahawk
MITCHELL (THE),	Tomahawk
Montreal House,	Tomahawk
Montreal House, Mill cor First,	Merrill
Parker House, Prospect nr Grand ave, (rates 1:00 per day)	W Merrill
Paul Peter,	Tomahawk
Rymond Joseph,	Tomahawk
Thatcher House, 412-414 w Main, (rates $1.00 per day),	W Merrill
Wolf River House,	Tomahawk

IRON AND STEEL.

FEHLAND H. R. & Co., 1221 Main,	Merrill

JUSTICES OF THE PEACE.

Gothia C. H., Ellis Court,	W Merrill
MARSHALL W. L.,	Tomahawk
Sanfear Peter,	Tomahawk
Townsend C. C., Sixth,	W Merrill
White O. P.,	Tomahawk

LAUNDRIES.

Boyer G. W., 100 Grand ave,	W Merrill
Morley Mary Mrs., 807 Main,	Merrill
Yep Sam, 1012 Main,	Merrill

LAWYERS.

ANDERSON J. P., 303 w Main,	W Merrill
BUMP E. L., 914 Main,	Merrill
CURTIS, CURTIS & REID, 1012 Main,	Merrill
FLEET & PORTER, 916 Main,	Merrill
HELMS A. A., 1014 Main,	Merrill
HETZEL H. C., Main cor Poplar,	Merrill
HOYT S. M., Main cor Poplar,	Merrill
VAN HECKE J., Mill cor Main,	Merrill
WOODBURY MILO,	Tomahawk
WOODWORTH A. H.,	Tomahawk

LIME AND CEMENT.

KALTENBORN R. V., Poplar bet Main and First,	Merrill
STEWART W. D., 315 w Main,	W Merrill

LIVERY, SALE AND EXCHANGE STABLES.

SCOTT J. W., Park nr River,	Merrill
Goetsch & Kiepke, Prospect cor Merrill,	W Merrill
Hilderbrand L.,	Tomahawk
West Louis, Prospect opp w Main,	W Merrill

LUMBER, LATH AND SHINGLES.

CHAMPAYNE LUMBER CO., Wolf nr w Third,	W Merrill
CRANE BROS.,	Tomahawk
FARMERS LUMBER CO.,	Tomahawk
GILKEY & ANSON CO., w Main,	W Merrill
SCOTT E. B. LUMBER CO., Main opp Mill,	Merrill
STANGE A. H., ft Prospect,	W Merrill
TOMAHAWK LUMBER CO.,	Tomahawk
UNITED STATES LUMBER CO.,	Tomahawk
Wisconsin Valley Lumber Co., w Main nr First, 6th w,	W Merrill
Wolf River Lumber Co., end of First, 6th w,	W Merrill
WRIGHT H. W. LUMBER CO. (THE), State nr w Main,	W Merrill

MACHINE SHOPS AND FOUNDRIES.

Christenson D. & Son, Genesee nr w Main,	W Merrill

MEAT MARKETS.

Barrett J. A., 312 w Main,	W Merrill
Marcouiller Phillip,	Tomahawk
McCarthy M., 1029 Main,	Merrill
Piper & Tipson,	Tomahawk
Theilman J., 910 Main,	Merrill
Theilman R.,	Tomahawk

MERCHANT TAILORS.

Brandel John, Grand ave at the bridge,	W Merrill
BOHN WM.,	Tomahawk
HANSON HANS, w Main cor State,	W Merrill
Heilman Bros., 1007 Main,	W Merrill
Smith D., Mill nr First,	Merrill
WOMER & POPHAL, 909 Main,	Merrill

MIDWIVES.

Raddatz A. F. Mrs., 105 Genesee,	W Merrill

MILLINERS.

Halverson E. Miss, 409 w Main,	W Merrill
Jaquith A. C. Mrs., Main nr Park,	Merrill
Nourse L. C. Mrs.,	Tomahawk
Pattinson Alice Miss, Main,	Merrill
Schmitt A. Miss & Co., Ellis Court opp w Main,	W Merrill
Shirk W. M. Mrs. and daughter,	Tomahawk

MUSICAL MERCHANDISE.

Searl C. E., 1001 Main,	Merrill
Searl E. E.,	Tomahawk

NOTARIES PUBLIC.

ALLEN H. R., 910 w Main,	W Merrill
ANDERSON J. P., 1013 Main,	W Merrill
BABCOCK J. R. & CO., 914 Main,	Merrill
BUMP E. L., 925 Main,	Merrill
CURTIS CURTIS & REID, 1012 Main,	Merrill
FLEET & PORTER, 916 Main,	Merrill
HELMS A. A., 1016 Main,	Merrill
HOYT S. M., Main cor Poplar,	Merrill

Bellis' Merrill and Tomahawk City Directory c. 1898

OILS—LUBRICATING.

STANDARD OIL CO., First nr C. M. & St. P. depot, Merrill

PAINTERS.

BRAZEE C. J., First nr Poplar, Merrill
Laces J. N., Grand ave nr Cottage, W Merrill

PAINTS, OILS AND GLASS.

KALTENBORN H. V., Poplar nr Main, Merrill
Macomber C. E., Tomahawk
STEWART W. D., 315 w Main, W Merrill

PHOTOGRAPHERS.

Duquette M., 412 Second, Merrill
Fleming E. G., Main cor Mill, Merrill
Moloney J. H., Tomahawk
REED & HOFFMAN, Main cor Court, Merrill
Seidle C. A., Tomahawk

PHYSICIANS AND SURGEONS.

Collier L. B., Main nr Mill, Merrill
CUTTER J. D., Tomahawk
Faerber J., 100 Poplar, Merrill
LA COUNT L. B., 914 Main, Merrill
LAMB D. H., Tomahawk
MICHAUD J., 909 Main, Merrill
Poirier J. E., Tomahawk
REINHART D. B., Main cor Court, Merrill
Walsh Charles C., 303 w Main, W Merrill
Wittman A. R., Ellis Court nr Prospect, W Merrill

PIANOS AND ORGANS.

Harrison L. A., 914 Main, Merrill
LITTLEJOHN H., 815-817 Main, Merrill

POP FACTORY.

Theiler Martin, Tomahawk

PRINTERS—BOOK AND JOB.

ADVOCATE PUB. CO., Main opp Lincoln House, Merrill
COON JED. W., Tomahawk
DUNN & JOHNSON, Main opp Lincoln House, Merrill
HONIGMANN C. W., Centre ave nr Main, Merrill
SHULK W. M. & SON, Tomahawk

PUMPS.

SIGLER H. C., Polk nr Second, Merrill

REAL ESTATE.

ALLEN H. R., 310 w Main, W Merrill
BABCOCK J. R. & CO., 914 Main, Merrill
Gothla C. H., Ellis Court, W Merrill
HEINEMANN SIGMOND, Heinemann's New Block, Merrill
MARSHALL W. L., Tomahawk
MATHEWS F. E., Main cor Poplar, Merrill
Werden F. O., Tomahawk

RESTAURANTS.

Allen E. Mrs., 315 Grand ave, W Merrill
BOYER MARY R., 1005 Main, Merrill
Burrington & Conkrite, Tomahawk
Dufrane S., Grand ave nr the bridge, W Merrill
Foote C., Tomahawk
Fuller H. M. Mrs., Park nr Main, Merrill
Marque J., Grand ave nr the bridge, W Merrill
Meunier J. N., Tomahawk
Rodenbush J., 1203 Main, Merrill

SALOONS.

Barrett Bros., 310 w Main, W Merrill
Berard P. E., 901 Main, Merrill
Berg Bros., Tomahawk
Brassard Wm., Mill cor First, Merrill
Daigle R., Tomahawk
Dawson R., Tomahawk
Day W. M., Tomahawk
Dole P., Tomahawk
Dunn W., Main, Merrill
Ebert & Maynard, 305 Grand ave, W Merrill
Flaischfresser A., 313 Grand ave, W Merrill
Fournier A., Tomahawk
Fuller H. M., 1027 Main, Merrill
Galligher T. B., 1025 Main, Merrill
Gibson F. M., 304 w Main, W Merrill
Gilman J. C., Tomahawk
Grimm & Muellen, Main, Merrill
HAMPEL H. J., 1215 Main, Merrill
Hebert L., Tomahawk
Hicker & Beard, Tomahawk
Hildebrand J. P., Tomahawk
Hoey W. E., Merrill
Hyman Bros., 902 Main, Tomahawk
Hyman Bros., Tomahawk
Jacques J.,

BELLIS' MERRILL & TOMAHAWK DIRECTORY.

Johnson Bros.	Tomahawk
KAMKE A., 1201 Main,	Merrill
Kelcher D. H., 1020 Main,	Merrill
Klevin H. W., 400 w Main,	W Merrill
Knauf J.,	Tomahawk
LANG ERNST, Grand ave nr Prospect,	W Merrill
La Plant W.,	Tomahawk
Larson Sam, Second nr C. M. & St. P. Ry. depot,	Merrill
Lawson F., Ellis Court cor Prospect,	W Merrill
Loomis & Rodden, Grand ave,	W Merrill
Lussier A., 6th w,	W Merrill
Loiseau & Paul, Grand ave,	W Merrill
Marque James, Grand ave nr the bridge,	Merrill
McBride James,	Tomahawk
Morency L.,	Tomahawk
Myro & Habert,	Tomahawk
Noel Frank, 810 First,	Merrill
Paul Peter,	Tomahawk
Picket & Sayres,	Tomahawk
Poirier M. L., Main nr Poplar,	Merrill
Polzin & Co., Main nr Court,	Merrill
Rosenbloom J., 1911 Main,	Merrill
Rusch C., 1313 Main,	Merrill
Rymond J.,	Tomahawk
Skattabo Ole, Second nr R R,	Merrill
Thatcher W. J., w Main cor Prospect,	W Merrill
Toelej Parkjam, 418 w Main,	W Merrill
Veaux Joseph, Grand ave cor Ellis Court,	W Merrill
York J., Scott cor First,	Merrill

SASH, DOORS AND BLINDS.

Central Mfg Co. (The) second cor Polk,	Merrill
CHAMPAYNE LUMBER CO., Wolf nr w Third,	W Merrill
KALTENBORN R. V., Poplar nr Main	Merrill
MERRILL LUMBER CO., First cor Clinton,	W Merrill
SCOTT T. B. LUMBER CO., Main opp Mill,	Merrill
STANGE A. H., n Prospect,	W Merrill
STEWART W. D., 315 w Main,	W Merrill
Wolf River Lumber Co., s end 6th w,	W Merrill
WRIGHT H. W. LUMBER CO., State nr w Main,	W Merrill

TINSMITHS.

FEHLAND H. R. & CO., Main cor Park,	Merrill
Gefer F., Grand ave nr Prospect,	W Merrill
Luedke L., Centre ave nr Main,	Merrill
Olson A. J.,	Tomahawk

BUSINESS DIRECTORY.

WEISS HARDWARE CO., Willard Block,	Merrill

UNDERTAKERS AND EMBALMERS.

HANKWITZ F., 110 Prospect,	W Merrill
LITTLEJOHN H., 315-317 Main,	Merrill
Nick Bros.,	Tomahawk

VETERINARY SURGEONS.

Richard A., Depot nr Sales,	Merrill

WATCHMAKERS AND JEWELERS.

HEATH D. P.,	Tomahawk
Moe Fred, 402 w Main,	W Merrill
PHINNEY DAVID M., Main nr Poplar,	Merrill
Shafer G. B., 1016 Main,	Merrill
Strickland George, Main cor Court,	Merrill
SEARL C. E., 1001 Main,	Merrill
Searl E. E.,	Tomahawk

WELL DIGGERS.

SIGLER H. C., Polk nr Second,	Merrill

TOMAHAWK DIRECTORY 1902

CLASSIFIED BUSINESS DIRECTORY

BARBERS

City Barber Shop, 117 Wisconsin av. (See ad)
Star Tonsorial Parlor, 406 Wisconsin av. (See ad)
Pioneer Barber Shop, cor. Tomahawk av. and Wisconsin av. (See ad)
Mitchell Tonsorial Parlor, cor. Tomahawk av. and Wisconsin av.
Slater's Tonsorial Parlor, Wisconsin av. btw. Tomahawk av. and Railway (See ad)

BAKERIES

Meunier, J. N., Wisconsin av. btw. Railway and Tomahawk av. (See ad)
Tremblay J., Wisconsin av. btw. 3d and 4th (See ad)

BREWERS' AGENTS

James O'Connel, cor. 3d and Lincoln av. (See ad)
John Solberg, Tomahawk av. btw. Somo av. and Washington av. (See ad)

1902 Tomahawk Business Directory

Tomahawk Directory

BRICK MANUFACTURERS
Tomahawk Brick Company, East Tomahawk

BOOK AND STATIONERY
Mrs. K. E. Clarke, Wisconsin av. btw. Tomahawk av. and 2d.
C. E. Macomber, Wisconsin av. btw. 2d and 3d
J. N. Meunier, Wisconsin av. btw. Railway and Tomahawk av. (See ad)

BOOTS AND SHOES
City Shoe Store, G. O. Newborg, prop., Wisconsin av. btw. 2d and 3d (See ad)
L. White, Wisconsin av. btw. Tomahawk av. and Railway

BLACKSMITHS
Fontaine Alex, Tomahawk av. btw. Rice av. and Spirit av. (See ad)
Schmitz M., 12 Spirit av.
Hanson C. J., 308 Spirit av.
Obey A., cor. 2d. and Spirit av.

BOARDING HOUSES
Chippewa House, 220 Tomahawk av.
Clarke House, cor. 4th and Washington av.
Commercial House, Railway, btw. Wisconsin av. and Spirit av.
Michigan House, Railway, btw. Somo av. and Washington av.
Norway House, 305 Tomahawk av.
Scandinavian Home, 315 Wisconsin av.
Somo House, Railway, btw. Somo av. and Washington av (See ad)
Scandia House, Tomahawk av. btw. Somo av. and Washington av. (See ad)
Tobin House, Railway, btw. Spirit av. and Rice av.
Maple Leaf House, Tomahawk av. btw. Somo av. and Washingington av.
Harrison House, cor. Railway and Somo av.
Wisconsin House, Wisconsin av. btw. Tomahawk av. and Railway

1902 Tomahawk Business Directory

Tomahawk Directory

CIGAR MANUFACTURERS
Kabat's Cigar Store, Railway btw. Spirit av. and Merrill av.
Edward E. Schultz, Tomahawk av. btw. Wisconsin av. and Spirit av.

DENTISTS
Dodd J. R., Wisconsin av. btw. 2d and 3d

DEPOTS
C., M. & St. P. Ry., west end of Wisconsin av.
M., T. & W. Ry., West Tomahawk

DRAYMEN
L. A. Hildebrand, cor. Rice av. and Railway (See ad)
Conkrite Bros., cor. Railway and Somo av. (See ad)

DRUGGISTS
C. E. Macomber, Wisconsin av. btw. 2d and 3d
Standard Mercantile Co., cor. Wisconsin av. and Tomahawk. av. (See ad)

EXPRESS COMPANIES
American, 217 Wisconsin av. btw. Tomahawk av. and 2d
United States, C., M. & St. P. Depot
Western, cor. Somo av. and Tomahawk av.

FURNITURE DEALERS
Jacob Nick, cor. Wisconsin av. and 3d
Standard Mercantile Co., Tomahawk av. btw. Somo and Wisconsin av.

HARDWARE DEALERS
Evenson Bros., cor. Wisconsin av. and 3d (See ad)
Koth R. F., 121 Wisconsin av. (See ad)
Olson A. J., Wisconsin av. btw. Tomahawk and 2d (See ad)
Standard Mercantile Co., cor. Tomahawk av. and Wisconsin av.

1902 Tomahawk Business Directory

Tomahawk Directory

HARNESS MAKERS
Standard Mercantile Co., cor. Wisconsin av. and Tomahawk av.
Koth, R. F., 121 Wisconsin av.

HOTELS
The Mitchell, cor. Tomahawk av. and Wisconsin av. (See ad)
The Irving, cor. Railway and Somo av.
The Lake Side, cor. 2d. and Somo av.
Tomahawk House, Railway btw. Wisconsin av. and Spirit av.

HOUSE MOVERS
Lambert John, cor. 4th and Prospect av.
Iotte Louis, Merrill av. btw. 2d and 3d
Eldridge James, Tomahawk av. btw. Wisconsin av. and Spirit av.

INSURANCE AGENTS
Bradley W. H. & J. W., cor. Wisconsin av. and Tomahawk av.
Olson A. J., Wisconsin av. btw. Tomahawk av. and 3d
Seth James A., cor. Tomahawk av. and Somo av.
Kelly James, cor. Somo av. and 2d

LAND COMPANIES
Tomahawk Land Co., Gen'l Office, West Tomahawk (See ad)
Smith & Sutliff, cor. Tomhawk av. and Somo av.
Whitson & Johnson, Wisconsin av. btw. 2d and 3d

LAUNDRIES
Tomahawk Steam Laundry, Somo av. btw. Tomahawk av. and Railway
Cong Wing, Tomahawk av. btw. Wisconsin av. and Spirit av.

LAWYERS
Woodworth A. H., Wisconsin av. btw. Tomahawk av. and 2d
O'Leary James, Wisconsin av. btw. Tomahawk av. and 3d
Sheldon G. M., Wisconsin av. btw. Tomahawk av. and 2d
Silverthorn W. V., Railway btw. Wisconsin av. and Somo av.

1902 Tomahawk Business Directory

Tomahawk Directory

LUMBER, LATH AND SHINGLES

Bradley Co., West Tomahawk (See ad)
Bangor Lumber Co., West Tomahawk
Farmers Lumber Co., West Tomahawk
Crane Bros., North Tomahawk

LIVERY STABLES

Hildebrand L. A., cor. Rice and Railway (See ad)
Londo O., Somo av. btw. Tomahawk av. and 2d (See ad)
Irving Stables, cor. Washington av. and 2d

MACHINE SHOPS

Tomahawk Iron Works, West Tomahawk (See ad)

MEAT MARKETS

Piper Packing Company, cor. Wisconsin av. and 3d
Thielman R. C., cor. Wisconsin av. and 2d (See ad)
Marcoullier Phillip, cor. Somo av. and 4th

MERCANT TAILORS

Bunde Fred, Wisconsin av. btw. Tomahawk av. and Railway (See ad)
Bohn William, Wisconsin av. btw. Tomahawk and Railway
Tomahawk Tailoring Co., Wisconsin av. btw. 2d and 3d (See ad)

MILLINERS

Nourse Mrs. L. C., cor. Wisconsin av. and 2d
Standard Mercantile Co., cor. Tomahawk av. and Wisconsin av.
Wangard Lena, cor. Wisconsin av. and 3d

NEWS DEALERS

Meunier, J. N., Wisconsin av. btw. Railway and Tomahawk av. (See ad)

OPTICIANS

Heath D. P., cor. Wisconsin av. and 3d

1902 Tomahawk Business Directory

Tomahawk Directory

PAPER MILLS
Tomahawk Pulp and Paper Co., South Tomahawk   (See ad)

PHOTOGRAPHERS
Seidel C. A., cor. 4th and Somo av.   (See ad)

PHYSICIANS
Jay Johnson, Wisconsin av. btw. Tomahawk av. and Railway
J. D. Cutter, Wisconsin av. btw. Tomahawk av. and 2d
G. R. Baker, Wisconsin av. btw. 2d and 3d

PLANING MILLS
Bradley Co., West Tomahawk   (See ad)

PLUMBERS
Evenson Bros., cor. Wisconsin av. and 3d
Koth R. F., 121 Wisconsin av.
Olson A. J., Wisconsin av. btw. Tomahawk av. and 2d
Tomahawk Iron Works, West Tomahawk

RAILROADS
C., M. & St. P., West end of Wisconsin av.
M., T. & W., West Tomahawk

RESTAURANTS
Gerwells J. H., Wisconsin av. btw. Tomahawk av. and Railway
Roberts Geo. E., Wisconsin av. btw. Railway and Tomahawk av.
Meunier, J. N., Wisconsin av. btw. Railway and Tomahawk av.
   (See ad)
Tremblay J., Wisconsin av. btw. 3d and 4th   (See ad)

SALOONS
Hyman M. C., Wisconsin av. btw. Tomahawk av. and 2d
Gokey Fred, 107 Wisconsin av.
Badger, Wm. Jeannot, prop., cor. Wisconsin av. and 4th

1902 Tomahawk Business Directory

Tomahawk Directory

SALOONS—Continued.

Poutre Jos., cor. Tomahawk av. and Somo av.
Office Sample Rooms, Felix Lambert, prop., cor. Wisconsin av. and Tomahawk av. (See ad)
Morency Louis, Wisconsin av. btw. Tomahawk av. and 2d.
McCutcheon David, Wisconsin av. btw. Tomahawk av. and Railway
Rooney M. J., cor. Railway and Wisconsin av.
Stenderson Thos., 309 Wisconsin av.
Riley Thos., 418 Wisconsin av. (See ad)
Chevrier Jos., cor. 4th and Somo av. (See ad)
Chevrier Peter, cor. Spirit av. and Tomahawk av.
Myer E., Tomahawk av. btw. Spirit av. and Rice av.
Ryan Chas., cor. Tomahawk av. and Lincoln av.
Doll Peter, Wisconsin av. btw. Railway and Tomahawk av.
Gahan Leo, Wisconsin av. btw. Railway and Tomahawk av.
Zastrow Aug., Wisconsin av. btw. Railway and Tomahawk av.
McCormick Robt., cor. Wisconsin av. and Railway
McBride Jr. Jas., cor. Somo av. and Railway
Twomey Timothy, Railway btw. Somo av. and Washington av.
McCarthy Harry, Wisconsin av. btw. 2d and and 3d
Johnson Bros., Wisconsin av. btw. 2d and 3d.
Tomahawk Hotel Co., cor. Wisconsin av. and Tomahawk av.
Bouchard Abel, Wisconsin av. btw. 3d and 4th

STORES

Gents' Clothing and Furnishings, C. A. Gessell, prop., Wisconsin av. btw. Tomahawk and 2d (See ad)
Standard Mercantile Co., cor. Tomahawk and Wisconsin avs.
Gents' Furnishings, J. Heacker, prop., Wisconsin av. btw. Tomahawk av. and 2d
The Pioneer, John Oelhafen, prop., 110 Wisconsin av (See ad)
New York Bargain House, Mrs. B. O'Leary, prop., 311 Wisconsin av.

1902 Tomahawk Business Directory

Tomahawk Directory

STORES—Continued.

General Store, Adam Thum, prop., Tomahawk av. btw Somo and Wisconsin avs.

Grocery Store, H. N. Burrington, prop., Wisconsin av. btw. Tomahawk av. and Railway

Grocery and Meat Market, Phillip Marcouiller, prop., cor. 4th and Somo av.

Dry Goods Store, C. H. Fairfield, prop., Wisconsin av. btw. 2d and 3d

Bay Mills Store, Bay Mills

The Bee Hive Grocery Store, 308 Wisconsin av.

General Store, Anton Wangard, prop., cor. Wisconsin av. and 3d

JEWELRY STORES

Standard Mercantile Co., cor. Tomahawk and Wisconsin avs.

Searl E. E., Wisconsin av., btw. Tomahawk av. and 2d

Kaepham Wm., Wisconsin av. btw. Tomahawk av. and Railway

VETERINARY SURGEONS

McCormick Charles, Tomahawk av. btw. Washington av. and Lincoln av.

POLES, CEDAR POSTS, ETC.

Brooks Hall L., Wisconsin av. btw. Tomahawk av. and 2d (See ad)

1902 Tomahawk Business Directory

IRONICALLY, BY THE TIME THE WEDDING ANNOUNCEMENT FOR WILLIAM H. BRADLEY AND MARIE HANNEMYER HAD BEEN PUBLISHED, BRADLEY HAD ALREADY PASSED AWAY.

Married:—At Milwaukee Monday January 5th. William H. Bradley and Miss Marie Hannemyer.

THE CITY OF TOMAHAWK, DETERMINED TO FORGE AHEAD, FORMED NEW BUSINESS ASSOCIATIONS AND FOCUSED ON 'TOURISM.' THE CITY WAS NOT ABOUT TO CRUMBLE EVEN THOUGH ITS' FOUNDING FATHER WAS GONE.

THE FOLLOWING NEWSPAPER ARTICLES FROM 'THE TOMAHAWK', FOLLOWING BRADLEY'S DEATH IN 1903 REVEAL THE CITY'S ABILITY TO MOVE AHEAD

The Tomahawk

Published for the People Now as Ever, for Good or for its Opposite, Regardless of Race, Color, Sex, Religion, or Politics.

Sixteenth Year.   Tomahawk, Lincoln County, Wisconsin, March 21, 1903.   Number 24.

Tomahawk Advancement Association

The Citizens of Tomahawk Meet and Organize a Strong Association

Most Notable Public Meeting Ever Held in the City of Tomahawk

IN ACCORDANCE with a call issued by Mayor Thielman last week, the citizens of Tomahawk met at The Mitchell Wednesday evening to discuss the formation of a business men's association. It was undoubtedly the most notable public meeting ever held in this city, on account of the unusually large attendance and the unanimity of action manifested in perfecting the organization. The right spirit was abroad; the spirit that is pushing its enterprises and improvements in every direction. It was a representative gathering—the men from the mills and the stores, the employer and the employee—all co-operated to make the meeting a grand success. The attendance spoke well for the future development of our city and surrounding country.

The meeting was called to order by Mayor Thielman who stated that the object of the meeting was to promote the welfare of the city, and to encourage the development of this immediate vicinity.

In response to an appeal by the mayor for suggestions, Mr. F. G. Stark said, "The old Business Men's Association having become only luke warm, I am glad to see the revival of the former interest shown here this evening. I think that good work can be accomplished at this time and now is the proper time to get at it with enthusiasm. All ought to go into it with whole sole and work to push the thing along. Interest immigrants to invest here and settle, and keep them from going west into Minnesota and Dakota. We can settle up our own country by this movement." Mr. Stark's remarks were effective and highly appreciated.

Ex-Mayor Hyman was next in order and said, "It is time to go at work. There are none who cannot help the city. Tomahawk can be made one of the most prosperous cities in Northern Wisconsin. There is no reason why industries and manufactories should not do better here than in other parts of Wisconsin. I would suggest to maintain the present association, but change the name to the Tomahawk Advancement Association. I think it a good suggestion because we might get more members, as many citizens are not in business."

Alderman McBride was the next speaker and expressed himself as being glad to see the revival of the good work. Mr. McBride suggested that the secretary of the association be allowed a little compensation, as that office involves considerable work.

Many other citizens contributed timely suggestions to the meeting.

Upon motion by M. C. Hyman the name of the association was changed to the Tomahawk Advancement Association.

The following officers were then elected: R. C. Thielman, president; F. G. Stark, vice-president; O. M. Smith, secretary; J. W. Froehlich, treasurer. Executive Board—M. C. Hyman, Morris Fitzgerald, F. J. McBride, J. F. Wilson. Committee to draft Constitution and By-Laws—A. H. Woolworth, G. M. Sheldon, James O'Leary. Committee to solicit membership—A. J. Olson, Fred McWithy, H. A. Atcherson.

The next meeting will be held at The Mitchell Wednesday evening, March 25th, and it is hoped that everybody will turn out and assist in carrying out the work so enthusiastically begun.

This city should, with all its great natural advantages, become one of the most prosperous cities in Northern Wisconsin. It offers every encouragement to the manufacturer with its unrivaled water-powers, and its surrounding forests, also its splendid railroad facilities; and to the immigrants, who, as Mr. Stark says are passing our door every day, the thousands of acres lying adjacent to the city, would prove a blessing to them. Here they can clear the forest, cultivate the fields and till the soil, and live a happy, industrial people, whose homes will nestle in every vale and gleam on every hillside.

We are glad to see this great revival of interest manifested by our citizens, who are working zealously for the betterment of present and future conditions. This is an age of progress so with hearts and heads put together, shoulder to shoulder, right hand to right, and no wrong hand to anybody, let us work that this movement be such that its influences shall assist in the upbuilding of our city, and promote interest in the many great natural advantages with which we are so abundantly blessed.

WHAT TOMAHAWK HAS

WE HAVE two reasons for publishing the following list. First, it is published for the information of those who are not familiar with our city, and secondly, we want to impress those that are here that they are living in one of the most prosperous and up-to-date towns in Northern Wisconsin.

A city hall.
Two banks.
Four rivers.
Five hotels.
One bakery.
One dentist.
Pretty girls.
Good streets.
Six churches.
A health park.
Three lawyers.
Three doctors.
Electric lights.
Two dray lines.
One brick yard.
A stave factory.
Good arc lights.
Two cemeteries.
Beautiful lakes.
One brass band.
A bright future.
Three saw mills.
One news dealer.
Two newspapers.
Two drug stores.
Two tailor shops.
Perfect drainage.
One opera house.
City government.
Four restaurants.
A city pest house.
Four barber shops.
One photographer.
One large hospital.
Excellent drainage.
Good sewer system.
Two harness shops.
Two fire companies.
Two cigar factories.
Prosperous farmers.
Three livery stables.
Three meat markets.
Progressive citizens.
Three jewelry stores.
An excelsior factory.
Two millinery stores.
Many fine residences.
Fine business blocks.
One large paper mill.
Free traveling library.
Pure invigorating air.
Four school buildings.
An excellent orchestra.
Three hardware stores.
Seven church societies.
Several pleasure boats.
Three furniture stores.
Three land companies.
Handsome young men.
Four insurance agents.
Competent city officers.
Two department stores.
One large planing mill.
An elegant high school.
One veterinary surgeon.
Unlimited water powers.
Home telephone system.
Fourteen general stores.
Three blacksmith shops.
Several boarding houses.
One large steam laundry.
Three express companies.
Two boot and shoe stores.
Electric fire-alarm system.
A steady influx of settlers.
$563,000.00 in bank deposits.
Three ladies' literary clubs.
Excellent hunting grounds.
One large electric light plant.
Unequalled railroad facilities.
A good system of water-works.
Two book and stationery stores.
Good fruit and vegetable stores.
Long distance telephone service.
Largest tannery in the northwest.
Twenty-six mill and factory sites.
An efficient corps of school teachers.
A large machine shop and foundry.
Largest hotel in Northern Wisconsin.
Fourteen secret and benevolent societies.
Best shipping point in Northern Wisconsin.
Good carpenters, masons, plumbers and gas-fitters.
A population of 3000 enterprising and energetic people.
Connections with four railroads and another in sight.
Great natural advantages and resources for advancement.

(Newspaper clipping transcribed)

WHAT TOMAHAWK HAS

A city hall
Two banks
Four rivers
Five hotels
One bakery
One dentist
Pretty girls
Good streets
Six churches
A health park
Three lawyers
Three doctors
Electric lights
Two dray lines
One brick yard
A stave factory
Good arc lights
Two cemeteries
Beautiful lakes
One brass band
A bright future
Three saw mills
One news dealer
Two newspapers
Two drug stores
Two tailor shops
Perfect drainage
One opera house
City government
Four restaurants
A city pest house
Four barber shops
One photographer
One large hospital
Excellent drainage
Good sewer system
Two harness shops
Two fire companies
Two cigar factories
Prosperous farmers

Three livery stables
Three meat markets
Progressive citizens
Three jewelry stores
An excelsior factory
Two millinery stores
Many fine residences
Nine business blocks
One large paper mill
Free traveling library
Pure invigorating air
Four school buildings
An excellent orchestra
Three hardware stores
Seven church societies
Several pleasure boats
Three furniture stores
Three land companies
Handsome young men
Four insurance agents
Competent city officers
Two department stores
One large planning mill
An elegant high school
One veterinary surgeon
Unlimited water powers
Home telephone system
Fourteen general stores
Three blacksmith shops
Several boarding houses
One large steam laundry
Three express companies
Two boot and shoe stores
Electric fire alarm system
A steady influx of settlers
$503,000.00 in bank deposits
Three ladies' literary clubs
Excellent hunting grounds
One large electric light plant
Unequalled railroad facilities

A good system of water works
Two book & stationery stores
Good fruit & vegetable stores
Long distance telephone service
Largest tannery in the NW
26 mill & factory sites
An efficient corps of school
   teachers
A large machine shop & foundry
Largest hotel in northern
   Wisconsin
14 secret & benevolent societies
Best shipping point in northern
   Wisconsin
Good carpenters, masons,
   plumbers and gas-fitters
A population of 3000 enter-
   prising & energetic people
Connections to four railroads &
   another in sight
Great natural advantages and
   resources for advancement

- That there are nineteen trains arriving and departing daily from Tomahawk which carry passengers.
- That seventeen crews stop in Tomahawk every night in the year.
- That there are on an average 6,000,000 pounds of freight moved in and out of Tomahawk daily.
- That the number of men employed by railroad companies in Tomahawk the year around is nearly one hundred fifty.
- That the railroads carry in and out of Tomahawk daily an average of one hundred twenty five passengers.
- That it is possible to leave Tomahawk at 8:50 or 9:50 o'clock in the morning and arrive in Milwaukee in time for supper.
- That freight rates and connections between Tomahawk and the rest of the world are as favorable and convenient as from any point in the United States similarly situated.
- That you can go, or come or stay in Tomahawk as easily and cheaply as in any city of its size in the world.
- That deliveries can be made from Tomahawk via the Chicago, Milwaukee & St. Paul Railway, the Marinette, Tomahawk & Western Railway, The Chicago & North-Western Railway, the Wisconsin Central and the Soo Line.
- That, taken all in all, Tomahawk has railroad transportation facilities which rank with those of the great railroad centers of the country.

The Tomahawk – April 26, 1903

The Tomahawk

Published for the People Now on Earth, for Cash or its Equivalent, Regardless of Race, Color, Sex, Religion or Politics.

Sixteenth Year.   Tomahawk, Lincoln County, Wisconsin, May 8, 1903.   **Number 31**

TOMAHAWK
AN IDEAL SPOT

THE natural beauties of the city of Tomahawk and the country immediately surrounding render it an ideal spot and our reader can scarcely be improved upon as a summer resort.

The question is asked and rightly, too, why don't some of Tomahawk's public-spirited citizens exert themselves and take the necessary steps to bring the city's claims more prominently before the visiting public.

Every year thousands and thousands of people in neighboring cities spend many weary days and nights racking their brains in the selection of some nice spot from which to radiate in search of summer enjoyment.

Is there any spot in Wisconsin better suited for this purpose than Tomahawk? That being the case, would it not be of untold benefit to the city if a circular if every citizen would take pains to make known its peculiar claims and hunting grounds and its beautiful scenery. It does not take the wisdom of a Solomon to see the vastness of Tomahawk's possibilities in this regard, situated as she is at the confluence of three beautiful rivers and in the midst of dozens of picturesque lakes.

No section of these great United States possesses any better natural resources and facilities for summer resort openings than Northern Wisconsin, and Tomahawk has, needing more, and more the year, more than her average share, with pure, bracing air and sparkling picturesque lakes and streams, water and bright sunny days, and a varied scope of plain and hill and valley, her pine and hemlock and shaded drives and sport with rod and gun and, more than all, the oak and birch and maple, and rest they can get here, more and more, basswood and spruce and tamarack, her splendid railway connections with the big and busy cities, better than anywhere else—the rest of the west, where the dense population for tired brains and nerves that all her varied forms.

All these things are pointed to with pride means a market for our farm as evidence of this section and in a hundred instances their influence is observable in the operating of resorts, products and fruit and cattle and that are patronized more largely butter and sheep and poultry and year after year and will continue to the railroads and lumbermen, and be until every lake and stream will and business of all kinds.

These things are all coming and coming pretty fast. The old ideas have its group of summer visitors of North Wisconsin is passing. In who bring with them the cash earn-its stead is a future that excels the ed in the rushing trade of the city, rapid development of the country and get value received in renewed in every possible direction. Here is a land of independent small farmers, of prosperous towns, of active and profitable industries, varied and numerous. Here will be thousands of delightful summer resorts, miles of good roadsy peaceful homes, intelligent and progressive citizens, and with it all the best in the civilization and development of the race.

These things can be brought a little if we all together don't get in each others way, but they are coming and all the

This is the Tomahawk.
It stands the Symbol of a busy town;
It does not mean, as once it did,
The weapon of a savage,
Used to strike men down.
It means today,
The sign by which men know
That a fair city has been built
In a fair land.
In a land where Mother Nature,
Ever lavish with her treasures,
Has strewn the earth with plenty,
Where pleasant rivers flow,
And mirrored lakes laugh back
The gladness of the sunshine;
Where men rear homes
And live in peace and happiness.

And unto men of other lands
This sign a greeting brings,
A word of hope and cheer.
Here there is virgin soil and pleasant days,
And toil brings sure reward.
And there is room for all,
And open, hearty welcome.
Opportunity is here - - -
By our open gates she stands
And bids you come.
We need the brawny arms and sturdy backs
Of men who toil,
And in returned our fields and forests yield
For them and theirs the best men seek.
No longer cling to worn out soils
And crowded streets,
Where all the avenues of life are full;
Here there is room,
Along these winding streams,
Upon these fertile hillsides,
Within these charming plains,
Besides these placid lakes, Where waters
ripple 'gainst empty shores,
Wide room is here to grow - - - To grow to
strong and sturdy manhood.

The Tomahawk – August 22, 1903

The Tomahawk

1887

Published for the People Bow on Earth, for Cash or its Equivalent, Regardless of Race, Color, Sex, Religion or Politics.

Sixteenth Year.   Tomahawk, Lincoln County, Wisconsin, May 16, 1903.   Number 32

NORTHERN WISCONSIN

A Kentucky stockman and sheep fancier, after traversing the hardwood districts of Northern Wisconsin and observing its adaptability as a sheep and cattle country, wrote the following description of it:

NO MAN knows where it may be or even was (Paradise), but if you mean a land where trout streams murmur and broad rivers gleam through walls of hardwoods, and the gold of buttercups is mingled with the white bloom of the clover, then I have seen the fair land of which you dream, a country gently undulated like the billows of the sea, fruitful and rich in all the grasses that a sheperd loves, free from harmful parasites, a soil composed of loam and clay, fertile as the valley of the Nile and beautiful as the garden of the Gods; a climate healthful alike for the shepard and his flocks; a land which has been covered with the waters of the lakes in the time long ago, and swept by the forest fires, in the ashes of which rape, roots and all the grasses grow in wild and rich luxuriance, and where even now among the wreck and ruin wrought by the flames, the blue grass covers the ground like a carpet and the bloom of the clover gleams in the valleys like the fall of snow.

Seventeenth Year. Tomahawk, Lincoln County, Wisconsin, January 2, 1904. **Number 12**

A Retrospective View of Tomahawk's Progress During the Year 1903 And the Outlook for Continued Prosperity During the Year 1904

DURING the year just passed many important changes have transpired in Tomahawk. In the death of the late William H. Bradley the city sustained a great loss and, for a time, there was a strain of uneasiness among business men as to the future of the city. But the lack of confidence soon gave way to a universal spirit of renewed energy and enterprise. Our business men had too much at stake to let their interests go by way of default and all rallied in one united effort to continue the good work started by the founder of the city, which, at the time of his death, was in the bud of maturity. What has been accomplished in this direction speaks well for the town and attests to the confidence and determination of its citizens. And the year of 1904 is ushered in with new business enterprises and bright prospects for a year of continued prosperity. The Tomahawk Excelsior Company and the Tomahawk Stave and Veneer Company, both capitalized and managed by Tomahawk business men, are examples of what can be accomplished if backed by the right spirit. It is probable that a year ago the stock-holders in these companies had no idea of going into the manufacturing business, but our many advantages for manufacturing pursuits invited their attention and they grasped the opportunity at the right time. Today their manufacturing plants are in operation and doing a thriving business—in fact, new machinery will be installed in both within a short time. The large tannery built by Mr. Bradley will also be in operation soon and with these three new enterprises to start in with, the year 1904 will be one of added prosperity. Besides these three new industries a large saw mill and several smaller manufacturing plants are promised and the prediction is safe that the year 1904 will be a banner year for this city. Coupled with all the natural advantages Tomahawk possesses, the city has a good variety of first-class business places, fine large stores with immense stocks of goods in all lines. The city is also fortunate in having competent and wide-awake professional men. There are good markets for every kind of farm produce with liberal cash prices. There are good wagon and blacksmith shops, one of the best foundries and iron works in this section of the state, good livery stables, hotels, restaurants and banks—in fact, the business interests of the city are many and varied and in the hands of progressive and painstaking business men. Tomahawk is one of the few cities that has a site and everything adapted to this locality would be sure of permanent success and enjoy all the modern advantages that are found in large up-to-date cities, electric lights, water works, sewer system, good schools, churches and a splendid city with beautiful surroundings. People coming here to live may feel sure that their property will increase in value and that their investments will be safe.

CITIZENS IN WWI

The city is justifiably proud of the record she established during the World War, both at home and abroad. At the front she was represented by Company A of the 119th Machine Gun Battalion, 32nd Division, which was made up of men from Tomahawk and vicinity and was organized here by John B. Fosnot in the spring of 1917. Mr. Fosnot, who was appointed captain and was the only man in the company with previous military experience, worked untirely to build up the organization and instill in its members the principles and spirit of military practice, and these efforts together with the excellent material of which the company was composed resulted in a thoroughly efficient military unit. The company was mustered into the Wisconsin National Guard on May 10, 1917, as the machine gun company of the 4th Regiment; it was mobilized July 15, 1917, and mustered into the Federal service August 5, leaving Camp Douglas for Waco, Texas, September 25th. On October 15, 1917, at Camp McArthur, Waco, it was made Company A, 119th Machine Gun Battalion, 32nd Division. On leaving Tomahawk it numbered 84 men, including noncommissioned officers, and its officers were: John B. Fosnot, captain; Jens Munthe, first lieutenant; and Roy T. Lyons and Eugene Meunier, second lieutenants; Ira I

Henry was first sergeant, Charles Stern, supply sergeant, and Ray M. Atcherson, mess sergeant. Upon reorganization at Waco, the company received 98 men and two officers from Stanley, Wisconsin. The officers were First Lieutenant Francis Phillips and Second Lieutenant John Galvraith. The company left Waco for Camp Merritt on February 7, 1918; February 18th it embarked at Hoboken for overseas duty, and it landed on European shores March 4th. A short time after arriving in Europe the unit was ordered into the Alsace sector, and it subsequently took part in all the activities of the 32nd Division throughout the war. The 119th Battalion was decorated as a unit for the services it performed, and two local men, Orville Scheffner and Robert Coey received individual decoration for bravery they displayed in going through a heavy barrage on the Soissons front near Rhiems to appraise the American artillery of the fact that its barrage was falling short and was causing casualties among American troops. Some of the high lights in the history of the 32nd Division as summed up by the joint war history commissions of Michigan and Wisconsin in the "32nd Division in the World War" are as follows: Six months under fire – from May to November 1918- with but 10 days in a rest area; fought on five fronts in three major offensives- the Aisne-Marne, Oise-Ainse, and Meuse-Argonne; met and vanquished 23 German divisions, from which 2,153 prisoners were taken; gained 38 kilometers in four attacks and repulsed every enemy counter-attack; marched 300 kilometers to the Rhine as front line element of the Third U.S. Army and occupied for four months in the center sector in the Coblenz bridge-head, holding 63 towns and 400 square kilometers of territory; were the first American troops to set foot on German soil; fought in the Oise-Aisne offensive as the only American unit in General Mangin's famous Tenth French Army, breaking the German line which protected the Chemin des Dames; twice the line in the Meuse-Argonne offensive, fighting continuously for 20 days, penetrating the Kriemhilde Stellung, crossing the Meuse and starting the drive to flank Metz; left Germany homeward bound in April 1919; arrived in the United States and was demobilized in May. The local company was discharged at Camp Grant June 2, 1919. Three of its members from Tomahawk, Henry Bronstad, Fred Martinson and Fred Berkland were killed in action.

  The honor roll of those from Tomahawk and vicinity who gave up their lives in the service of the country in this great conflict is as follows: Fred A. Berkland; Henry Bronstad; Louis Jorgenson; Frank Liberty; Fred Martinson; William Morris; Leon Paradise; Patrick A. Robarge; Vernon C. Switzer; Gordon Tozer; Edward Trimburger; Hiram Woodruff; William Wurl.

PIONEERS

The Tomahawk Old Settlers Association was established in 1908 with the following members, each of whom came to this section of the country in the year indicated. The association ceased activity in the fall of 1917.

Mr/Mrs Germaine Bouchard – 1863

Alex Robarge – 1882

Mrs. M. LeRoy Parshall – 1885

Mr/Mrs O. K. Welty – 1887

Mr/Mrs John Oelhafen – 1887

Mr/Mrs R. Dawson – 1887

F. A. Larson – 1887

Mrs. C. C. Stiff – 1887

J. O. Seth – 1887

Mrs. V. Sager – 1887

Mr/Mrs L. A. Hildebrant – 1887

Mr/Mrs H. P. Stevens – 1887

Mr/Mrs Martin Theiler – 1887

Mrs. Thomas Murphy – 1887

Mr/Mrs Albert Olson – 1887

J. McCarthy – 1887

Ed Evenson – 1887

Mr/Mrs Charles E. Macomber – 1887

H. H. Johnson – 1887

August Lasbreau – 1887

Mrs. Moyer – 1887

Mr/Mrs T. Toomey – 1887

Mr/Mrs Joseph Trimberger – 1887

William Oelhafen – 1887

Mr/Mrs B. Gahan – 1887

Mrs. Fred Copes – 1887

Mrs. Paul Laton – 1887

Mr/Mrs Robert Russell – 1887

William Schmitt – 1887

Mrs. Tobin Ball – 1887

Dr. & Mrs. J. D. Cutter – 1887

Mr/Mrs Herb Cronkrite & Mrs. Jennie (Dibbs) Cronkrite – 1887

Mr/Mrs Howard Burrington – 1887

Mr/Mrs John Lambert, Sr. – 1887

J. W. Gahan – 1888

Mr/Mrs Martin Deering – 1888

Mr/Mrs J. L. McCarthy – 1888

Mrs. Johanna Gigler and husband – 1888

Mrs. J. Joyce – 1888

Mr. John W. Oelhafen – 1888

B. D. McCarthy – 1888

Mr/Mrs Jerry McCarthy – 1888

John Ecklund – 1888

Mr/Mrs Anton J. Olson – 1889

Mrs. O. M. Smith – 1889

Mr/Mrs John Lambert – 1894

PIONEER PASSES AWAY

GERMAIN BOUCHARD, the oldest inhabitant of this section of the Wisconsin Valley, died at his home at Spirit Falls last Monday, after a lingering illness. He came to this section of the state from Canada some fifty years ago and was 73 years of age at the time of his death. Long before the city of Tomahawk was even thought of he had a fine farm where Lake Tomahawk now lies and owned the site upon which the city is built, but after the Wisconsin river dam was completed he was compelled to abandon his farm as the back water from the dam completely flooded it. He then purchased some land in the vicinity of Spirit Falls which he developed into a farm and where he has since resided.

The remains were brought to this city Tuesday and the funeral services were held from St. Mary's Catholic church Wednesday morning.

The Tomahawk – February 6, 1903

BIOGRAPHIES

Books documenting the history of counties and local communities such as those published in the late 1880's early 1900's were very popular. Even more popular was the opportunity for local individuals to submit their own family information in the form of biographies, to be included in these history books; often paying as much as $2.00 for the chance to boast a little about their accomplishments! The following were included in the 'History of Lincoln, Oneida, and Vilas Counties Wisconsin published in 1924.' The biographies include early settlers, prominent citizens, and some ordinary folks, who lived and worked in and around Tomahawk. Keep in mind that a biography could have been written and submitted by a friend, and may contain information that was not always verified by a family member. Updated information was included by the author as it was discovered.

Ernest B. Conkrite, manager of the Standard Oil Co.'s station in Rhinelander, was born in Clarence MO., December 23, 1870, son of Charles H.S. and Elizabeth (FURMAN) CONKRITE. The parents were natives of New York, where the father taught school. About 1866 the family moved to Freeport, IL., where Charles was employed for four years as bookkeeper in a department store. In 1870 he went to Clarence, MO., and in 1892 he came to Lincoln County, Wisconsin and subsequently lived practically retired until his death in 1918. His wife passed away in 1921. Of their seven children, Hattie (Mrs. ROYCRAFT) is dead; so also is Herbert S.; Anna is Mrs. H. D. STEELE, of Washburn, Wisconsin; Sibyl is Mrs C. M. STEELE of Tomahawk; William H. lives in Virginia, MN.; Nellie is the wife of Victor WILSON of Virginia, MN. Ernest B. CONKRITE acquired his education in the state of Missouri and first began industrial life as a common laborer. In 1887 he came to Lincoln County, locating at Tomahawk, where he was connected with a retail lumber and flour and feed business. Later he was agent for the Standard Oil Company with his brother Herbert and continued there until 1907. He then made a trip to the Pacific coast, visiting Oregon and Washington, and in the following year came to Rhinelander, Wisconsin as manager for the Standard Oil Company. Mr. CONKRITE is a member of the local Masonic lodge and of the Methodist Church. He was first married January 10, 1892, in Tomahawk to Jennie DIBBS. Five children were born to them as follows: Ether, who married John WELCH and resides in Lincoln County; Charles of Eveleth, MN; Sibyl, who is married and lives in Milwaukee; and Earl and May, who live in Tomahawk. Mr. CONKRITE was married secondly at Rhinelander, March 26, 1917, to Bertha GUMS.

Paul R. Philleo, of Rhinelander, Oneida County, who has had a varied business career and is now manager for the Daniels Manufacturing Co., of this city, was born June 29, 1879, in Grand Rapids (now Wisconsin Rapids), Wisconsin, of which city the parents, Hart B. and Isabelle (INGRAHAM) PHILLEO, were pioneer settlers. The father died in 1869 and became one of the proprietors of the Wood County Reporter, published in Grand Rapids and afterwards for some time had full control of the paper, which he edited. He subsequently died there, but his widow is still living in Wisconsin Rapids, being now 83 years old. Their children were: I. Erving, of Wisconsin Rapids; Hattie, who married Solon PRESTON and died February 7, 1923; Dean B., Edward J. and Charles A. all of Wisconsin Rapids; Helen B., now wife of Dr. J. D. CUTTER of Tomahawk; Florence, who is the wife of Guy NASH of Wisconsin Rapids; and Paul R. of Rhinelander. Paul R. PHILLEO acquired his education in Grand Rapids, having graduated from high school there in 1899. In the same year he went to Tomahawk, Lincoln County, where he became clerk in the drug department of the Standard Mercantile Company. A year later he was transferred to the lumber department, in an office position. When Wm. H. BRADLEY died, Mr. PHILLEO was transferred to the Tomahawk Iron Co., which was later known as the Tomahawk Steel & Iron Co., as secretary and office manager, and remained there until 1911. In that year he came to Rhinelander and established himself in the insurance business, having the district agency for the Travelers Insurance Co. In 1912 he gave up that occupation and purchased the Bijou Theatre, in February the same year became cost accountant for the Rhinelander Paper Co., in which position he remained for 14 months. The theatre he continued to operate until September, 1915, when he sold it and became office manager for the Brown Bros. Land & Lumber Co. In the following year he entered the employ of the Flambeau Paper Co. of Park Falls and remained there until July , 1917, when he became auditor for the Oneida Gas Company. Later he became manager for the Daniels Manufacturing Co., in which position he is now serving. Mr. Philleo is a member of the Masonic order, belonging to the lodge in Tomahawk, of which he is a past master, and he also belongs to the Rhinelander lodge of Elks. He was married at Tomahawk, June 24, 1904, to Beatrice BURRITT, daughter of Roland and Mary (KEARNS) BURRITT; the parents are now deceased. Mr. and Mrs. PHILLEO have one child, Helen, who was born July 20, 1905, and is a senior in the Rhinelander High School. Mrs. PHILLEO is an active and useful member of several societies in Rhinelander, including Woman's Club and the Ladies' Aid Society of the Congregational Church; also of the Eastern Star Chapter at Tomahawk.

Larson, Bennett president and general manager of the Larson Machine Factory, of Rhinelander, was born in Waupaca County, Wisconsin, May 23, 1860, son of Ole and Gurina (BENSON) LARSON. He acquired his education in the common schools and remained at home with his parents until 22 years old. He then began working in the woods, winters at logging and in the summers was employed in sawmills, following these closely related occupations until 1886, when he came to Oneida County, locating in Rhinelander. Here he entered the employ of the Brown Brothers Lumber Co., and was with them two years, working both in the woods and sawmills. At the end of that time he went to Tomahawk, Lincoln County, which at that time contained but three houses of almost primitive construction. He was thus one of the early residents of that place and for two years thereafter he continued to work in the woods. He then became millwright for the paper mill there, a position which he held for two years. The next year he was otherwise employed, after which he returned to the paper mill and was millwright and mechanic there for 14 years. His next change of base was to Rhinelander, where he obtained a position as millwright and mechanic that he held subsequently for nine years, being recognized as master mechanic. It was during that time that he conceived the idea of a collapsible shaft, on which he obtained a patent and in the manufacture of which he is now engaged. This shaft automatically opens before being placed in boxes, thus eliminating the costly annoyance of tearing off and remaking of the paper. Though the lightest shaft on the market, it is the most durable and efficient and will last for years without bilging at the ends. Mr. LARSON knows its qualities so well that he will send a standard size Larson shaft on 30 days trial to any reasonable firm. The shaft is provided with journals to fit any box and has satisfied customers throughout the United States and Canada, being now used in over 100 mills. These include every paper-mill in the countries above mentioned; his sales in Canada covering territory from Newfoundland to British Columbia, and some have been made in European countries. Mr. Larson's factory, located at No. 503 W. Davenport Street, is fully equipped for carrying on his business in the most thorough and satisfactory manner. On November 15, 1889, Mr. LARSON was married in Merrill, Wisconsin to Martha WEBSTER, who was born in Winnebago County, Wisconsin, November 30, 1864. The children of this marriage are as follows: Lenora, born August 19, 1890, who holds the position of secretary in the Tomahawk Steel and Iron Works; James, deceased; Walter, born December 19, 1896, now at home, who was in the United States service in the World War; Charles, born September 12, 1900, who is a resident of Vancouver, B.C.; and Elmer, deceased. The family attends the M. E. Church and Mr. LARSON is a member of the Equitable Fraternal Union.

Larson, Albert C. secretary and treasurer of the Larson Lumber Company, whose headquarters are in the village of Jeffris, Lincoln County, was born in Wexford County, Michigan, Sept. 19, 1892. His parents were Ole and Augusta (BOOSTROM) LARSON, natives of Sweden who came to the United States in 1887, settling in Osceola County, Michigan, where Ole LARSON found work in logging camps. For many years thereafter he was connected with the lumbering industry in its various branches, and in 1912, with his son Albert C., he purchased the town site of Jeffris, consisting of 115 acres of land and all the buildings in the village, which they bought from the Bundy Lumber Company, who had previously purchased it from D. K. JEFFRIS, who had started the village in 1891. In 1913 the Larson Lumber Co. was incorporated with Ole LARSON, president; Albert C. LARSON, secretary and treasurer; and J. C. WORDEN, vice president. The concern is now one of the important and representative industries of Lincoln County and is doing an extensive business. In the winter of 1913-14 they erected a large sawmill which they have since kept in continuous operation, their output of lumber being sold in wholesale lots, principally in Milwaukee and Chicago, though quite an amount goes to Michigan and the far East. They manufacture pine, hemlock and all northern hardwood lumber and also spruce and cedar poles and pulp wood. In addition to this they conduct a large general store, in which the post office was kept until 1921. The 115 acres comprising the site of Jeffris village are contained in Lots 6 and 7, Section 24, town of Harrison (Township 35 north, Range 8 east). While the Bundy Lumber Company was here the village and post office was known as Bundy, the original name, however, being subsequently resumed. In addition to the large store building and sawmill, there are a warehouse, schoolhouse, and 24 residences. It is on a branch of the Chicago & Northwestern Railway, which gives it good shipping facilities. Mr. Ole LARSON, president of the company, is one of the solid business men and widely known residents of Lincoln County. His faithful wife passed away on Aug. 6, 1915. Albert C. LARSON was educated in the public schools of Osceola County, Michigan, and in the Ferris Institute at Grand Rapids, Mich. For three years thereafter he was stenographer in the employ of the Grand Trunk Railway with headquarters at Battle Creek, Mich. At the end of that time he became associated with his father in the lumber business at Jeffris, as already mentioned, and since then he has established an excellent business reputation in the county. For six years he was postmaster at Jeffris. He was married April 30, 1917, to Hazel AMOE of Jeffris, and he and his wife are the parents of two children: Irene Jeanne, born Feb. 19, 1918, and Dorothy Nancy, born Aug. 8, 1921. They are affiliated religiously with the Methodist Episcopal Church.

Jones, David C. a leading merchant of Tomahawk, also conducting a brokerage business in land, lumber and logs, was born on a farm near Monticello, Marquette County, Wis., Jan. 15, 1862, son of John and Jane (PRITCHARD) JONES. The parents were natives of Wales who came to this country as young people and were married in Newark, Ohio. It was about 1853 that they came to Wisconsin, settling on the Marquette County farm, which was their subsequent home. Their family numbered ten children: John, now deceased; Richard, of Monticello, Wis.; Anna, who married E. W. WHITSEN of Tomahawk but is now deceased; Margaret REYNOLDS of Tomahawk; William, of Jim Jalls, Chippewa County, Wis.; Eli, of Luverne, Minn.; David C., of Tomahawk; Robert, of Biard Island, Minn.; Edward, who is living in Monticello, Wis., and Ellen Jane, deceased, who was the wife of Robert LUKE. David C. JONES acquired his elementary education in rural schools and for a year and a half subsequently attended the Monticello High School. He resided on the home farm until he was 19 and then went to Castleton, N. D., where he engaged in a meat business, conducting a shop for two years, at the end of which time he sold out and entered the employ of the McCormick Harvester Co. as salesman and collector at Castleton. After two years in that occupation he came to Tomahawk and entered the mercantile business, opening a store on Wisconsin Avenue, where he carries a full line to staple and fancy groceries. Since 1921 he has been engaged in the brokerage business, as already intimated, dealing in land, lumber and logs. A Republican since he first took an interest in politics, Mr. JONES has served his ward several times as alderman and is still in that office. He also served on the county board of supervisors several terms and in 1912 was a delegate to the LaFollette Republican Congressional Convention at Chicago. Fraternally he belongs to the Masonic Blue Lodge, the Odd Fellows and the Modern Woodmen of America in Tomahawk, and to the Elks lodge in Merrill. He is a stockholder in and a member of the board of directors of the Tomahawk State Bank. Mr. JONES was married July 4, 1898, to Saloma PEPPLER, of Reed City, Michigan, where she was born July 7, 1874, daughter of John and Clara PEPPLER. There were six children born of this union, namely: Reva, who died; Grace, who is the wife of Harold EITTRIEN of Tomahawk and has two children, Harold and Willis; Richard and Raymond (twins), both of whom died in infancy; Willis, who died at the age of seven years; and David, who is a pupil in the high school. Besides losing four children, Mr. JONES suffered another bereavement in the death of his wife, who passed away Oct. 19, 1919. He affiliated with the Methodist Episcopal Church, and helps to support both that church and others, though not a member of any. His surviving children are members of the Congregational Church.

Johnson, Charles M. a well known citizen of Tomahawk, Lincoln County, where for many years he has been engaged in the hotel business, was born in Sweden, March 8, 1856, son of John and Christina CARLSON, the parents being also natives of Sweden, where they spend their active lives engaged in farming. Of their eight children there are four now living, namely: Reka, wife of Anton PAULSON, residing in Sweden; Charles M., of Tomahawk, Wis.; Anton, who was associated in business in Tomahawk with his brother Charles for 15 years, but who returned to Sweden where he now lives, having married there; and Alfred, who also lives in Sweden. Those deceased are Olaus, Mary, Adolph and Caroline. Charles M. JOHNSON was reared in Sweden, where he attended school. He subsequently worked as a common laborer and also to some extent as a sailor. In 1882 he came to the United States, locating first in Minnesota, where he found work on farms, and later settling in Wausau, Wis., where he remained seven years. In 1890 he came to Tomahawk and engaged in the hotel business, operating a bar in connection with it. It was in the busiest days of the lumber industry, when the village was building up and men were constantly coming here, or passing through, to work in the mills or woods, and Mr. JOHNSON got a good share of their patronage. He is still conducting the hotel and also a soft drink parlor in connection with it. He has also bought timber lands, logged the timber from it, and then sold the stump land for farms. While in Wausau he worked in the mills, and he remembers that when he first came to Tomahawk, also this entire region was covered with heavy timber, with a small clearing here and there made by a homesteader, while stumps were still standing in the main street, and there were no sidewalks. There was a small lake on Main Street and another where the Community Building now stands, both of which were subsequently filled in. Mr. JOHNSON is a stockholder in the Bank of Tomahawk, also in the Bradley Bank and in the Tomahawk Iron Works. He is fraternally affiliated with the order of Eagles. He was married in 1890 to Matilda HANSON, who was born in Sweden and came to Wausau with her parents, who are both now deceased. She died in 1918, having been the mother of six children, all now living, namely: Mary, alfred, Ada, Hulda, Alvira and Elna. Alfred is married and lives at Madison, Wis., where he is foreman in the roundhouse of the C. M. & St. P. Railway. Ada lives in Nebraska and is the wife of Prof. W. P. HARNES. Mary is now keeping house for her father.

Kelley, John W. district attorney for Oneida County, was born in Oshkosh, Wis., Jan. 13, 1887, son of John and Mary E. (MONAGHAN) KELLEY. Both parents were from the East, the father being a native of St. Johns, N. B., and the mother of Calais, Me. The father came west to Oshkosh in 1880 and in that city he and his wife were married. He was a prominent lumberman in that part of the state and so continued until his death on July 31, 1922. His wife, who is still living, resides on the farm with a daughter in the town of Little Rice, Oneida County. Their children are: Thomas J., proprietor of an ice cream business in Tomahawk; John W., of Rhinelander; Mary E., wife of Robert NETZEL, a farmer in the town of Little Rice, Oneida County; George E., also a farmer in that town, and Charles P., who is with the Tomahawk Motor Co. John W. KELLEY as a boy attended school in Tomahawk, his education being afterward supplemented by a course at the Rhinelander Business College and a law course at Marquette University. On May 14, 1917, he enlisted in the United States' service at the officers' training camp at Fort Sheridan, Ill., where he remained until Nov. 27, 1917. He then received a commission as second lieutenant in the Officers' Reserve Corp, Field Artillery, and one Dec. 27, 1917, sailed for France. January to February 1, 1918 he attended the artillery school at Saumur, and from Feb. 1 to March 1 the same year the artillery school at Vincennes, France. Then until July 16 was stationed at Suumur; and from the latter date to Aug. 27, 1919, was with the field artillery of the Second Division, during which time he saw action on several different fronts. He received a citation for bravery in action Oct. 4, 1918, and was awarded the Croix du Guerre, and a few days afterwards, Oct. 10, he was commissioned first lieutenant. On Dec. 13, 1918, he started with the army of occupation for Germany and served with that army until July 30, 1919, returning to the United States early in August, and being discharged at Camp Grant Aug. 27, 1919. His division was cited for bravery in the Argonne sector. In July, 1920, Mr. KELLEY successfully passed the Wisconsin state bar examination at Madison, and in October the same year he opened a law office in Rhinelander. He soon proved himself an able lawyer in November, 1922 was elected to his present office as district attorney for Oneida County. He is chairman of the Oneida County Soldiers' Relief Commission and belongs to various societies including the Law Fraternity at Milwaukee the Delta Theta Phi college fraternity, the American Legion, the Knights of Columbus and the Eagles. He has made a good impression on the people of Rhinelander both professionally and socially and has numerous friends. Mr. KELLEY was married in Tomahawk, Wis., Oct. 7, 1920, to Helen M. DWYER, daughter of Patrick and Mary (GLYNN) DWYER, now residents of Prentice, Wis. He and his wife are the parents of one child, Mary Eileen, who was born July 19, 1921.

Johnson, Julius a well known resident of Tomahawk, of which city he was one of the pioneer settlers, was born in Christiania, Norway, Nov. 4, 1865, son of John and Sophie JOHNSON, who were natives of that country, the father being a blacksmith by trade. Neither he nor his wife ever visited America, but both spent their lives in their native land. There were at least five sons in the family in addition to the subject of this sketch, but their names are not now remembered. Julius JOHNSON as a boy attended school in Norway and remained in that country until 1882, when he came to the United States. He first located in Minnesota, where he worked at farming, and from that state went to Iowa, where he was similarly employed, also working for a time in a brick yard in Mason City. When the city of Tomahawk, Wis., was stated in 1887 Mr. JOHNSON was among the crowd who rushed in seeking profitable employment in the mills or woods, or in the construction of the various buildings which were rapidly put up. The "Soo" railway over which he traveled from Iowa only ran as far as Bradley, from which place he walked to Tomahawk. He found the town site covered with timber, and there were two stores, one saloon and another building on Fourth Street. His first employment was on the dam of the Tomahawk Boom Company, and after it was completed he worked in the lumber camp on the site of the present Mohr lumber plant, from which land he helped to cut the timber, and he was also employed for some time in the Bradley mill. For many years he has followed the occupation of saw filer during the last five years having been in the employ of Frank THIELER. He is a member of the Lutheran Church and belongs to several fraternal orders, including the Maccabees, the Odd

Fellows and the Equitable Fraternal Union. Mr. JOHNSON was married in 1898 to Anna LOFTUS, whose parents, Thomas and Anna LOFTUS, now deceased, were farmers at Sand Creek, Dunn County, Wis. Of this union three children have been born: Alice and Helen, who reside with their parents, and Julia, who is the wife of Carl BRONSTED of Tomahawk.

Johnson, Henry A. a respected pioneer of the city of Tomahawk, where he is now living, was born at Newberg, Washington County, Wis., Nov. 24, 1857, son of Alonzo W. and Harriett (TAYLOR) JOHNSON. The father, Alonzo W. JOHNSON, who was born in New Hampshire, was a bridge carpenter, as also was his father, Nathan JOHNSON and together they built many bridges in the state of Maine. In 1856 Alonzo came to Wisconsin, settling in Washington County, where he engaged in carpenter work and farming. In 1858 he moved to Waupaca County, being one of its early settlers, and in order to reach the land he had bought he had to cut a road to it for six miles through the timber. After the Civil War broke out he joined the Sixth Wisconsin Regiment, which formed a part of the "Iron Brigade," serving under General Bragg of Wisconsin and being present at the surrender of General LEE. He and his wife spent the rest of their lives on their farm in Waupaca County, where he died May 25, 1899, at the age of 63 years. His wife, who was a native of New York State, survived him some years, passing away in 1912. They were the parents of 13 children, of whom nine are now living: Charlie, of Waupaca County; Jesse, residing in Waupaca County; Ella, wife of Henry BINGHAM of Crandon, Wis.; Estella, now Mrs. Urial FLETCHER of Clintonville, Wis.; May, wife of Than SMITH of Forest County, Wis.; Sylvia, wife of Nels JURGENSON of Waupaca County; Maggie, wife of Bud WILCOX, residing in Sacramento, Calif.; and Henry A. Of the four deceased, three died in infancy, and the other was Henrietta, a twin sister of Henry A. Henry A. JOHNSON was reared on his parents' farm and as a boy attended the rural school of his district. The surroundings were very wild and Indians were numerous in the neighborhood. The schoolhouse partook of the general credity, being built of logs, with a long pine desk running the length of the room, at which the pupils sat on hewed log benches. When 21 years old young JOHNSON left the home farm and went to Royalton, Wis., where he worked a farm on his own account and conducted a store. In 1887 he came to Tomahawk before any buildings had been erected on the town site. Putting up a building and a brick oven, he started the first bakery, in town, a most necessary place of business, since eating is the first thing that everyone has to do. Later he sold his bakery and engaged in logging, the industry most extensively followed here at that time. He would buy land, cut off the timber, and then sell the land to prospective farmers, settlers or speculators, and in that way he was employed for some 15 years. After that he spent ten years in cruising for the State, and since the end of that period has been retired. He has served as a member of the local school board and for two terms was a member of the county board. His fraternal affiliations are with the Masonic order. Mr. JOHNSON was married at Royalton, Wis., Dec. 23, 1878, to Sarah FLETCHER, daughter of John and Evelyn (MOORE) FLETCHER, the parents being natives of New York State, of English ancestry, and early settlers and farmers in Waupaca County, Wis. The father, John FLETCHER, fought for the Union in the Wisconsin regiment. Of their ten children two died in infancy, while those who grew to maturity were William H., Sarah, Uriah, Cyrus W., Harriett M., Eva, John, Jr., and George. Mr. and Mrs. Henry A. JOHNSON are the parents of one daughter, Jennie B., who is now the wife of William I. MACFARLANE, a well known dentist of Tomahawk.

Kummer, Peter J. who holds the responsible position of general superintendent in the Tomahawk Pulp and Paper Mill, is a veteran in the paper manufacturing industry, having been engaged in it for the last 30 years. He was born in Austro-Hungary, June 25, 1877, son of Joseph Franz and Marie (GREGOTCH) KUMMER. In 1888 the family came from Hungary to the United States, and directly to Stevens Point, Wis., where they settled. The father worked in saw mills and on the railroad, in order to earn a little ready money. Mr. and Mrs. Joseph F. KUMMER had in all 11 children, of whom the first born, Marie, died in Hungary. Peter J. was the second born and there were two in addition to Marie who died in infancy. The others included Mary (second); Peter J. of Tomahawk, John and Mike (twins), both deceased; Joseph, who met an accidental death; Paul J., of Des Plaines, Ill.; and Elizabeth, now Mrs. A. J. BRADY of Stevens Point. Peter J. KUMMER acquired his education at Stevens Point in public and parochial schools, which he attended up to the age of 13 or 14 years. When 14 he became industrially active, finding employment in the stave mill where, he worked 12 hours a day. After two seasons in that mill he entered the employ of the Wisconsin River Pulp & Paper Mill Co. at Stevens Point and remained with that concern there until 1905, except for one year spent in Wisconsin Rapids, with the "Consolidated" mills. Beginning at the bottom of the ladder, he advanced step by step, learning every detail of the business. In 1905 he came to Tomahawk and entered the employ of the Tomahawk Pulp and Paper Co. as a machine man; in 1907 he was made foreman of the plant, in 1917 he was promoted to the position of interior superintendent, and in 1919 to his present position as general superintendent of the entire works, which he has well earned by his capacity and close attention to duty. For three years Mr. KUMMER served as treasurer of School District No. 1, town of Bradley. He is fraternally affiliated with the modern Woodmen of America and with the United Order of Foresters. On Sept. 29, 1901 Mr. KUMMER was united in marriage with Frances LANG, who was born in Germany Feb. 22, 1880, daughter of Matthew and Frances (MEYER) LANG. She came to Stevens Point, Wis., with her parents as an infant, in 1882, and it was there that the family made their home. The mother is still living there, the father having died in 1915. Mrs. KUMMER was the eldest of four daughters, the others being: Bertha, now Mrs. O. M. JOHNSON of North Fond du Lac, Wis.; Rose, wife of Herman LEVERENCE of Tomahawk, and Mary, wife of John GORMAN of Milwaukee. Mr. and Mrs. KUMMER'S children are two daughters, Marie R., born at Stevens Point, Aug. 29, 1902, and Irene, born at Grand Rapids, Wis. (now Wisconsin Rapids), July 15, 1904. Marie was graduated from the Tomahawk High School in the Class of 1921, and having taken a business course, is now with the Tomahawk Drug Co. Irene took the same course of study, being graduated in 1922, and is now in the employ of the Ball & Lambert Electric Co. of Tomahawk. The family are members of St. Mary's Catholic Congregation. They occupy a nice residence at 124 N. Third Street, owned by the parents.

Kilroe, Thomas H. one of the best known citizens of Tomahawk, of which city he is a pioneer, and also a prominent representative of the logging and lumber industry, and as such known far beyond the bounds of this city, was born at Liberty Falls, Sullivan County, N. Y., Aug. 2, 1863. His parents, Patrick and Mary (REDDINGTON) KILROE, were natives of Ireland, the former born in 1832 and the latter in 1842. Both came to the United States in the latter 40's-- Patrick in 1849-- and they were married in New York State in 1862. His active career was spent as a tanner and he and his wife Mary finally died in Sullivan County, New York. Their children were Thomas H., James, Edward, Mary, John, Margaret, Agnes and Catherine, the two last mentioned being twins. All are living except Catherine. James, Mary, John and Agnes reside in Monticello, N. Y. Edward also resides in New York State; Margaret lives in Brooklyn. The surviving daughters are unmarried. Thomas H. KILROE in his boyhood attended rural school up to the age of 15. He then left home to shift for himself, finding employment in logging camps in New York State. After a years' experience there, he went to Potter County, Pennsylvania, where until July, 1887, he was engaged in the same industry. It was at that time that he heard of the logging operations that had been started in the vicinity of Tomahawk, Wis., and of the founding of this settlement, and realizing that this was likely to be a busy place for some time to come, he turned his face in this direction and arrived here, a strong young man nearly 24 years of age, on July 7, 1887. There wasn't much in Tomahawk at that time but a couple of stores, but employments was easy to obtain for those who were not afraid of hard work and Mr. KILROE not being troubled that way, he soon found plenty to do in the great industry that was rapidly transforming the northwest from a wild expanse of forest, lake and stream to a cultivated and thickly settled region. In this work he took a prominent and active part, finding his previous experience in the east highly useful, and he has remained in the harness up to the present time, though he no longer does the hard and rough work, but is employed by the Twoomey-Williams Company, large jobbers doing a brokerage business in logs and timber, as their logging engineer, estimating timber tracts, the cost of cutting and marketing and in laying out the right of way for their log railways, etc. At present they have large interests in northern Minnesota and in Canada, where his work now lies. In September, 1893 Mr. KILROE was united in marriage with Mary Exilda, daughter of John and Margaret (FILEX) LAMBERT of Tomahawk, and who was born at Chippewa Falls, Wis., Feb. 14, 1873 and had come to Tomahawk with her parents. Previous to his marriage Mr. KILROE had bought a lot at 127 E. Somo Avenue and put up a small house on it, where he and his wife began domestic life together. Later at the same locate he erected one of the best homes in the city, which is the present family home. After nearly 30 years of happy married life, Mrs. Mary KILROE passed away on Jan. 6, 1922, deeply mourned by her husband and surviving children, besides numerour friends. The children (including those deceased) were born and named as follows: Madge, born Sept. 21, 1894; John Edward, June 18, 1895; Agnes D., February, 1897; Thomas E., June 14, 1899; Helen E., Feb. 7, 1901; Winnefred M., June 12, 1904; William P. (date note remembered); Harriett C., June 21, 1908; and Dorothy L., Feb. 21, 1909. William P. died in infancy and Dorothy L. at the age of five years in March, 1914. The children who grew up were all afforded good educational advantages, and all have graduated from the Tomahawk High School, except Harriet C., who is now a pupil in her second year there. The eldest daughters act as housekeepers. Mr. KILROE is a substantial citizen and although born in the United States, possesses all the best qualities of the race from which he sprung, their quick wit, optimistic disposition, earnest application to any task to which they set their hands, regard for family and friends and love of the ancient church of which the great majority of them are members. He and his family belong to St. Mary's Catholic Congregation in Tomahawk. In politics he is a broad minded Democrat and at times he has served his city and town in various public capacities; but whether in office or out he has always had the best interest of the community at heart and been ready to promote them.

    Lewerenz, William one of the most notable pioneers of Lincoln County, who as builder of railroads, schools and highways, was for many years an important factor in its development, and who is now living retired on his farm in Section 9, town of Bradley, was born in Pommern, Germany, March 28, 1854, son of Mr. and Mrs. Karl LEWERENZ, the father being a miller and baker by occupation. In his boyhood William attended school up to the age of nine years, when he had to quit owing to failing eye sight. Between the ages of 13 and 14 he worked in his father's grist mill, and having learned not only that trade but also that of baker, he followed them until he was 22. He then had to enter the army, serving first one year and three months in the infantry. As he spoke not only his native tongue, but also English and Polish, together with a little Norwegian, his usefulness was recognized; he was made an officer, advanced to the position of lieutenant and drew a good salary. After serving four years and a half in the army he was allowed to return home and resumed his work in the mill and bakery. He also married his first wife, Minnie KNUTH, and had started a resort hotel of 100 rooms, when, after only a year and a half of freedom, he was again called into the army, to serve an additional period of six months. This completely ruined him, as he had to sell his business at a great loss, and to make matters worse, his wife died while he was away and on his return he found himself a widower, with little or no money and nothing but his trade to depend on. Quite disgusted, he resolved to leave his native land and try is fortunes in America; so in 1882 he crossed the ocean, and after landing in the United States came west to Mauston, Wisconsin, where he found employment at his trade with Ben BORMAN, with whom he remained until Mr. BORMAN died. The business was then sold and for a short time Mr. LEWERENZ worked for the new proprietor. About that time he married his second wife, Elizabeth BLAAS, who was born in New york in 1851, and whose father, Diebold BLAAS, was in the grocery and restaurant business in Mauston. For this father-in-law he went to work, leaving the mill. In the same year (1887) he obtained a contract to haul materials for Mauston's new schoolhouse, for which purpose he had to buy wagons and teams. Thus began a new era of his life, for while in the German army he had learned the art of railroad building, and being now equipped for construction work, he was ready, when he got through with the schoolhouse to take on another and larger contract, which was to built the C. M. & St. P. Railroad from Irma through Tomahawk to Heafford Junction, where it connected with the "Soo." On taking this contract he established his home in Tomahawk, where his family was among the first arrivals after the founding of that place, and which was his home until 1892, for his work for the St. Paul road covered a period of five years. He cleared the 160 acres for "flowage land," and during his labors lived in a tent not far from the site of the Tomahawk depot, employing 160 men. Since his new start in life in a new country Mr. LEWERENZ had been making some progress, but fortune was now about to deal him another hard blow. In 1890 he contracted to build the roadbed of the Wisconsin Central Railway from near Marshfield to Greenwood in Clark County. For this work he employed 150 men, but the season proved a very west one, which so greatly increased the difficulties of construction that he not only lost all he had but found himself $1200 in debt besides. To borrow the language of the ring, he was "down and out." But Mr. LEWERENZ was not the man to stay down long. He could always made a living at his trade, but he wishes to pay his debts and get ahead in the world, and so kept his eyes wide open for another opportunity. The next that presented itself launched him on an agricultural career. In 1891 the government put the water reserve land on the market, with the sale office at Wausau. To that place, therefore, Mr. LEWERENZ hurried, finding when he got there an immense throng of 700 to 800 people in line before the office. He showed his patience and determination by standing in the line for 24 hours, by the end of which time it was Saturday night, the office was closed and the people told to go home. By chance he found that a piece of 120 acres on Section 9, Township 35 North, Range 6 east, four and a half miles from Tomahawk, had not been filed on; and on the next day, Sunday, securing the help from some friends, he hastened there and put up a shack of poles and brush. Then he hurried back to Wausau to be the first in line when the office should open again on Monday morning. Two o'clock in the morning found him in place on the office steps, and there he waited until seven until the office was opened and he entered and filed on the land which is his present home. If Mr. LEWERENZ hadn't got up early enough that morning to beat the birds by several house he would have "got left," for as he was coming out of the office he passed a man who was entering to file on the same piece of land. This was the 24th of December, 1891, and the next day Mr. LEWERENZ celebrated Christmas with a joyful spirit, for he had made a third new start in life, which was to prove more fortunate than the previous ones-he had got onto the land. There is much talk just now of the hardships the farmer has to endure, but there are many who would be glad to exchange their lot for his. He is the monarch of all he surveys in the broad acres which stretch out in teeming richness from his door step. Though once in a while his bank balance may be low, he never has to wonder where the next meal is coming from, for on his own place he can raise far more than he and his family can consume, of meats, grain and vegetables, to say nothing of milk and dairy products, orchard fruits, and the wild berries, which he can have for the picking but for which the city dweller must pay a good price per quart. In getting started on his farm Mr. LEWERENZ was aided by the late W. H. BRADLEY, who gave him enough lumber to built a home of 16x18 feet. That he put up in the spring of 1892 and immediately moved his family into it. During the first 18 months he had no team, and in bringing supplies from Tomahawk had to follow a trail, there being no road. When he had secured a team he had to grub out a road for it. In the surrounding timber he cut many a cord of jack pine, which he hauled through the woods to Tomahawk, where he was paid $1.25 a cord for it. It was money hardly earned and was not squandered, for every cent was needed for the running expenses of the household before the farm had begun to be profitable. Mr. LEWERENZ was also helped again by Mr. BRADLEY, who gave him a job of foreman in the woods, cutting wood, clearing land and building road beds for his logging railroads. In this work he was engaged for eight years, by the end of which time he had got on his feet again. In the meanwhile he was gradually developing his farm, clearing and improving the land and from time to time putting up new buildings and he now has 120 acres under the plow. He is doing general farming and dairying, keeping registered Holstein-Freisian cattle, with a registered sire at the head of his herd. Formerly for eight and a half years he had a milk route in Tomahawk and did a good business, building it up to large proportions. It would seem that Mr. LEWERENZ'S activities, as heretofore related, would have been enough to keep any ordinary man fully employed, but he has crowded much more action into his life. He served as supervisor for the towns of Rock Falls and Bradley, in all 16 years, being chairman 9 years, and so for the latter period being a member of the county board. For nine years also he was secretary of schools, when there were 16 schools in one district under the town system. He built or had to do with the building of every schoolhouse in the towns of Rock Falls, Bradley, Tomahawk, Somo and a part of Harrison. He also built or superintended the building of nearly every main road in the territory above mentioned. He, with Judge Hurley of Wausau, William H. BRADLEY of Tomahawk and Governor HOARD of Madison held the first "good road meeting" in Milwaukee. Later a public meeting was held at Wausau to discuss the same subject, and for an object lesson Mr. LEWERENZ built a short sample of surface road out of Wausau. He also secured the first subscriptions for the first surface road from Tomahawk north to McGuinness corners. Mr. LEWERENZ'S second wife Elizabeth died July 1, 1920. She had been the mother of two children: Roy B., born Feb. 25, 1886, and Mada, born Aug. 24, 1887. The birthplace of Roy was Mauston, while Mada was born in the family tent in Tomahawk that has been previously mentioned, and was the first white child born in the infant village. Roy B., who for some time operated the home farm, is now living three miles away on a farm in the town of Bradley. Mada is employed as manager of the normal school at Whitewater, Wis. Since the death of his second wife Mr. LEWERENZ has married Mrs. Ella STRENGE, of the 'town of Bradley, who was born at Elmore, Ohio, Aug. 27, 1871, and who is the widow the Louis STRENGE. By whom she had three children, all now living, namely: Elmer, now in the state of Washington; Oscar, residing in Chicago, and Fred, who is on the Lewerenz farm. All things considered, Mr. LEWERENZ has been a successful man, and the success has been well deserved because it has been strenuously worked for. His work has been done with the thoroughness characteristic of those of his race, and he has never spared himself when he had a worthy purpose to achieve. During his active career, for he retired from active work in 1917, he made the acquaintance of men of note, all of whom appreciated his sterling qualities. He has interest as a bank stockholder and in other directions, and is a member of the German Lutheran Church.

Lambert, John B. land owner and farmer, who has also other business activities, and whose home is in Tomahawk, Lincoln County, was born in Canada, Aug. 9, 1855, son of John and Margaret LAMBERT. The parents were natives of the Dominion and of French descent. John LAMBERT (Sr.) followed logging in Upper Canada and came to the United States in 1864, locating at Chippewa Falls, Wis., where he was engaged in logging and river work, building bridges and house moving. He came to Tomahawk in 1887 to work on the dam then being built by the Tomahawk Boom Company. He also moved the first sawmill to Tomahawk from Chippewa Falls for W. H. BRADLEY and subsequently engaged in logging on the Somo River. In 1908 he died, having survived his wife three years. They had in all a family of 13 children, of whom John, Paul, Leo, William, Parmelia and George are now living. Of those deceased, three died in infancy, the others being Exilda, Felix, Peter and Addis. Exilda, who became the wife of Thomas KILROE, is now deceased.

John B. LAMBERT was nine years old when he moved with his parents to Chippewa Falls. After attending school there he began industrial life, working in the woods and river drives and rafting lumber down the Chippewa River to Beef Slough, and he was thus employed until he came to Tomahawk in 1889. Here for 13 years he was engaged in logging and in sorting logs for W. H. BRADLEY, working on the Somo, Tomahawk and Wisconsin rivers. He then bought timber land and cut the timber, disposing subsequently of some of the land, though he still owns 280 acres of cut-over land, of which he has 40 acres cleared and under cultivation. He also moves houses when his services are called for in that capacity. A member of the Catholic Church, his fraternal society affiliations are with the Catholic Foresters. Mr. LAMBERT was married at Eau Claire, Wis., Nov. 15, 1880, to Carrie KINGSLAND, daughter of Isaac and Harriett (PHILLIPS) KINGSLAND, the parents being natives of New York State. They settled in Wisconsin before the Civil War, and after it broke out Isaac KINGLAND enlisted at Two Rivers and subsequently served three years, or until his term had expired. He then re-enlisted but did not survive the war, dying from a wound received in battle. He and his wife had two children, Ira J. and Carrie. After her husband's death Mrs. KINGSLAND married Joseph KING of Eau Claire, Wis., by whom she had one child, Rebecca, who is now dead. Mr. and Mrs. LAMBERT have had three children: J. Eugene of Tomahawk; Edna M., wife of Elliot BRADY of Tomahawk; and Mabel, who is deceased.

Lambert, George a well known resident of the city of Tomahawk engaged in the electrical business, and who has resided here since infancy, was born at Chippewa Falls, Wis., Aug. 8, 1886, son of John and Margaret LAMBERT. The parents, natives of Canada, came to the United States and to Chippewa Falls in 1865, and in that vicinity John LAMBERT, the father, worked in the woods at logging until he came with his family to Tomahawk in 1887, the year the village was laid out. Here he worked on the dam, which was then in process of construction, and after its construction helped to move a saw mill from Chippewa Falls to Tomahawk for William H. BRADLEY, this being the first mill set up in the latter city. After that and during the rest of his active period he was occupied in house moving and general jobbing. His death occurred in 1908 and that of his wife Margaret in 1905. They had a family of 13 children, of whom six are now living, namely: John, Paul, Leo, William, Parmelia and George. Felix and Exhilda are dead and five others died in infancy. George LAMBERT was two years old when his parents settled in Tomahawk. Here in time he attended grade and high school, after which he worked for six years in a printing office and six years for the city light company. In the fall of 1918, in association with William H. BALL, he opened an electrical store and shop, which he and his partner are still conducting with good success. He is assistant chief of the Tomahawk fire department and is also a member of the Commerical Club, having closely identified himself with the interests of the city which has been his home since early childhood. Mr. LAMBERT was married in Tomahawk in 1911 to Nellie REYNOLDS, daughter of Frank and Jennie REYNOLDS. Her parents, former residents of Wausau, Wis., where for some years Mr. REYNOLDS operated dye works, are now living on a farm in the southern part of Wisconsin. Mr. and Mrs. LAMBERT are the parents of three children: Lorma and Donald, living, and one who died in infancy.

Lambert, Leo L. a trusted employee of the Tomahawk Pulp and Paper Co., was born at Chippewa Falls, Wis., Oct. 25, 1874, son of John and Margaret LAMBERT. The parents were French-Canadians, and the father for some years in early life followed the occupation of logger in Upper Canada. He and his family moved to Chippewa Falls, Wis., in 1864, and there he followed logging, and various others kinds of work until 1887, when he came to Tomahawk among the pioneers of this place. He worked on the dam built by the Tomahawk Boom Company, moved a saw mill from Chippewa Falls to Tomahawk for W. H. BRADLEY, and was afterwards engaged in logging on the Somo River. He died in 1908, his wife Margaret having passed away in 1905. Their children who are now living are John, Paul, Leo, William, Parmelia and George. Three died in infancy, and four others are also deceased, Exilda (Mrs. Thomas KILROE), Felix, Peter and Addis. Leo L. LAMBERT acquired his education in the schools of Chippewa Falls and then became connected with the lumber industry, working in the woods in that vicinity until 1888 (or 1887) when he came to Tomahawk with his parents. Here he was employed on the river rafting lumber and also in the woods at logging, following those occupations until 1919, at frequent internals assisting his father at house moving and other kinds of contracting. In 1919 he went to work for the Tomahawk Pulp and Paper Co., working as foreman of construction in summer and of the chain gain in winter, which is the position he now holds. He is a member of two fraternal societies - the Eagles and the Catholic Foresters. On Jan. 14, 1902, Mr. LAMBERT was united in marriage in Tomahawk to Lena DOLL, who came to Tomahawk in 1887, and whose parents are now deceased. Mr. and Mrs. LAMBERT have had one child, Norman, who died at the age of three years.

Koth, Reinhold F. proprietor of the Winchester Store in Tomahawk, was born at Reeseville, Dodge County, Wis., April 20, 1871, son of August and Louise KOTH. The parents were natives of Germany who came to the United States in the late 60's, Mr. KOTH after settling in Reesevile being engaged in farming and blacksmithing, having a shop on his farm. There he subsequently died, and his wife, who survived him, passed away at Lowell, in the same county, in 1915. She had married for her second husband Carl ROGGA, by whom she had a daughter, Dora, who married Charles RAILER and lives in California. Her children by August KOTH were: Herman residing in Merrill; Edward, in Milwaukee; Anna, wife of John HUEBNER of Doyelestown, Wis., Reinhold F., of Tomahawk; George, of Des Moines, Ia.; Oscar, of Milwaukee; Martha, wife of August LASS of Milwaukee, and Louis of Gary, Ind. Reinhold F. KOTH was reared on the home farm and educated in the district school. His summers up to the age of 18 were spent in agricultural employment, and then, in 1889, he left home and coming to Tomahawk began to learn the tinsmith's trade with Lamb & Moore, for whom he worked for two years. During the next seven years he was in the employ of Axel OLSON, after which he engaged in business for himself, starting a tin and plumbing shop, six months later adding hardware to his stock. This place he sold to the Northern Hardware Co. and was their manager for three years. Then he once more started in for himself and has since continued in the business. He carries a complete line of light and heavy hardware, McCormick and Deering farm implements, trucks, tractors, automobiles and accessories, all kinds of building materials, barn equipment, sewing machines, victrolas, clocks, watches, silverware, pipe and fittings, fertilizer and many other things, and is doing a large business. He also owns a plot of ground 300 x 1330 feet, lying close to Tomahawk, which he has platted as Koth's Addition, and on which this season he will build cottages for rent and sale. He is a stockholder in the Bank of Tomahawk, the Tomahawk Shoe Manufacturing Co. and the Winchester Firearms Co. His fraternal society affiliations are with the Equitable Fraternal Union and the Maccabees. Mr. KOTH was married in Tomahawk, April 19, 1896, to Allie Fogerty, daughter of Mr. and Mrs. James FOGERTY, long time residents of Tomahawk. Their married life lasted only about 10 years, as Mrs. Allie KOTH died in 1906, leaving one son, Lloyd, born in 1898. The latter entered the naval service of the United States in the World War and trained at Great Lakes, where he was stationed. In 1909 Mr. KOTH married secondly, at Des Moines, Ia., Louise BOESE, whose father died in Germany and whose mother resides in Iowa.

REINHOLD F. KOTH

Klade, Fred C. proprietor of a successful merchant tailoring establishment in Tomahawk, in association with his sons, Robert and Fred, was born in Germany Dec. 25, 1855, son of August and Amelia KLADE. Having learned the tailor's trade in his native land, he came tin 1882 to the United States, locating in Wausau, Wis., where he opened a shop. The venture proved successful and he conducted the business there for many subsequent years. In 1905 he opened a small branch shop in Tomahawk, which also proved successful, and his trade so increased that in 1911 he erected a two-story brick building here, 25 x 60 feet in dimensions, moving his equipment from Wausau to Tomahawk and giving up his business in the former place. It is now conducted in Tomahawk under the firm name of F. C. Klade & Sons, Robert and Fred, both skilled tailors, being the actual managers, as Mr. Fred C. KLADE retired from active work in 1922. They carry on a general merchant tailoring business, doing repairing, cleaning and pressing, and also carry a general line of men's caps. Mr. KLADE was married at Wausau to Matilda GRUENWALD, a native of Germany whose parents were early settlers in Wausau. Of this union seven children were born, of whom five are now living, Robert, Fred, Henry, Esther and Margaret. Matilda and Webster were the two who died. Esther is the wife of D. T. SWIFT of St. Paul, Minn. The three sons were all in the United States' service in the World War. Robert, who was born in Wausau in 1890, was inducted into the military service in 1918, trained at Camp Grant, and was there assigned to Ammunition Train No. 311, 86th Division, being one of 48 men of the train selected to drive four-wheel trucks. He went to Kenosha, Wis., and from there to New York, and on Sept. 27, 1918 sailed for France. Returning to the United States after the armistice, he was discharged at Camp Grant in February, 1919. He belongs to several fraternal orders, including the Elks, Odd Fellows and Eagles. Fred KLADE, who was born in Wausau in 1891, was inducted into the army service July 21, 1918 and assigned to Tank Corps No. 305. He was stationed at Raleigh, North Carolina and was discharged in December, 1918. He married Margaret COEY of Tomahawk. His fraternal affiliations are with the Masons. Henry enlisted in Tomahawk in 1917 in a machine gun company belonging to the 32d Division. He trained at Waco, Texas and was discharged after one year's service on account of disability. He then joined the mounted police in Canada, but is now a U. S. revenue afficer stationed in Michigan.

Kuehling, Herman H. county highway commissioner for Lincoln County, was born in the province of Saxony, Germany, Jan. 9, 1879, son of Henry and Marie (ENGELMAN) KUEHLING, and came to the United States with his parents when he was nine years old. Here the family settled near Unity, in Marathon County, Wis., where the father was subsequently engaged in the operation of a large farm until his death in 1919. The mother is still living at Unity. Of the seven children born of these parents, the four eldest were born in Germany before the family's removal to the United States; the three youngest were American born. The children were as follows: Herman H., subject of this sketch; William, now of Tomahawk; Walter, also of Tomahawk; Emma, who is Mrs. Albert BERNITZ of Pittsburg, Pa.; Sophia, now Mrs. Richard JAHRMAN of Tomahawk, Wis.; Louisa, now deceased, formerly Mrs. L. MARTZ of Tomahawk; and Anna, also deceased, who was Mrs. Gustav SIEPERT of Milwaukee. Herman H. KUEHLING attended school at Unity and graduated from the high school there with the class of 1896, after which he enlisted in the United States regular army as a member of the 14th U. S. Cavalry, Troop G, serving for three years and four days, eleven months of which time he spent in the Philippine Islands. While in the military service in the United States he was stationed at Fort Wingate, N. M., helping to erect this fort and gaining a great deal of experience in road construction there. After returning from the Philippine Islands he was discharged at San Francisco on March 14, 1903, and after a short stay at the family home in Unity he then went to Tomahawk, Lincoln County, and engaged in the steam laundry business. Selling that business after three years, he then established the Tomahawk Bakery and Grocery Co., building the store in which this enterprise was housed and being senior partner of the firm for the following three years. He then purchased 200 acres of cut-over land in the town of King, 12 miles east of Tomahawk and proceeded to develop the property, being so engaged until Jan. 1, 1920, at which time the farm was rated as one of the finest in Lincoln County. Mr. KUEHLING cleared 135 acres of the land, fenced the entire tract, and erected a fine set of modern buildings, thus making a most valuable contribution to the agricultural development of the region. In 1913 he was appointed to the position of county highway commissioner by the Lincoln County board of supervisors and has continued in that office ever since. He moved to Merrill in 1921, and now owns a comfortable modern home here. Mr. KUEHLING was first married on Feb. 20, 1909, and on May 2, 1922, he was united with his present wife, who was born in Merrill, Wis., Dec. 11, 1893, daughter of Mr. and Mrs. Gus E. POPHAL of Merrill, Wis. Mr. and Mrs. KUEHLING affiliate with St. John's Lutheran Church of Merrill and are highly respected throughout the community. Mr. KUEHLING is president of the Merrill Buick Co., and owns a half-interest in this concern, which has one of the most up-to-date garages in this section of the state, located at 1007 East Main St., Merrill. He has always commanded respect and esteem in the communities in which he has lived, and has been recognized as a man of marked ability. He was a member of the Lincoln County board of supervisors for two years, having been elected chairman of the town board; he was city supervisor of Tomahawk for two years, and during his residence in the town of King he was clerk of his school district there for six years.

Kuehling, William F. representative in Tomahawk, Lincoln County, of the Standard Oil Company, was born in Saxony, Germany, May 3, 1887, son of Herman and Marie KUEHLING, whom he accompanied to American when he was six months old. The family settled on a farm at Unity, Clark County, Wis., where William F. was reared, and where he attended school, finally passing the eighth grade. There his father died in 1921, but Mrs. Herman KUEHLING is still residing there, with her daughter, Emma (Mrs. Albert BERNITZ) and Frieda who is Mrs. Edwin TESMAR of Colby, Wis.

William F. remained on the home farm until the spring of 1906, when, a young man of 19, he went to North Dakota and was there employed in construction work on the Garrison extension of the "Soo" Railway. In the fall of the same year he came to Tomahawk and during that season and in the following winter worked for his brother Herman in the latter's bakery. In May, 1907, he went to work for the Northern Hardware Co. of Tomahawk as clerk and salesman, and was with that concern for two years, at the end of which time the company closed out the business. Mr. KUEHLING, with Leo MARTZ, then bought the company's plumbing department and subsequently operated a shop on Wisconsin Avenue under the firm name of Martz & Kuehling, in which business he continued until July 8, 1919, when he sold his interest in it to Mr. MARTZ and engaged in his present occupation, becoming agent and local manager for the Standard Oil Company. He has built up a fine business, his territory covering a radius of 20 miles in and about Tomahawk. In politics he rather favors the Republican party but first considered the candidates when casting his ballot. On Feb. 19, 1912, Mr. KUEHLING was united in marriage with Martha E. BARTZ, who was born in Wausau, Wis., Feb. 23, 1893, daughter of Herman and Bertha (LITZSCHWATER) BARTZ, and was brought to Tomahawk by her parents when three months old. She was educated in the public schools here, passing the grades. In 1917 her parents moved to a farm about two miles from Tomahawk. Mr. and Mrs. KUEHLING has one child, Eileen, born Oct. 24, 1916. Their residence, which they own, is a comfortable bungalow at 217 Third Street South. Mr. KUEHLING belongs to the Masonic Blue Lodge in Tomahawk, also at the Eastern Star Chapter, and to Lodge No. 696, B. P. O. E. Mrs. KEUHLING is a member of the Eastern Star.

Labbe, Victor E. who is engaged in the general insurance business in Tomahawk, Lincoln County, of which city he has been a resident for 22 years or more, was born in

Redford, N. Y., August 17, 1878, son of Albert and Mary (TREMBLAY) LABBE. The father, a native of Canada, moved to New York State when 18 years of age and was there purchasing agent for the Chauteaugay Ore & Iron Co. Subsequently he returned to Canada and engaged in the furniture business in Montreal, where he is still living. It was in New York State that he was married to Mary TREMBLAY, who was born in that state of French ancestry. Their family numbered six children, Victor E., Diana, Adelard, Ernestine and Ernest (twins) and Elmo. All are now living but Ernest. Victor E. LABBE attended school in New York State until eight years old and then went with his parents to Montreal, where he finished his schooling. He then started business life as office boy for a lumber firm, a job at which he remained for a year and a half, after which he spent five years as assistant bookkeeper in a hardware store. Then for 14 months he worked as bookkeeper for his uncle, George H. LABBE, head of the firm of Geo. H. Labbe & Co., furniture manufacturers. On April 10, 1901, he came to Tomahawk and became clerk in the Mitchell Hotel, where he remained for six months. He then became bookkeeper in the Bradley Bank, being thus occupied for two years and a half, after which he entered the employ of the Tomahawk Pulp & Paper Co. With that concern he remained as bookkeeper for 11 1/2 years, and in that position he continued until Jan. 1, 1923, when he engaged in his present business. He is a stockholder in the Bradley Bank and takes an active part in various civic affairs, in business and social circles being recognized as a man of ability and good citizenship and being popular among his associates. Mr. LABBE was married in Tomahawk, July 19, 1902, to Delia LEVEILLE, daughter of Joseph and Delphine (LABBE) LEVEILLE. Her father was one of the pioneers of Tomahawk, coming here before the railroad was built, and being a carpenter by trade he helped to put up many of the early buildings here. He and his wife spent the rest of their lives in this city, his death occurring in 1901 and hers in 1913. Mr.

and Mrs. LABBE are the parents of five children, Muriel, Paul, Robert, and John and Daniel.

Londo, Orville one of the few surviving pioneers of the city of Tomahawk, Lincoln County, was born in the province of Quebec, Canada, March 11, 1861, of Canadian-French parentage. When he was nine years old, the family having lost all they had by fire, the father came to Wisconsin, found work in Wausau, and as soon as they had accumulated a little money, returned to Canada for his family. On his return with them they all located on a homestead in Marathon County, 11 miles from Wausau, which they began to develop, and though very poor and suffering many privations, in time they cleared up the place and found themselves the owners of a fairly good farm. There in time both parents died. Orville LONDO had but little schooling but from a very early age has been engaged in the active pursuits of life with the main object of making a living, which he has done practically since the age of 11 years, at which time he used to ride race horses. At 12 he hauled logs for his father with an ox team, and it was not long before he was contributing out of his earnings to the support of the family. On May 4, 1887, he was married at Duck Creek, near Green Bay, Wis., to Rose CORBEY, daughter of John L. and Delphine (ARSONBEAU) CORBEY, and who was born at Green Bay March 16, 1861. A few months later, in July that year, he and his wife came to Tomahawk with a wagon and team, bringing their few personal belongings with them, and buckling down to hard work as pioneer settlers of the little village, which had just then been founded. It was on Bradley's first plat of the town, known as the "Forks" and three miles south of the present site of Tomahawk that they first located, residing for the first year in a small log shanty with a trough roof. It was a poor dwelling-place, especially in winter, as it was not storm-proof and leaked badly, so that icicles would even form on the stovepipe. It was there that their first child, Elroy, was born, without the assistance of a doctor or nurse, and soon after its birth it was found necessary to remove the mother and child to a more comfortable location. This child was born in February and during the following winter work was very scarce, but Mr. LONDO secured a job working for a lumber and mill many, for whom he hauled logs at the rate of $2.50 per 1000 feet, "finding" both himself and the team. It was small pay even for those days, and by the time he got the job he was entirely out of money and had to get supplies from the camp store on the strength of it. This was about all he got, for his employer, it seems, was also in embarrassed circumstances, and when spring came told him he could not pay him, but allowed him to take the remaining supplies in the store and such lumber as he might need to build a house. Those early years were very hard ones for the family, but gradually times improved for them and Mr. LONDO finally became prosperous. Today he owns four large farms in this vicinity, three of which are occupied by renters, the other being operated by him. He has fair sets of buildings on all the farms. The one he operates, which lies close to the city, is well stocked with dairy cattle and is well equipped with all necessary tools and machinery. He is also engaged in logging timber from his own lands, carrying on this work continually, and he owns a comfortable residence at No. 104 Soma Avenue, Tomahawk. Mr. LONDO was reared a Catholic and in politics has always been independent. He and his wife have been the parents of four children, Elroy A., Louis M., Josephine J., and George E., whose record in brief is as follows: Elroy A., born Feb. 26, 1888, is married and is now doing dental laboratory work in Chicago. Louis N., born Oct. 22, 1889, is living at home and is assisting his father in logging. He was the first child baptized among the members of St. Mary's Catholic Church, then a small congregation worshipping in the building now known as Foresters' Hall. Josephine J., born June 24, 1895, is a bookkeeper in the employ of Blum Bros., of Marshfield, Wis., where she resides.

George E., born Sept. 8, 1896, is residing at home, and, like his brother Louis, is assisting his father in the latter's logging enterprises. Elroy and George were both in the United States service during the World War. Elroy, who entered the navy and trained at Great Lakes, was en route for France when the armistice was signed and the vessel turned back. George, who was in the ambulance corps of the army, went overseas and saw active service for 11 months in France.

Lee, John P. who for 15 or 16 years has been pleasantly and profitably engaged in the culture of small fruits within the limits of the city of Tomahawk, was born at Delafield, Waukesha County, Wis., son of Peter and Elizabeth LEE. The parents were natives of Ireland who came to the United States in 1848 while yet single, locating in Brooklyn, N. Y., where they were married. It was in the early 50's that they came to Wisconsin, settling in Waukesha County, where Peter LEE died in 1869. His wife Elizabeth died at the age of 74 in the year 1900. Their family numbered eight children in all, of whom six are living, namely: Michael B., Mary, James, Frank, Kate and John P. Mary is the wife of Thomas NAKINS of North Dakota, James and Frank reside in Chicago, and Kate is the wife of William SHEEHAN of West Allis, Wis. The two deceased are Joseph and James. John P. LEE was reared at Delafield, Wis., where he attended common school. When 12 years old he was hired by a man who conducted a small farm to work for him eight months (the active farm season) for 50 dollars. After doing so he returned home for a while. Altogether he worked for that man eight years, during which time he received a thorough training in agriculture and horticulture, his employer being a man who conducted his place in accordance with modern scientific methods. After he left that farm Mr. LEE went successively to Marinette and Menomonie and was engaged for two years in logging. He next went to the Dakotas as a farm laborer, returning to Wisconsin in 1882 and locating at Wausau where for the next five years he was engaged in logging. In 1887 he came to Tomahawk, that being the year in which the village was founded, and here he continued in the same occupation, for 20 years handling the mill wood. At the end of that period Mr. LEE bought six acres of land within the city limits of Tomahawk and engaged in horticulture, in which occupation he has since continued, raising berries and small fruits, and making a specialty of ever-bearing strawberries, for which he finds a ready home market. He occupies a neat and comfortable residence of Kellystone finish outside and with good modern equipment. Mr. LEE is one of the representative citizens of Tomahawk and for 20 years served as such on the county board. He is a charter member of the Commerical Club and was one of a committee of three on agriculture that was instrumental in organizing the Tomahawk Agricultural Society. He has always been strongly progressive and is as widely respected as he is well known. In 1889 Mr. LEE was married at Madison, Wis., to Sophronia WINTERS, daughter of James and Mary (ASHCRAFT) WINTERS. Her parents, both now deceased, were native of Missouri, and in 1861-62 James ASHCRAFT engaged in fighting the Indians at Ft. Ridgely and New Ulm in the great Sioux outbreak. Mr. and Mrs. LEE are the parents of two children, Joy and Lowell.

Jacks, Henry D. representative of Tomahawk and elsewhere, of the Metropolitan Life Insurance Company, was born at Howard City, Mich., Jan. 7, 1891, son of Thomas and Ellen (HOWE) JACKS. The father, born in Glasgow, Scotland, June 1, 1824, came to the United States when a young man, and settling in the vicinity of Howard City, Mich., engaged in the logging and lumbering business. He died there when nearly 87 years old, on May 28, 1911. His wife Ellen, mother of Henry D., was born in Montcalm County, Mich., Nov. 2, 1859, her parents having come to his country from England. She is still living and now resides with the subject of this sketch. The children in the family were: Tena, now Mrs.

William HEMMINGER of Tomahawk; Henry D., of Tomahawk; Emory of Cleveland, Ohio; William, who died in Tomahawk, April 1, 1920, and Albert of Tomahawk. Henry D. JACKS as a boy attended a grade school in Howard City, Mich. He first came to Tomahawk in 1906, but subsequently went back to Michigan and for two years was engaged in taking a business course in the Ferres Institute at Big Rapids, that state, and from there, when to Cleveland, Ohio, where he was in the tailor business for eight years. He then returned to Tomahawk and entered the employ of Henry EUBLE, proprietor of a tailor's shop, with whom he remained two years. Then on Dec. 17, 1917, he took his present position with the Metropolitan Life Insurance Co., as their representative in Tomahawk, and Merrill in Lincoln County, and Minocqua in Oneida County; and in addition to this, he is also salesman for the Chevrolet Automobile Co. Mr. JACKS was married June 4, 1916, to Emma H., daughter of Arthur and Ida (LAUZ) LAMBS, of Wausau, Wis., in which city she was born. The parents were of German nativity, the father born Jan 22, 1856, and the mother in December, 1867. The latter died in Wausau Nov. 28, 1919 but the former is still residing there. They came to this country when quite young with their respective parents at a time when the site of Wausau was yet unoccupied except by Indian savages. Mr. and Mrs. Henry D. JACKS own a comfortable residence at No. 128 Lincoln Avenue. They are the parents of two children: Anita L., born March 1, 1920, and Arline E., born March 22, 1921. The religious affiliations of the family are with the Methodist Episcopal Church, of which Mr. and Mrs. JACKS are members, while Mr. JACKS is also a member of the local Odd Fellows Lodge.

Atcherson, Herbert A. of the H.A. & R. M. Atcherson Co., of Tomahawk, proprietors of a flour and feed mill, and successfully operating both a wholesale and retail business, was born in Charleston, N. H., Feb. 8, 1854, son of

Thomas and Lorinda (STODDARD) ATCHERSON. The parents were both of English ancestry, the father a native of New Hampshire and the mother of Massachusetts, and they were married in the former state. Thomas ATCHERSON, who was a farmer by occupation, in 1856 brought his family to Wisconsin, settling in Adams County. He and his wife both died in Plainville, that county. They were the parents of seven children, as follows: Henry, now deceased; Charlotte, widow of Martin SPURBECK and now postmistress at Plainville; Minerva, who married Horace LA BAR and died in Kansas City, Mo.; Josephine, the widow of Henry BARRETT and now living in New Hampshire; Oscar, a resident of Plainville, Wis.; Walter, who lives in Friendship, Wis., and Herbert A. of Tomahawk. Herbert A. ATCHERSON was educated in the public schools of Kilbourn City, Wis., being graduated from the high school. He then returned to the home farm to care for his parents, and was engaged in its operation for some years, giving it up in order to take charge of the lumber yard at Kilbourn City belonging to the Goodyear Lumber Co. of Tomah. This he did very successfully for three years and was thereupon made mill superintendent for the company and sent to Sperbeck, Wis., to take charge of their interests there, remaining until the timber was exhausted. From that place he came to Tomahawk in 1889 and has since resided here, one of the pioneers of that city. On his arrival in Tomahawk Mr. ATCHERSON started a retail lumber business, but later branched out into the wholesale trade and as a manufacturer, being thus engaged until 1907, when he sold out his lumber interests and entered into the flour and feed business, erecting his present feed mill. As above mentioned, he is operating both a wholesale and retail business, and is associated with his son, Ray Morse, whom he took into partnership. They have been very successful and are numbered among the leading business men of the city. In addition to his milling interests Mr. ATCHERSON owns extensive timber lands, and also some farms, one of which he operates, and he and his son each own a good modern residence at the corner of Fifth and Somo Streets. At various times he has also rendered efficient public service. He was a member of the commission to establish ward lines for Tomahawk City; served on the school board for 16 years, one term as its president, and was for years a member of the Lincoln County Board of Supervisors. His fraternal society affiliations are with the local Masonic lodge which he has served as master. Mr. ATCHERSON was married June 25, 1883, to Estella MORSE, daughter of Uri and Marinda MORSE of Big Spring, Adams County, Wis., and of this union has been born the son above mentioned, Ray Morse, on Feb. 18, 1891. The latter, was graduated from the Tomahawk High School and from Ripon College. On June 23, 1920 he married Mary Vance MEADOWS, daughter of Samuel and Minne MEADOWS of Wausau, Wis., and they have one child, Elizabeth Vance, born June 11, 1922. Mrs. H. A. ATCHERSON is a member of the Congregational Church, which Mr. ATCHERSON attends and helps to support. The family occupies a high social station in Tomahawk.

Baker M.D., George Rowe for more than 20 years a resident of Tomahawk, Lincoln County, and prominent in his profession, was born at Thompsonville, Racine County, Wis., Dec. 27, 1873, son of George and Mary Anne (SMITH) BAKER. The parents were natives of that county and farmers by occupation, owning a farm of 260 acres. The father died in 1913, but the mother is still living and has now attained the age of 78 years. They had three children, Abram H., George R., and Mary E. George Rowe BAKER was reared on the home farm, which he helped to operate, and, when young attended district school. His education was carried farther at the Beloit Academy, where he was graduated in 1895. He then entered the medical department of Marquette University, Milwaukee, where he was graduated and received his degree of M.D. in 1900. After that he took a course in the

Post-graduate School in Chicago and spent five months in Columbus Memorial Laboratory. During his last year at Marquette he taught pathology under Dr. EVANS. He spent one year at Trinity Hospital, Milwaukee, and was there closely connected with Drs. NOBLES and MALONE, for four months taking charge of Dr. MALONE'S practice in Milwaukee. In 1900 he came to Tomahawk and engaged in general practice, specializing, however, in surgery. He has since been intimately connected with the growth and development of Sacred Heart Hospital; all his surgical activities have been carried on there. This institution has attained a very enviable reputation in northern Wisconsin and stands high among those of its kind in the state. It is also recognized by the National College of Surgeons. In 1916 Dr. BAKER became associated with Dr. William C. MCCORMICK and they have since practiced together under the firm name of Baker & McCormick, winning a fine reputation and enjoying an ample measure of success. Dr. BAKER is a member of the county and state medical societies, the American Medical Association and the Wisconsin Surgical Association. He enlisted for World War service, being commissioned in June, 1917, and called for service in the medical corps Aug. 7, 1917. After training at Ft. Riley, Kans., two and a half months, he was assigned to the 355th infantry, 89th Division, and in June, 1918, crossed over to France, after his arrival there being stationed in the Lucy Sector, Grande France, as regimental surgeon, and was with the troops in all engagements participated in by the 89th Division. While attending a wounded soldier in the Argonne he was wounded in the ankle by a piece from a high explosive shell, which broke his leg, destroyed a large section of bone and severed the main nerve, after which he was confined to the hospital for ten months. He then returned to the United States and was discharged in August, 1919, at Ft. Sheridan, Ill. He is a member of the American Legion and is also a 32d degree Mason, Scottish Rite. Dr. BAKER was married in Milwaukee, April 25, 1900, to Martha C. NEARY, daughter of John and Ellen NEARY, the father being a native of Ireland and the mother of Milwaukee; both parents are now deceased. Dr. and Mrs. BAKER have one son, Rowe George, who is also a student of medicine. He has finished a four-year course at Wisconsin State University and is now finishing his course at Rush Medical College.

GEO. R. BAKER, M. D.

Ball, William H. an active young business man of Tomahawk, engaged in the electrical business in partnership with George LAMBERT, was born at Proctor, Penn., Dec. 28, 1890, son of James and Hettie BALL. The parents were natives of New York State who came to Tomahawk in 1904, where James BALL, organized a company and built a stave mill, which he operated for three years. He later became a manufacturer of cigars but finally sold his business and is now living retired. When he first came west he was associated with the United States Leather Co., and was superintendent of their tanneries at Prentice, Rib Lake, Medford, Phillips, and

Mellen, Wis. He and his wife Hettie were the parents of seven children, of whom those now living are Emerson, Evelyn, Nellie and William H., Nellie being the wife of E. M. WAKEFIELD of Chicago. Those who died were James, Lester and Howard. William H. BALL attended school in Pennsylvania, also at Phillips, Wis., where the family spent three years, and in Tomahawk, being graduated from the high school here in 1909. He then became an employee of the electric company, at that time operated by the Bradley Co., and was thus occupied for some years. Afterwards he worked a short time for A. M. PRIDE, and then in the fall of 1918 he formed his present partnership with George LAMBERT. They do all kinds of electric work, keep a good line of electric supplies and sell the Delco lighting plants. Mr. BALL is also manager for the Tomahawk Baseball Association, and, like his partner, Mr. LAMBERT, is a member of the Commercial Club, being always ready to promote the interests of his adopted city. He was married in Tomahawk in 1914 to Angie SMITH, daughter of James W. and Hulda SMITH, her father being a well known citizen of Tomahawk engaged in the logging business, who is now living; her mother has passed away. Mr. and Mrs. BALL are the parents of a son, William Robert.

Bauer, J. August engineer of the Tomahawk city waterworks, and a well known and popular citizen, was born in Germany, Jan. 25, 1857, son of Carl and Elizabeth BAUER, the father being a shoemaker by trade. The children of Carl BAUER were William, J. August, Libby and Christian, of whom the two latter are deceased. Christian having been killed by a fall from a tree which he was trimming. Both parents spent their lives in Germany. J. August BAUER was reared and education in his native land, and subsequently worked for the government as stage driver until he was 21. On June 25, 1880 he came to the United States, settling at Montego, Mich., where he found employment in a sawmill for a while. After that he loaded steamboats one summer, and afterwards until 1889 he worked during the summers in mills and during the winters in the woods at logging. Then coming to Tomahawk, he opened the hotel known then as the Muskegan House, which he conducted for ten years, at the end of that time selling out. During the next five years he was street commissioner, subsequently being appointed to his present position, which he has held for 18 years up to May 1, 1923, having rendered the city skilful and satisfactory service. He is a member of the Methodist Episcopal Church and, fraternally, of the Independent order of Odd Fellows. In 1884, at Montego, Mich., Mr. BAUER was married to Johanna AILEY, daughter of William and Caroline AILEY, both parents being now deceased. Of this marriage four children were born, of whom three are now living, Ralph, Carrie, and Ernest. Ralph, who is employed as foreman of the chain-gang in the paper-mill, enlisted during the war in the Tomahawk Machine Gun Company, trained at Waco, Texas; then went to France as sergeant and saw service in the 32d Division at Chateau Thierry and in the Argonne, where he was gassed. He was also with the army of occupation, and after two years' service returned to the United States and was discharged in 1919. Carrie is the wife of Albert BISHOP and is keeping house for her father; she has two children, Bauer A. and Elizabeth. Ernest is now living on his father's farm of 160 acres.

Bauman, William G. vice president and general manager of the Tomahawk Steel & Iron Works, was born in Chicago, Ill., Nov. 22, 1888, son of Adam and Sophia (SCHULTZ) BAUMAN. The father, a boiler maker by trade, was a native of Bavaria, Germany, and the mother of Chicago, in which city they were married. Their children, who are now living, in addition to the subject of this sketch, are: Emma, now Mrs. Charles PECKAT of Chicago; Amanda, wife of M. G. NEUBACHER of La Grange, ill., and Lillian, who is unmarried. William G. BAUMAN acquired his education in his native city of

Chicago, passing from the grade school into the high school, but his last two years of high school studies were taken in an evening school, as he had to work during the day time. It was in the steel mills of South Chicago that he learned the practical part of the iron and steel industry and while working there he took a night course in mathematics and metallurgy in the Armour Institute of Technology. In 1911 he entered the construction department of the Scully Iron & Steel Co. of Chicago, and worked there for a while, later becoming a traveling salesman for the company and continuing as such until April, 1917. On April 10, four days after the United States declared war on Germany, he enlisted in the regular army, becoming a private in the light artillery, and after a brief training went overseas. He served in France for 19 months being discharged July 2, 1919, with the rank of first lieutenant. On his return home he resumed his old employment as traveling salesman with the Scully Iron & Steel Co., and so continued Nov. 29, 1920, when he gave it up to become vice president and general manager of the Tomahawk Iron & Steel Works, in which he had purchased an interest. On March 18, 1920, Mr. BAUMAN was united in marriage with Margaret C. DREVER, who was born in Tomahawk, Wis., March 17, 1898, daughter of William and Elizabeth (HALL) DREVER, with whom he and his wife reside. Mr. and Mrs. BAUMAN are the parents of one child, William Drever, who was born Aug. 22, 1922. They affiliate religiously with the Congregational Church, and Mr. BAUMAN is a member of Lagrange Post, No. 41. In politics he is independent.

Baumgartner, William C. proprietor of a modern steam laundry plant at Tomahawk, was born on a farm in Stephenson County, Ill., near the city of Freeport, in 1866, son of John and Mary BAUMGARTNER. The father was a native of Ohio and the mother of Pennsylvania; the parents came west as children, their respective families driving overland and settling on farms near Freeport, Ill. at a time when Indians were still numerous in that section. John and Mary BAUMGARTNER remained there after their marriage until 1882, in which year they moved to Naperville, Ills., where they spent the remainder of their lives, the husband and father being engaged in carpenter work; he died in April of 1911 and his wife in March of the same year, leaving three children living: Samuel, who lives at Naperville and is a painter by trade; Anna, also of Naperville, wife of John BENTZ; and William C. William C. BAUMGARTNER attended district school near Freeport, and when 16 years of age removed with his parents to Naperville. He continued his education at the latter place, subsequently attending Northwestern College, and then for some time worked at painting with his brother Samuel and at carpenter work with his father. He next operated a hand laundry for two years, and after selling that enterprise went to Batavia, Ill, where he conducted a similar business for a time. From Batavia he went to Waukegan, Ill., and from there in 1902 he came to Tomahawk, remaining here only briefly at that time, however, before going to Wisconsin Rapids, where he subsequently spent four years in the hand laundry business. For the five years following this period he was head laundryman for the state of Wisconsin, and after leaving that position he returned to Tomahawk and purchased the laundry here, which he has since operated. He has improved the property and equipment and has built it up into a thoroughly modern steam laundry, employing five people and constituting a fine addition to the conveniences of life in the city of Tomahawk. Mr. BAUMGARTNER has been in the laundry business for 30 years, and the city is very fortunate in having a man of his type connect with the enterprise. He is a member of the Tomahawk Commercial Club, and his fraternal affiliations are with the Woodmen of the World. Mr. BAUMGARTNER was married at Naperville, Ill., in 1890 to Mary A. SHAFFER, daughter of Aaron and Alice SHAFFER, who were engaged in farming near that place; Mrs.

BAUMGARTNER'S parents are both deceased. Mr. and Mrs. BAUMGARTNER are the parents of three children: Ruth A., now Mrs. Michael HICKEY of Antigo, Wis.; Charles W., associated in business with his father; and Ralph E., who is employed in the Searles feed business in Tomahawk. Charles W. and Ralph E. both made excellent records for themselves in the World War enlisting 1917 in the Tomahawk Machine Gun Company; they trained at Waco, Texas, and went to France attached to the 119th Machine Gun Battalion, 32nd Division, serving 16 months and taking part in the operations at Chateau Thierry, on the Soissons front, and in the Argonne, with the 10th Army Corps. At the conclusion of hostilities they were with the army of occupation on the Rhine. Both are members of the American Legion at Tomahawk.

Bradley, W. H. who was responsible for much of the development of Tomahawk and surrounding territory was born at Bangor, Me., Feb. 25, 1838, and died at Milwaukee, Wis., Jan. 7, 1903. He came west with his father Daniel W. BRADLEY in 1855, and during the following winter they were on the Au sable River in Michigan. In 1860 they commenced buying timber on the Red River, hiring it sawed at Oshkosh until, in 1862, with others they erected a mill at that point. In 1865 they went to Muskegon, Mich., from which place they operated on the Muskegon, Manistee, and Pete Marquette rivers, erecting a mill at Muskegon in connection with Wheeler, Hopkins, & Co. in 1867. In 1877 W. H. BRADLEY returned to Wisconsin, locating in Milwaukee and from 1880 to 1886 Bradley Bros. & Co. operated on the Chippewa River, the latter part of the time under the name of the State Lumber Co. Mr. BRADLEY also operated on the Wisconsin River waters as the Bradley Co. and the United States Lumber Co., with principal offices at Tomahawk. He was interested in mills here with a brother, J. W. and a cousin, Levi BRADLEY, and he carried on very extensive operations. In 1886, in connection with the C. M. & St. P. Railway he organized the Tomahawk Land & Boom Co., built a large dam here, and in 1888 erected his first Tomahawk mill. He was connected in a financial way with most of the town's enterprises, was the largest owner of the Marinette, Tomahawk & Western railroad with its 62 miles of main line, and was a heavy stockholder in the "Soo" and Milwaukee roads, being at the time of his death one of the board of directors of the "Soo." He organized a company conducting a large department store at Tomahawk, with six branch stores along the line of his railroad, and was interested in a large number of lumber concerns and timber and land companies. He was instrumental in securing for Tomahawk the splendid schools and hospital there, and every church in Tomahawk was well supported by him. A man of fine public spirit, he was as well known for his strict integrity, and his word was as good as his bond. He left Tomahawk four weeks previous to his death, being conscious that his end was approaching, and he passed away at his home in Milwaukee. Two days before his death he married Miss Marie HANNEMEYER, his private secretary for 20 years, and one-third of his wealth went to the bride of two days, and one third to his adopted son, William T. BRADLEY, and other third being divided between his two brothers, Edward and James W. BRADLEY.

W. H. BRADLEY

Bronsted, Henry E. and Martinson, Fred were the first of Tomahawk's sons to fall at the front in the World War, and in both life and death they were closely united. Both were born in Tomahawk, BRONSTED on June 26, 1898 and MARTINSON on September 15, 1895. The former was the son of John M. and Bertha (WALLER) BRONSTED and was a graduate of the Tomahawk High School, while MARTINSON was the son of Christian and Christine MARTINSON and had acquired his education in the grade school. They had been playmates, schoolmates and comrades, and both enlisted in the Wisconsin National Guards in 1917, being member of the Fourth Infantry. After preliminary training at Camp Douglas,

Wisconsin, they went with they company to Camp McArthur at Waco, Texas, where the regiment was broken up and the company to which the boys belonged became Company A, 119th Machine Gun Battalion, 32d Division. On Feb. 18, 1918 they embarked at Hoboken for overseas and arrived at Brest, France March 4. Within four days they were advanced to within six kilometers of the front at Cuperly, near Chalons, and on June 2 they were into the trenches. They served on four fronts, in Alsace Lorraine at Chateau Thierry and at Juvigny. MARTINSON was wounded on the Juvigny front his lung being pierced by a machine-gun bullet, and died later in the hospital. It was on the same front that Henry E. BRONSTED was killed, Aug. 31, 1918, being struck in the heart by the fragment of a shell. Their remains were brought home, arriving at Tomahawk Jan. 1, 1921, and their joint funeral services were held at Maccabee Hall, the entire community turning out to pay them the last tribute. They were buried with military honors. Both being exemplary young men and Post No. 93 of the American Legion has been named in honor of Henry E. BRONSTED.

Bronsted, John for the last 25 years a resident of the city of Tomahawk, Lincoln County, and the father of two sons who served in this country's ranks in the World War, one of whom made the supreme sacrifice, was born in Kongesberg, Norway, Nov. 1, 1864, son of Lars and Ingeborg (TOLLEFSON) BRONSTED. The father, who was a smelter working in silver mines, died when the subject of this sketch was three months old, and many years later, in 1898, his widow crossed the ocean to make her last home with her children who had previously emigrated. There were five children in the family: Olaf, the first to come to America, who is now deceased; Josephine, now Mrs. Charles ANDERSON of Brule, Wis.; Gustave, residing in Chicago; Laura, wife of John JACOBSON of Wisconsin Rapids, and John of Tomahawk. John BRONSTED who had but a limited education, located in what is now the city of Wisconsin Rapids in 1882. At that time it [Wisconsin Rapids] consisted of the two cities of Grand Rapids and Centralia. Having remained there until 1896, he then moved to Harshaw, Oneida County, then a small settlement dependent upon the logging industry which was carried on in the vicinity, and in which Mr. BRONSTED was employed. When the surrounding timber had been cut the place declined, and in 1898 Mr. BRONSTED moved to Tomahawk, where he has since made his home. He has always been employed in one department or another of the lumbering industry, much of the time working in the sawmills. He was married on Aug. 26, 1891, at Arkdale, Adams County, Wis., to Bertha WALLER, who was born in that place Feb. 1, 1862, daughter of Tolaf and Helen (NELSON) WALLER, who were farmers by occupation, and both of whom are now deceased. To Mr. and Mrs. BRONSTED have been born four children, Carl J., Leonard T., Amel and Henry E. Carl J., who was born at Wisconsin Rapids, May 24, 1892, is now office manager and bookkeeper for Frank THEILER, lumberman. He was married Sept. 17, 1922 to Julia T. JOHNSON of Tomahawk in which city she was born Jan. 2, 1904. Leonard T. BRONSTED, born at Dancy, Wis., May 24, 1893, was married Oct. 25, 1920 to Anna MOE of Tomahawk, who was born here April 3, 1891. He is now in partnership with his father-in-law, Hans MOE, they being proprietors of an ice business in this city. Amel A. BRONSTED, born at Harshaw, Wis., Jan. 27, 1896, is employed as clerk in the hardware store of A. J. OLSON of Tomahawk. On May 10, 1917, he enlisted in the Wisconsin National Guard, becoming a member of Machine Gun Company Fourth Wis., Inf. Having trained first at Camp Douglas, he was sent thence to Camp McArthur, where the regiment was split up, his entire company being transferred to Co. A., 119th Machine Gun Battalion, 32d Division. He entrained for Hoboken, N.J., Feb. 2, 1918 and 16 days later embarked for overseas, landing at Brest, France, March 4. Four days later his battalion was at

Cuperly, near Chalons, which was within six kilometers of the front, and on June 2 they were in the trenches. They served on four fronts - in Alsace-Lorraine, at Chateau Thierry and at Juvigny, and it was in the battle at the place last mentioned that his brother Henry was killed. Amel later served in the Argonne Forest and when the armistice was signed he was in the trenches fronting the Meuse River. His company subsequently marched through Luxemburg and on Dec. 1 crossed the Rhine at Coblence, entering Germany with the army of occupation. He was stationed in Issenberg, Germany for four and a half months, and sailed about the middle of May for home, being discharged at Camp Grant, Illinois, June 1, 1919. Although in active servied on the war front for a year and three months he escaped without a scratch. Henry E. BRONSTED, who was born June 26, 1898 in Tomahawk, Wis., served in the same battalion and division and was killed at Juvigny. His record is separately given in connection with that of his friend, Fred MARTINSON, who was skilled at the same time. The Bronsted family are affiliated religously with the Norwegian Lutheran Church, and are highly respected in the community.

Brooks, Hal L. postmaster of the city of Tomahawk, where he has resided for the last 25 years, and who for many years has been active in the lumber industry as a jobber and dealer in forest products, was born in the town of Medford, Mass., Oct. 1, 1864, son of Luther and Georgiana (DYER) BROOKS. The parents were of English puritan stock, the father a manufacturing jeweler by occupation; they died years ago in Massachusetts. Hall L. BROOKS in his youth attended the common schools up to the age of 14 years. At the age of 17 he went to work in lumber camps in the state of Georgia and henceforth supports himself and was independent of the home folks. He followed that occupation for a number of years, learning it thoroughly, and in 1885 came to Wisconsin, locating at Schofield, Marathon County, where he followed lumbering until 1897 for others, and since then has operated on his own account as a jobber and dealer in various forest products. It was in 1898 that he located permanently in Tomahawk, where he soon became well known as a man of good business ability and reliable character, so that it was not long before he was called upon to take part in the affairs of local government. From 1907 to 1922 he was a member of the Lincoln County Board of Supervisors, and served three terms as its chairman, which position he was occupying when appointed postmaster of Tomahawk in October, 1922. He has always been a Republican in politics and in the winter of 1905-06 represented his district in the state legislature. Previous to that for seven years he was a member of the Langlade County board. He did good patriotic service during the World War as a member of the board of defense. Mr. BROOKS was married Oct. 21, 1891, to Edith A. BELANGER, daughter of Frank and Mary BELANGER of Wisconsin Rapids, Wis. During the war Mrs. BROOKS was active in Red Cross work.

Ball, Mrs. Joseph A. who was the first white woman to settle in Tomahawk, of which place she is still a resident, was born in Portage County, Wisconsin. Nov. 28, 1856, daughter of Bartholomew and Helen (FLEMMING) MAHANNA. Her parents were from the east, having been married in Malone, N.Y., on June 1, 1854, immediately after which they had set out to make a home for themselves in the wilds of Wisconsin, traveling by boat over the Great Lakes to Sheboygan and from there overland to Portage County. It took courage to say good bye to all old friends and associations and make up their minds to suffer years of privation in a country consisting mostly of forest inhabited by savages, and with white neighbors few and far between. But they both possessed this courage and bravely and steadfastly played their humble parts in the drama of the West. Mr. MAHANNA'S part in it lasted some 16 years, for he died on the Portage county farm on Aug. 13, 1871. His wife Helen survived him many years, passing away in Tomahawk Oct. 8, 1912. She had witnessed many wonderful changes; seen the passing of the Indian, the clearing of the forests, and the growth of towns, villages and cities, and the coming of the railroad and the automobile. Through it all she had done her part as a good wife and mother. Her children were: Wallace, who died Oct. 29, 1923; Ella, a twin sister of Wallace, deceased; Helen, also deceased; Mary, the subject of this sketch, and Louise who is deceased. Mary MAHANNA grew up on her parents' farm, and was instructed by her mother in household duties. On Oct. 7, 1877, she was united in marriage with John TOBIN of Portage County, Wis., son of Mr. and Mrs. James TOBIN, who had come to Wisconsin at an early day from Connecticut. Mr. MAHANNA was a California pioneer, having joined the rush of gold seekers to that territory soon after the discovery of the yellow metal there in 1849. He had the trip by way of Cape Horn and met with some success in his search. His wedding ring was made from a gold nugget that he brought home with him. John TOBIN was 21 when he began farming for himself, having previously lived on the home farm and assisted his father. He acquired a tract of 200 acres and put up a good set of buildings and by 1887 it was regarded as one of the best in that part of the country. In the spring of that year, leaving his wife on the farm, he came to Tomahawk to examine this locality, as it was the time when the village was just starting. Not wishing to decide upon removal too hastily, he got a job driving a stage between Tomahawk and Merrill, and after being thus engaged for a month he sent for this wife. On her arrival they located in a log shanty at a point on the Wisconsin River west of the Tomahawk town site, and just opposite Rodgers Island, and it was thus that Mrs. TOBIN, now Mrs. BALL became the original women pioneer of Tomahawk. It was above a month before the second white woman appeared. Mr. TOBIN cleared 125 acres west of the town site for the Tomahawk Land &

Boom Company for flowage ground, after which he launched out into business for himself, buying lots on S. Railway Street, corner of Spirit Avenue, and erecting a frame building into which he and his wife moved, turning it into a boarding-house as well as a residence. It was a good move to make, as the railroad was then building in, bring many workers to the place during its construction, and, after its completion many new settlers. Mr. TOBIN did not depend upon the boarding-house for a living entirely, however, for he became active in various other occupations, including the cord wood business, the dairy business and the ice business, building a large ice house. Later he became local agent for the Miller Brewing Co. of Milwaukee and the Badger State Bottling Co. of Watertown, and altogether he built up a large business and was successful so long as his health lasted, but on March 17, 1894 he died, and his widow took up the care of his business interests, including the farm, and conducting the boarding-house also until 1911. Some years previous to this latter date she had married for her second husband Joseph A. BALL of Tomahawk. Mr. BALL was born at Defiance, Ohio, and in 1900 came to Tomahawk, entering the employ of the C. M. and St. P. Railway in the car department, of which he is now foreman. In 1911 they gave up the boarding-house and they now have a comfortable residence on Spirit Avenue. Mrs. BALL had three children by her first husband, J. Leroy, Raymond J. and Mercedes. J. Leroy was born Aug. 7, 1880 and is now living in the west. Raymond J., born July 6, 1884, is in Seattle, Wash. Mercedes, born April 2, 1893, was married July 7, 1916 to Raymond J. WEIK, a traveling salesman, and she has had two children: Raymond J. Jr., born April 5, 1821, who died Jan. 19, 1922, and another who died in infancy. She was educated partly in the Tomahawk High School, where she spent one year, and partly in St. Mary's College in Prairie du Chien, which she entered in 1906, being graduated from the academic course in 1911 and in music in 1913. She is a lady of culture and refinement, and, though bereaved of her children, of an amiable disposition, resigning herself to the will of Providence.

Eklund, John a respected resident of Tomahawk, Lincoln County, of which he is a pioneer, was born in Sweden, Aug. 5, 1857, son of John and Ingelborg EKLUND. The parents spent their lives in Sweden, the father following the occupation of carpenter. They had four children, two of whom are now deceased, John and Gustav being the two living. John EKLUND was reared in his native land and attended school there. At the age of 15 he began to learn the carpenter's trade under his father's instruction and he subsequently followed it in Sweden until he was 25 years old. He then came to the United States, locating first in Providence, R. I., where he spent a year working at his trade; but at the end of that time he felt the attraction of the Northwest, where he knew many of his countrymen had settled, and came to Minneapolis, of which city he was a resident for seven years. During all that time he continued to work at his trade, and in 1888 found a new field for it in Tomahawk, which place had been laid out and practically started in that previous year, and which almost immediately became a busy hive of industry. Getting off the train at Heafford Junction, Mr. EKLUND rode by stage the rest of the way to Tomahawk, and on his arrival here found the town site covered by timber, but building had commenced and he found no lack of employment at his trade. He helped to build the Mitchell Hotel, the school, hospital and quite a few houses. Since then he had been closely identified with the industrial activities of the place and has taken a good citizen's interest in its development. He is a member of the Commercial Club and is also affiliated with the local lodges of Independent Order of Odd Fellows and Modern Woodmen of America, and he and his family attend the Congregational Church. Mr. EKLUND was married in Tomahawk in 1894 to Mary OLSON, daughter of Mr. and Mrs. Arvid OLSON, who came to Tomahawk from Sweden. Both her parents are now deceased. Mr. and Mrs. ECKLUND have four sons, Elmer Victor, Oscar A., Lawrence C. and Carl. When the United States entered into the World War, Elmer V. enlisted in the Navy Medical Corps, and was assigned to a hospital ship on which he served 27 months, except for three winter months which he spent in a hospital in Ireland. He is now working in Canada for Robert THIELMAN. Oscar A. is employed in the Ford plant in Minneapolis. Lawrence C. is attending the University of Wisconsin at Madison, and Carl is living at home with his parents.

Emerich, Erwin R. manager of the Tomahawk store of the Emerich Mercantile Co. of Merrill was born in Merrill, Wis., June 5, 1897, son of John A. and Anne (WESTPHAL) EMERICH. He was educated in the public schools of his native city, being graduated from the high school in the class of 1915. He then entered the company's store in Merrill to learn the business, and was thus occupied for several years, or until Sept. 15, 1918, when he entered the United States service and was sent to Beloit College at Beloit, Wis., for radio training in the S.A.T. Corps. The signing of the armistice less than two months later precluded any possibility of his getting into active service in the World War, and on Dec. 14, 1918, he received his discharge. He then re-entered his father's store and soon after he and his brother, Lyndon B., were sent out by the company to visit Tomahawk and other localities, carrying with them a stock of goods for sale, and this itinerant trade proving successful, the company in February, 1921, as elsewhere related, opened a branch store in Tomahawk, of which Erwin R. EMERICH was made manager. The business has justified the best hopes of its founders and Mr. EMERICH has shown himself an able manager, and taken his place among the successful business men of this city. On June 15, 1921, Mr. EMERICH was united in marriage with Irene E. EDSTROM, daughter of Gust and Sarah EDSTROM of

Merrill, Wis. She was born in La Crosse, Wis., May 15, 1898, and it was not long after that the family moved to Merrill. In the latter city she was a co-graduate with her husband in the high school class of 1915, subsequently attending the La Crosse Normal School, from which she was graduated in 1917. After that and until her marriage she taught in the grade schools of Merrill. Mr. and Mrs. EMERICH affiliate with the Congregational Church of Tomahawk. In politics Mr. EMERICH votes independently, though his political leanings are towards the Republican party.

Foss, Charles E. a respected citizen of Tomahawk in the employ of the Mohr Lumber Co., was born in Jackson County, Minnesota, in 1867, son of George D. and Catherine (ORR) FOSS. The father was born in New York State and when a young man enlisted for service in the Civil War in the 167th New York Volunteer Infantry. He was in the army four years, and it was after the war and his return home that he married Catherine ORR, who was a native of Canada. With an ox team they set out for Minnesota and on their arrival they took a homestead in Jackson County. Later Mr. FOSS secured another claim under the Soldier's Rights act in Cottonwood County. After farming in Minnesota until 1884 he and his wife moved to Wisconsin and bought a farm at Wild Rose, Waushara County, where he is still living, Mrs. FOSS having died in 1916. They had a family of six children: George M., now in North Dakota; Nellie, now Mrs. Wilder of Tomahawk; Jesse J., of Tomahawk; Herbert of Wild Rose, Wis.; Charles E. of Tomahawk, and one who died in infancy. Charles E. FOSS attended school in Minnesota and was reared on his parents' farm in Minnesota, which he helped his father to cultivate. He was a youth of 17 when he accompanied his parents to Wild Rose, Wis., and he remained on their farm there until he was 21. After that he ran a threshing-machine each fall and continued to work on farms until 1907. In that year he came to Oneida County and worked in the woods with a sawmill outfit as engineer, having learned that trade while operating threshing-machines. He remained there four years and then came to Tomahawk, where he worked two years at odd jobs and was three years with the Oelhafen Lumber Co. in their warehouse. Since then he has been with the Mohr Lumber Co. as millwright and engineer. Mr. FOSS was married at Stevens Point in April 1890, to Orrilla MAUPIN, daughter of R. B. and Marie (WYCHOFF) MAUPIN. Her father, like his own, had fought for the Union in the Civil war, having served in an Illinois regiment. After the war he settled with his family in Missouri, later moving to Portage County, Wis. Both he and his wife have passed away. Mr. and Mrs. FOSS have had six children, four of whom are now living: Mrs. Walter WELCH of Tomahawk; Edward R. of Antigo; May of Chicago and Ruth of Stevens Point. Those deceased are Myron and Leslie. In 1918 Edward was inducted into the U.S. service from Antigo and attached to the Railroad Transportation Corps. He went overseas and was stationed 11 months at St. Sulpice, France, returning to the United States and receiving his discharge in 1919.

Foster, Elmer D. partner in the Foster Lumber Company of Tomahawk, was born at Ironwood, Mich., Feb. 14, 1888, son of George H. and Emma (LAWSON) FOSTER. The parents were natives of Maine and the father, formerly an engineer on steamboats plying on the St. Lawrence River and Atlantic coasts running to Portland, Maine, is now a locomotive engineer on the Marinette, Tomahawk & Western Railway. They settled in Ironwood in 1886, from which place they moved to Tomahawk in 1890. Their children were Elmer D., John, Grace, Lawrence and Herman, of whom Herman is now deceased. Elmer D. FOSTER was two years old when his parents settled in Tomahawk, where he later attended school, being graduated from the high school in 1907. After that he kept books two years for the Somo River Lumber Co. Then with his brother Herman he engaged in the wholesale lumber business, the firm buying lumber from the mills in blocks and selling it in car load lots to the trade in the Middle West markets. The original style of the firm was Foster Bros., but was changed after Herman FOSTER'S death and is now the Foster Lumber Co., Leo BOURCIER being associated in the business with the subject of this sketch. They handle principally hardwood lumber in the rough. Mr. FOSTER is a stockholder in the Bradley Bank and a member of the Local Elks lodge. He was married in Chicago, Sept. 3, 1914, to Ruth Gray FIELD, daughter of Eugene and Julia S. FIELD. The well known Eugene FIELD is now dead but his wife is still living. Mr. and Mrs. FOSTER are the parents of two children, Jean FIELD and William Engler. The family have a pleasant cottage on the Wisconsin River, where they spend the summer months.

Foster, George H. a well known and respected citizen of Tomahawk, now in the employ of the Marinette, Tomahawk & Western Railway, was born in Portland, Maine, Nov. 14, 1860, son of Jefferson and Lucy Foster. The father a native of Scotland, came to America when a young man, locating in Quebec, where he found work on the docks loading timber vessels. Before the breaking out of the American Civil War he crossed the border into the state of Maine, where he later enlisted in a Maine regiment, went to the front and was killed in action. His wife, who was a native of Canada of French descent, died when her son George was born in 1860. George H. FOSTER, being thus left an orphan while yet an infant, was reared by his material grandparents in Canada, where he grew up and attended school. He started work at an early age, when 15 years old being engaged in firing an engine of a steamboat plying between Montreal and Portland, Me. When 18 he settled in Bedford, Maine, where he worked in cotton mills for a time, and from there went to Menominee, Mich., where he worked one year for the Curley-Carpenter Lumber Co. - in the woods in winter and on their farm in summer. Then in 1882 he came west to Stevens

Point, Wis., buying land in the town of Plover, Portage County, which he cleared and improved and on which he lived for five years required by the homestead law. That done, he went to Ironwood, Mich., where he ran a hoisting-engine for the Ashland Mine Co. It was in 1888 that he came to Tomahawk, soon after the place was started. He found things busy here and at first did carpenter work for the Bradley Company, erecting several buildings at Jersey City, after which he ran the engine on the Bradley tug boat which hauled the family Bradley pleasure train on the Wisconsin and Soma rivers. Subsequently he became locomotive engineer for Mr. BRADLEY on the Wisconsin & Chippewa Railway, later the M. T. W., and has since remained with that road. He is a member of the Brotherhood of Locomotive Engineers, and also of the Catholic Order of Foresters. Mr. FOSTER was married in the town of Plover, Portage County, Wis., in 1883, to Emma LAWSON, by whom he had two sons, Herman and Elmer. Herman is now dead, Elmer is the proprietor of the Foster Lumber Co., of Tomahawk. On Feb. 15, 1904 Mr. FOSTER was married secondly to Mary O'NEILL, daughter of Patrick and Elizabeth (BONCHARD) O'NEILL, the father being a native of Hartford, Wis., and of Irish descent, and the mother of Fond du Lac, Wis. The O'NEILL family lived on a farm in Lincoln County, one mile north of Grandfather Falls, where Mr. O'NEILL died in 1915 and Mrs. O'NEILL in 1900. Of their ten children six daughters are living, namely: Mary, Margaret, Della, Josephine, Rosa and Lucy. Margaret is the wife of Albert DAVIS, Della the wife of William DONALDSON, Josephine married Charles KIBLER, Rosa is now Mrs. Edward CASSELL and Lucy also married. Mr. and Mrs. FOSTER are the parents of two children: Grace A., a graduate of Tomahawk High School, is now a student in the Oshkosh State Normal School and Lawrence a student in the Tomahawk High School.

Foster, Herman G. in former years a well known business man of Tomahawk, but who passed away some five years ago, was born in Plover, Portage County, Wis., June 10, 1886, son of Mr. and Mrs. George FOSTER. After graduating from the Tomahawk High School, he entered the office of the Gillett Lumber Co., a brokerage concern, with whom he acquired knowledge of the business. Then with his brother Elmer, he engaged in the same business himself, having an office in the post office block, and a successful business was done up to the time of Mr. FOSTER'S death, which occurred Nov. 3, 1918. In addition to the lumber business he and his brother operated a gravel pit, selling their gravel to the highway commission. On March 19, 1903, Mr. FOSTER was united in marriage with Lillian ZASTROW, who was born in Tomahawk, Wis., Sept. 22, 1888, daughter of August and Elizabeth (OELHAFEN) ZASTROW, who now resides on S. Tomahawk Avenue. Mrs. FOSTER was educated in this city, being graduated from the high school with the class of 1908. In 1921 she purchased the Princess Theatre, a moving-picture theatre on W. Wisconsin Avenue, which she is now operating, and in other ways also she has shown good business ability, as in 1918 before her husband's death, she purchased 200 acres of wild land in the town of King, hired eight men with whose help she cleared 90 acres of it, and having sowed it with winter rye, sold the tract to Foster Bros. She was reared a German Lutheran but is not now affiliated with any church. Mr. FOSTER was a member of St. Mary's Catholic congregation and belonged also to the Knights of Columbus Council and to the Knights of Pythias lodge in Tomahawk. They had no children of their own but adopted a son, Hugh W., who was born Sept. 21, 1917.

Conant, Herbert L. a well known citizen of Tomahawk, for many years in the employ of the C. M. & St. P. Railway, was born near Viroqua, Vernon County, Wis., Aug. 8, 1861, son of Truman and Melissa (SANFORD) CONANT. The father was born in Pennsylvania of Dutch parentage, or ancestry, and the mother in New York state of English-Dutch ancestry. Having settled in Vernon County, Wis., after their marriage, they resided there some years, or until their son Herbert was about six years old, when they moved to Sparta, Monroe County, where they resided for six years. Then Truman CONANT'S health failing, he moved with his wife about 1885 to a farm near Tunnel City in the same county, where Mrs. Melissa CONANT died in 1893, and Mr. CONANT subsequently resided with his son Herbert in Tomahawk until his death in 1898. Herbert L. CONANT as a boy attended school at Tunnel City. At the age of 16 he began to earn his livelihood, working in sawmills in summer and in the woods in winter and was thus occupied up to 1883. In that year he entered the employ of the C. M. & St. P. Railway Co., and in various capacities has worked for it ever since. By 1899 he had been advanced to the position of locomotive engineer. He followed the railroad into Tomahawk in 1887 and in 1895 moved his family to this city. Mr. CONANT was married Augl. 8, 1882, to Abigail C. WOODARD, daughter of Silas and Lucinda WOODARD of Tunnel City, Wis. She was born in Ontario, Canada, April 5, 1864; at four years of age she accompanied her parents to New York State and later to Tunnel City, Wis. She died at Tomahawk Nov. 8, 1919 as the result of being struck by an automobile while she was crossing Fourth Street on foot. Mr. and Mrs. CONANT were the parents of five children: Roy A., born March 14, 1884, at Tunnel City, who is now living on a farm at Bradley, Wis.; Percy, born March 17, 1886, at Tunnel City, who died Nov. 12, 1886; Lloyd W., born Sept. 3, 1887, at Tunnel City, who resides in Bradley; Alma P., born March 27, 1890, at Wausau, Wis., who is the wife of Harry THEILER of Tomahawk; and Archie T., born June 12, 1894, in Tomahawk, who is residing in this city. Up to 1921 Mr. CONANT was a very active man. Since his wife's death he has been living with his daughter, Mrs. Harry THEILER at No. 7 East Spirit Avenue. In politics he votes independently but has leanings toward the Republican party. In New Lisbon, Wis. the family were members of the

Baptist Church, but as there is no church of that denomination in Tomahawk, they attend the Methodist Episcopal Church, in which Mrs. CONANT was a very active worker.

Cutter M.D., John D. one of the very few original pioneers of the city of Tomahawk who are yet living, and a man well and favorably known throughout Lincoln County, was born in the city of Bangor, Maine, Jan. 26, 1858, son of William and Harriett (BENJAMIN) CUTTER. The father was also a native of the Pine Tree State, having been born in the town of Greene Sept. 20, 1913. During his active career he was engaged in the land and lumber business, the pine forests of Maine being then a considerable source of wealth. In the early 30's he visited Wisconsin, perhaps to get some idea of its timber resources, but did not remain. He died in Brewer, Maine, Feb. 10, 1869. His wife Harriett was born at East Livermore, Maine, Nov. 24, 1823. After his death she came west to Milwaukee, where she passed away some 28 years later, on Jan 28, 1897. They were the parents of seven children. John D. CUTTER acquired his elementary education in the public schools of Bangor, Maine, after which he entered the State College, now the State University of Maine, at Orono, from which he was graduated in 1879 with the degree of Bachelor of Science. He then entered the Medical University of New York City, where he received his degree of M. D. in 1881. Thus equipped he located in Big Rapids, Mich., where he began the practice of medicine, and there he remained until 1886, when he came to "The Forks", now Tomahawk, and opened an office. It was on Dec. 19, 1886 that the stage on which Dr. CUTTER was riding rolled up to the site of the present flourishing city, but which at that time was anything but an attractive prospect. Indeed, it was not until the following year that the village was laid out and an effort made to give it the appearance of a civilized community. But Dr. CUTTER has remained ever since and has shared the fortunes of the place. He has been successful in his profession and bult up a good practice, now occupying commodious offices in the upper part of the post office building. From time to time he has rendered efficient public service to other matters. He served four years as superintendent of the Tomahawk schools when that office was elective, and he served four terms as mayor of the city. In politics he has always been a Democrat. There is probably no man in Tomahawk better informed in regard to the history of the city and country and his knowledge of it is personal and not depending upon hearsay. He was one of the charter members of Tomahawk Lodge No. 243, F & A. M., and was its master for five terms. He was also a charter member of Wisconsin Valley Lodge, K. P., and served two years as its chancellor. On Aug. 14, 1895, Dr. CUTTER was united in marriage with Helen B. PHILLEO, who was born at Grand Rapids, Wis., (now Wisconsin Rapids), on Feb. 9, 1873, daughter of Benton and Isabelle PHILLEO. She was graduated from the high school of her native city and for some time before her marriage was a teacher. She is a member of the Congregational Church, of which Dr. CUTTER, though not a member, is a liberal supporter.

JOHN D. CUTTER, M. D.

Danielson, Daniel a well known resident of Tomahawk and a trusted employee of the Mohr Lumber Co., was born in Norway, Aug. 9, 1863, son of Daniel and Elizabeth DANIELSON. The parents were farmers who spent their lives in their native land. They had six children, Daniel, Nels, Margaret, Magnus, Ellen and Johanna, of whom Nels and Margaret are now deceased. Magnus lives in Eagle, Alaska, and Ellen and Johanna are in Norway. Daniel DANIELSON grew up in his native land, where he went to school and afterwards worked at farming, fishing, sailing and as a tinsmith. It was in 1885 that he came to the United States, locating at Waupaca, Wis., where he worked in the woods one year. Thence he went to Milwaukee and for five years was a sailor in the U.S. revenue service on the Great Lakes. Subsequently returning to Waupaca County, Wisconsin, he worked in the woods at logging and also in saw mills. After a while he moved to Marathon County, where he helped to organize the town of Francin and was its first treasurer, holding office 12 years. While there he worked in saw mills, and also in partnership with Ole LEKLAM started a saw mill, which was sold to C. H. MOHR and Samuel STATCER of Portage, Wis. He also helped to organize the Mohr Statcer Lumber Co., which was later moved to Wausau and reorganized as the Mohr Lumber Co., in which he is a stockholder. He lived three years at Russell, Portage County, where he conducted a hardware store, in which he still has an interest. In 1918 Mr. DANIELSON came to Tomahawk and has since had charge of the Mohr Lumber Co. planing-mill. He is also a professional filer and has filed many mill saws. He was married in the town of Albin, Portage County, Wis., in 1903, to Marie DOBBEE, daughter of Peter and Anna DOBBEE, her parents being early settlers in Portage County, where the mother is still living, Peter DOBBEE having passed away. Mr. and Mrs. DANIELSON are the parents of two children; Delia, now attending St. Olaf's College in Minnesota, and Donald, who is attending the Tomahawk High School.

Draeger, William J. who is successfully engaged in the garage and auto repair business in Tomahawk, which he entered three years ago after a long career as a locomotive engineer, was born on a farm in the town of Wolf River, Winnebago County, Wis., Oct. 8, 1872, son of William and Hermina DRAEGER. The father was born in Germany, from which country he came to this when five years old, subsequently residing with a brother in Chicago until he was 17. It was then that he settled in Winnebago, where he engaged in farming. On Jan. 28, 1872, he was married to Hermina DRAEGER, a native of Oshkosh, Wis. Twelve years later, in 1884, he and his family became pioneers of Antigo, Wis., where for a number of years he followed the occupation of gardener, at times also being engaged in railroad work. In 1922, Jan. 28, he and his wife celebrated their Golden Wedding-a privilege granted to few married couples, and one which he did not long survive, as he passed away in the following year. His wife is still living and makes her home with her daughter, Mr. Ed FROELICH of Antigo, whose given name is Verona. Of the other children in the family two died in infancy, Alfred is employed by his brother William in Tomahawk, Jake resides in Minneapolis, Charles is in Antigo, and William J. is the subject of this sketch. William J. DRAEGER was reared on his parents' farm in Winnebago County, Wisconsin, and acquired his education in the district school. He was 12 years old when he accompanied his parents to Antigo, in which place he finished his schooling. He began railroad work as a water-boy at the age of 16. When 17 he became a locomotive fireman and at the age of 21 a locomotive engineer on the Milwaukee, Lake Shore & Western Railway, which is now a part of the Northwestern System. In 1897, Mr. DRAEGER came to Tomahawk as an engineer on the M., T., & W. Railway, known as the Bradley railroad, and that position he subsequently held for 22 years. Then in 1920 he engaged in the automobile business and is now proprietor of the Draeger Garage, providing storage, carrying a general line of accessories and doing general repair work. He belongs to the Brotherhood of Locomotive Engineers and also to the local lodge of Elks and that of the Masons. It was in this city that Mr. DRAEGER was married in 1900 to Cora HICKEY, daughter of James and Alice HICKEY, her father being a native of Canada and her mother of Prairie Farm, Barron County, Wis. Mr. and Mrs. HICKEY were residents of Prentice, Wis., for a time, and later of Rice Lake, Barron County, from which place they moved to Tomahawk, where Mr. HICKEY died in 1921, being survived by his wife, who is still living. Mr. and Mrs. DRAEGER are the parents of four children, Evelyn, Alice, Moebell and Henry.

Drever, William president and treasurer of the Tomahawk Steel & Iron Works, Tomahawk, Lincoln County, was born in Hamilton, Ontario, Oct. 30, 1858, son of Thomas and Mary (CHINNOCK) DREVER. The parents were married in England, of which country the mother was a native, the father having been born in Scotland. Immediately after their marriage they set out for Canada, their journey to the Dominion, therefore, having somewhat the character of a honeymoon trip, and after their arrival they made their home in Hamilton. In course of time they became the parents of seven children, three of whom are now living, namely: Thomas, of Burlington, Ont.; Mary, who married Isaac RIGGS of Stratford, Ont., and is now a widow; and William, of Tomahawk, Wis. William DREVER was educated in Hamilton, attending common school up to the age of 13 years. At 16 he began an apprenticeship to the machinist's trade and served at it for four years, his wages for the first year being $2.00 per week, for the second year, $3.00, and so on in the same ratio, so that during his last years' service he was receiving $5.00 a week. His employers were the Joe Kelly Iron Works Co., of Hamilton, and he finished learning his trade with them in 1878, remaining with them subsequently as a journeyman up to 1880. He then came to the States, locating first in Detroit, Mich., where he remained a year, and from there moving to Muskegon, in which city he entered the employ of Alexander RODGERS, the same Mr. RODGERS who in 1888 founded the Tomahawk Iron Woods, of which the Tomahawk Steel & Iron Works are a later development. Mr. DREVER who came to Tomahawk with Mr. RODGERS, continued in his employ here, the latter soon becoming associated with W. H. BRADLEY. On Mr. RODGERS' death in, or about, the year 1904, the Bradley interests acquired the plant and Mr. DREVER was made manager, continuing in that position until he purchased the concern at the time of Mr. BRADLEY'S death. Its more detailed history may be found in the chapter dealing with that of the city of Tomahawk. Mr. DREVER may be numbered among the pioneers of the city, since it was but a year or two old when he first made his home here. He soon became one of its best known citizens and served for some time as alderman from his ward subsequently to its incorporation. He was married June 1, 1888 to Elizabeth HALL of Muskegon, Mich., but who was born in Brampton, Ont., in April, 1861, and accompanied her parents, John and Elizabeth HALL, to Muskegon when a babe. Mr. and Mrs. DREVER have had but one child, Margaret C., who was born in Tomahawk March 17, 1898, and is now the wife of William G. BAUMAN, vice president and general manager of the Tomahawk Steel & Iron Works. The family are members of the Congregational Church. In politics Mr. DREVER is independent, while his fraternal society affiliations are with the local Masonic lodge, the I. O. O. F., the Beavers and the Equitable Fraternal Union.

WILLIAM DREVER

Gahan, Benjamin J. a prominent citizen of Tomahawk, engaged in the furniture and undertaking business, was born in the town of Springfield, Adams County, Aug. 3, 1865, on the farm of his parents, Benjamin and Nora (JAMES) GAHAN. The parents were of Canadian birth, the father born on Prince Edward Island in 1811 and the mother in Ontario in 1843. Their families came to Wisconsin in 1855, the two families settling in the same neighborhood. After their marriage at Mauston, Wis., the parents of our subject settled on the farm in Adams County on which the latter was subsequently born. There they made their home for some 30 years, or until 1895, when they came to Tomahawk to live. Here Benjamin GAHAN, the father, died in 1902; his wife, surviving him twelve years, passed away in 1914. Their own family numbered in all ten children, namely: Margaret, now deceased, who was the wife of C. B. DEWING of Tomahawk; Thomas residing in Gilbert, Minn.; Elizabeth, now Mrs. Frank

ERICKSON of Grand Rapids, Mich.; Benjamin J. and John W., (twins) of Tomahawk; Mary, deceased, who was the wife of John MINN of Milwaukee; Isabella, also deceased, who was Mrs. Dana BILLINGS of Mapes. N. Dak.; Mae, deceased; George, of Grand Rapids, Mich.; and Leo of Milwaukee. Benjamin J. GAHAN remained on the home farm until about 16 years of age, at which time he began working as a farm hand for others. For nine years, or until his marriage, he was employed in the lumber industry, working in the woods in winter and log driving in spring. Then on June 30, 1891, at Mauston, Wis., he was married to Mary L. NOONAN, daughter of Patrick and Anne (FOX) NOONAN. She was born Sept. 8, 1865, on a farm near Elroy, Wis. There her father, who was a native of Ireland, subsequently died, and his wife Anne remained on the farm until 1894, when she came to Tomahawk; here she passed away in 1909. It was in this city that Mr. and Mrs. Benjamin J. GAHAN began their home life, and for the first two years they conducted the Tomahawk Hotel on Tomahawk Avenue. In the spring of 1893 he bought the Lakeside hotel, which he conducted with the assistance of his wife until 1900. He then rented and subsequently followed the carpenter's trade in and about Tomahawk until the spring of 1909, when he laid the foundation of his present business by going to Chicago and taking a course in embalming and undertaking. In September, the same year, in partnership with his brother, John W., he opened his present furniture and undertaking business at the corner of Wisconsin Avenue and Third Street, under the firm name of Gahan Bros. The business proved successful and the partnership was continued up to May, 1921, when Benjamin bought his brother's interest and is now the sole proprietor. He owns and occupies a good house at 123 Somo Avenue. In politics he is more or less independent, voting for the man rather than for the party, and he was alderman four terms from the Third Ward. Mr. and Mrs. GAHAN have had six children, Joseph, Benjamin P., William A., Genevieve M., M. Collette and

Andrew J. Of these children, the first, Joseph, born Dec. 2, 1897, died in May, 1905. William A., born Feb. 19, 1901, was graduated from the Tomahawk High School, and is now employed in his father's store. Genevieve M., born Jan. 15, 1903, was also graduated from the Tomahawk High School, and in 1920 from the Merrill Business College and is now bookkeeper in her father's store. M. Collette, born in February, 1906, is a graduate of the Tomahawk High School, and Andrew J., born May 16, 1910, is a student in the same school. Benjamin P., born March 1, 1899, has a longer record including service in the World War. He entered the army on May 10, 1917, as a member of the Wisconsin National Guards, and was assigned to Company A., 119th Machine Gun Battery. After training at Camp Douglas, Wis., he went from there with his company to Waco, Texas, where he was transferred to the 32d Division, and in February, 1918 he went over seas, being landed at Brest March 4, and sent to a hospital, as, while on the vessel he was attacked with scarlet fever. On his recovery two or three weeks later he rejoined his division and was soon engaged in actual fighting. He saw service in Alsace-Lorraine, in the Argonne forest, on the Meuse and at Chateau Thierry. During the battle at the last mentioned place he and a comrade were sent back to headquarters for reinforcements and on their return were cut off by the enemy and reported missing, but in three days he rejoined his company. After the armistice he served with his company with the army of occupation on the Rhine until May 1919, when he embarked at Brest for home, being landed at Hoboken, N. J. After resting there a few days the company came west to Camp Grant, at Rockford, Ill., where they were discharged May 28, 1919. On the same day Benjamine P. GAHAN enlisted in the regular army and was assigned to the aviation department. He served at Camp Bragg till Oct. 14, 1920, and was then transferred to Fayetteville, N. C. In the middle of December, 1921 he came home and remained until June, 1922, when he return to North Carolina. At present he is in a hospital at Camp Grant. The Gahan family are members of the Catholic church and of St. Mary's congregation in Tomahawk, which Benjamin J. served as trustee for twelve years. He is a member of Tomahawk Council No. 2066, K.C., and of Lodge No. 216, C. O. F.

Gillett, Harry Grant a resident of Tomahawk for 16 years, whose main activities have been connected with railroad construction and lumbering, was born in Necedah, Wis., Feb. 28, 1882, son of Andrew J. and Frances (HASTINGS) GILLETT. The father, who was born in Oconomowoc, Wis., was engaged for a part of his active period in railroad contracting and was also for 30 years in the hotel business. In 1907 he came to Tomahawk and remained here for two years subsequently, being associated with the Bradley Company. He then returned to Necedah, where he died in 1921, and where his wife is still living. She was born in New York State and married Mr. GILLETT in Oconomowoc, Wis. Of their union five sons and one daughter were born and five of the children are still living, namely, Lottie, Fred, William, Harry and Mina, Charles being the one deceased. Mina is the wife of R. H. JANNEST, superintendent for the R. and D. Division of the Chicago, Milwaukee & St. Paul Railway at Mason City, Iowa. Harry Grant GILLETT after acquiring his education in the Necedah schools, became industrially active in association with his father, who was then engaged in general contract work, gravelling, building railroads and logging. Coming to Tomahawk in 1907, at the same time as his father, he engaged in contract logging for the Bradley Company, being this employed for six years. During the next four years he bought standing timber and logged for himself. Then he took up another branch of contracting, building roads and highways running through Spirit Falls, Hazelhurst and Tripoli. After that he left this part of the country temporarily and spent the next two years logging in Virginia. He then returned to Tomahawk and for a year was engaged in buying spruce timber for the Grandfather Falls Paper Co., and was subsequently engaged in logging with Robert THIELMAN. He is now helping to build the new dam and has cut one and a half million feet of logs for the company. His fraternal society affiliations are with the Elks and Woodmen. Mr. GILLETT was married at Mauston, Wis., May 10, 1901, to Rena WEATHERBURY, daughter of Mr. and Mrs. Dean WEATHERBURY, her parents having settled in that place many years ago and being still residents there. Mr. and Mrs. GILLETT have four children: Raymond, a former student in Wisconsin State University, now associated with his father in the latter's business enterprises; Frank, who is studying medicine in the State University; and Donald and Harriett, residing at home with their parents.

Gillie, Robert J. who has proved himself a live factor in the development of the manufacturing interests of the city of Tomahawk by the erection of a saw mill and wood working establishment which he is operating successfully, was born at Twinsburg, Ohio, Feb. 20, 1876, son of Robert and Jessie (HAMILTON) GILLIE. The father, was born in Scotland, Sept. 3, 1840, and the mother in Hamilton, Ontario, Oct. 25, 1851. They came to the United States in 1857, settling in Ohio, where he conducted a saw and grist mill, besides farming. After living there until 1905, he retired and moved with his wife to Cleveland, where he died Jan. 22, 1909; his wife died Aug. 11, 1914. They had six children, Robert, Edith, William, Jean, James and Hattie. Robert J. GILLIE was reared and educated in Ohio, attending common and high school. In 1896, at the age of 20, he came to Rhinelander, Wis., where for two years he worked in mills and factories. In 1898 he came to Tomahawk, entering the employ of W. H. BRADLEY as greaser in Mill No. 2. After that he took up carpenter work, being employed by others, and so continued until 1904, when he started contracting and building on his own account. It was in 1910 that he founded his present establishment, erecting a building which he equipped with saws, planers and other machinery, and in which he began the manufacture of frames, sash and doors and mouldings. In 1916 he bought a portable saw mill, which he operated in various places sawing logs, but later installed in a building erected for the purpose close to his original plant, and in it he now saws the lumber to supply his wood-working plant as well as lumber for general distribution. He also owns a farm of 160 acres which he is devoting to general farming and dairying, having 40 acres under the plow, the balance being in cut-over and pasture land. He is meeting with good success in both his enterprises and is a well known and respected citizen of Lincoln County. On Ja. 29, 1901, Mr. GILLIE was married in Tomahawk to Laura JARVIS, who came to this place with her parents, John and Sophie JARVIS, before the advent of the railroad, when they had to travel by stage from Heaford Junction. Both her parents are now deceased. Mr. and Mrs. GILLIE are the parents of three children, all sons, namely: Robert Johnston, born Aug. 20, 1904; John Newell, born Sept. 29, 1913, and Warren Harding, born March 3, 1921.

MR. AND MRS. ROBERT J. GILLIE

Greggorie, George proprietor of a picturesque summer resort on the Wisconsin River, seven and a half miles northeast of Tomahawk, in Lincoln County, and who is also widely known as an artist of ability, was born in the city of Quebec, Canada, March 28, 1866, son of Charles and Adelle (JELLECAR) GREGGORIE. The parents were also natives of that city and it was there that they passed away, the father in 1886 and the mother in 1888. Their family numbered 13 children, seven sons and six daughters, of whom only four are now living. Of those who are, one son, Thomas, is now in the Klondick, and another, Joseph, is in Chicago. George GREGGORIE as a boy attended school in Quebec, his native place, where he resided up to the age of 19. At an early age he developed a taste for art which took the direction of painting and in time, with good instruction and practice he produced some highly praised pictures. Then coming to the States, he located in Chicago, where he was numbered among the well known artists and remained until 1906, in which year he came to Tomahawk and has since made his regular home in this vicinity, though each summer for 13 years after coming here he returned to Chicago and followed painting there. In the spring of 1922 he bought 40 acres of land on the Wisconsin River, seven and a half miles northeast of Tomahawk, and known as Pine Grove Resort. This is a beautiful rustic location providing abundant opportunities for both rest and sport. There is good fishing and hunting and Mr. GREGGORIE has four cottages and a number of boats, including a launch. No more attractive spot can be found in this section. Mr. GREGGORIE was for six years a director on the school board of District No. 48, in the town of Bradley. In politics he is not a partisan but votes for the man whom he regard as the best fitted for office. In his younger days he saw service in the Canadian army during the Riel rebellion, and when the United States went into the World War he enlisted as a state guard, being stationed at Tomahawk. In religion he was reared a Catholic. He was married in November, 1885, to

Adella LENNE of Quebec, who died soon after they came to the United States. Of this union one child was born, Oscar, who is now a painter and contractor of Rhinelander, Oneida County, Wis. He is married and has two children.

Griffith, John S. secretary and manager of the Mohr Lumber Co. of Tomahawk, Lincoln County, was born at Batavia, Ohio, in 1873, the second in order of four children, son of Thomas and Anna M. (EBERSOLL) GRIFFITH, both of whom were born in the Ohio Country like John S. The father died in 1885 and the mother on March 19, 1923. The subject of this sketch was educated in his native state, attending common and high school. He came to Wisconsin in 1890, and was married in 1902 to Maude M. MOHR, daughter of C. F. MOHR, president of the Mohr Lumber Co. Mr. MOHR had settled in Portage, Wis., in 1855 and was engaged in farming and mercantile business until 1893. He then entered into the lumber business, in which he continued until his death in 1923. Mrs. MOHR, whose maiden name was Mary EIKE, and who was reared near Baraboo, Wis., died in 1913. Mr. GRIFFITH became connected with the Mohr Lumber Co. in 1900. He has identified himself closely with the best interests of the city. His fraternal society affiliations are with the Masons. He and his wife are the parents of two children, Robert Mohr and Mary Virginia.

Hildebrand, Henry L. a well known and popular citizen of Tomahawk, in the employ of the C. M. & St. P. Railway, was born at Lyle, Minn., Oct. 24, 1876, son of Louis A. and Henrietta (MILLER) HILDEBRAND. The parents were of German ancestry but American birth; the father being born in Canada in 1847 while his parents were on the way from Germany to the United States, while the mother was born on the ocean in 1852 as the ship on which her parents were emigrant was approaching the shore of this country. Both families crossed the ocean on sailing vessels, which took six weeks to make the passage, and both settled at Lyle, Minn., where Louis A. HILDEBRAND and Henrietta MILLER grew up and were subsequently married. In 1879 the parents of the subject of this sketch moved to Merrill, Lincoln County, Wis., where the father engaged in the bus and dray business, in which he continued until 1884, for the last five years of that period operating the stage line between Merrill and "The Forks," a point near Tomahawk. They then moved to Tomahawk and was engaged in the livery and dray business here until he sold out to William SCHROEDER in 1906. His death occurred in this city on Sept. 11, 1909. He was survived by his wife, who is still residing here. They had a family of ten children, two of whom have passed away, the full list being as follows: William, deceased; Elizabeth, now Mrs. H. P. STIVERS of Delcona, Wash.; Marie, wife of John DOLAN of Rhinelander; Henry L., of Tomahawk; Ida, wife of R. A. NEWALL of Wausau, Wis.; Raymond, deceased; Emma, now Mrs. A. E. GRAVES of Tomahawk; Huldah, now Mrs. Walter HANSON of Tomahawk; Edward, of Tomahawk, and Esther, wife of Thomas CALLAHAN of Wausau. Henry L. HILDEBRAND in his youth attended school both in Merrill and Tomahawk and after passing through the grades began working for his father, in whose employ he remained until 1906 when the latter gave up business. He then engaged in the livery and dray business for himself, continuing in it subsequently until 1918, when he sold out and entered the employ of the C. M. & St. P. Railway as office clerk, in which position he is still serving at Tomahawk. He owns a farm of 160 acres in the town of Wilson, Lincoln County, of which he has 40 acres cleared. Fraternally he is affiliated with the Masonic order, as a member of the local Blue Lodge, and also with the Maccabees. Politically a Democrat, in 1916 Mr. HILDEBRAND became a candidate for the office of county sheriff, but was defeated. He served, however, as deputy under Emil KNOOR, a former sheriff, and also under Edward PATZER, who had defeated him. On Feb. 8, 1905, Mr. HILDEBRAND was united in marriage with Angelene HIGGINS, who was born at De Pere, Brown County, Wis., March 8, 1881, and who when a young girl had accompanied her parents to Merrill, where her father is still living, the mother having passed away. Mr. and Mrs. HILDEBRAND have two sons: Edward L., born April 27, 1906, who will graduate from the Tomahawk High School in 1924, and Louis T., born May 23, 1908, who is now a pupil in the high school. The family attends and helps to support the Congregational Church.

Houlahan, Edward a pioneer of the city of Tomahawk, and one of it principal business citizens today, and who has been closely connected with various phases of its growth and development, was born on a farm in Fond du Lac County, Wisconsin, son of James and Mararget HOULAHAN. The parents came to the United States from Ireland in the early 40's, while still single, taking passage on the ship "Baltic," which took six weeks to cross the Atlantic. They landed in New York, being doubtless glad to set foot on solid ground once more, and for awhile remained in that city, where they were married. It was in 1845 that they came west to Wisconsin, settling on land in Fond du Lac County, where they engaged in farming. On retiring from active work many years later they took up their residence in Stevens Point, where James HOULAHAN died Nov. 26, 1893. His wife subsequently made her home with her son Edward and daughters until her death Dec. 11, 1903. There were eight children in the family, of whom seven are now living, namely, Mary, Kate, Ellen, Richard, Edward, Bernard and George; the one deceased is John. George is a dentist at Stevens Point, Wis.; Mary married Daniel MCCULLOUGH of that city; Kate is the widow of Mike DOYLE, formerly of Belfield, N. D.; Ellen, the wife of Robert PHELAN of Stevens Point; Richard, lives in Madison, Wis., and Bernard lives in Hurley. Edward HOULAHAN was reared on his parents' farm in Fond du Lac County, Wisconsin, attending district school when young and assisting his father until he was 20 years old. He then drifted into the lumber industry, in which he was busy for some years, working in the woods near Mosinee as chopper and felling timber on the Wisconsin, Yellow and Black rivers; also rafting and driving logs on the Wisconsin River, which he did altogether at intervals for 12 years. In addition to this he worked in the mills at Mosinee. In 1886 he went to Hurley, Wis., where he conducted a hotel for two years, and then in 1888 he came to Tomahawk, which place was just starting out on its career of prosperity, having been platted in the previous year. Here or in this vicinity he engaged in logging, buying timber land, which he sold after cutting and logging the timber, and in that business he has been engaged up to the present time. In early days he did his freighting on the old "tote" road connecting Merrill and Otter Rapids, taking one week for the trip and sleeping on the ground under wagons. He still has considerable cut-over land for sale. Mr. HOULAHAN is one of the best known citizens in Tomahawk, having at various times prominently served the public in official capacities. He helped to write the original charter of the city and was one of its alderman when its general charter was adopted. At different times he has capably filled various municipal offices, having been a member of the Police and Fire Commission, member of the County Jury Commission, assessor, which office he has filled for 18 years, and a member of the Park Board, of which he is now president. He is a stockholder in the Bank of Tomahawk and is a member of two fraternal orders, the Knights of Columbus and the Catholic Knights. Mr. HOULAHAN was married at Stevens Point, Wis., on Nov. 11, 1885, to Nora SHEA, who was born at Erin, Wis., April 21, 1856, daughter of Thomas and Elizabeth SHEA. Her parents, now deceased, were natives of Ireland, and at one time Thomas SHEA was a school teacher at Hartford, Wis., and also a merchant. Mr. and Mrs. SHEA had four sons and four daughters and six of the children are now living. Nora SHEA, who was one of a family of eight children, was reared to young womanhood at Stevens Point. In 1888 she came with her husband to the then new city of Tomahawk, which was her subsequent home until her death on June 29, 1923. She was a most worthy woman, whose life was devoted to her home and family and to her Christian duties as a member of the Catholic Church and of its Altar Society, she taking an active part both in its services and in its outside activities. She had long been a patient invalid, and her passing brought keen sorrow to her family and numerous friends. Mr. and Mrs. Edward HOULAHAN were the parents of eight children, of whom the four now living are: Edward S., a graduate of Wisconsin University, who is employed in the office of the paper-mill in Rhinelander; Mida, wife of W. D. SUTLIFF of Tomahawk; Thomas J., superintendent for the Ashland Leather Co., of Ashland, Ky., and Rosella, who resides at home with her parents. Two children died in infancy and two others, Marguerite and Loretta, are also deceased. Mr. and Mrs. HOULAHAN also reared a daughter of the former's brother, Katherine HOULAHAN, who is a graduate of the Tomahawk High School. Besides her husband and children Mrs. HOULAHAN was survived by two sisters and two brothers: Mrs. Ed ESKER and Mrs. Margaret MULLEN of Stevens Point, Thomas SHEA of Chicago and Frank SHEA of Montana; also by eight grand-children.

Hansen, Hans P. one of that useful class of citizens who are building up the agricultural resources of Lincoln County by turning wild land into good farms, and whose place is located in Section 9 in the town of King, was born in Denmark, May 28, 1848, his parents, Hans Jensen and Marie HANSON, being natives of that country and the father a farmer by occupation. They came to the United States in 1870, settling in Michigan, where Hans JENSEN bought a farm, which he operated until he was killed in 1882 by a falling tree. His widow continued to reside on the place for a while but finally went to South Dakota with a son, where she died in 1920 at an advanced age. Mr. and Mrs. Hans JENSEN had seven sons, of whom four are living; Jens in Michigan, Nels in Ashland, Wis., Ole in Minneapolis and Hans P., the subject of this sketch. Those who died were Fred, George and Lars. Hans P. HANSEN, who after the Scandinavian custom, took his father's first name, with the addition of "sen" (or son), as a boy went to school in Denmark, where he later worked as a common laborer until reaching the age of 20 years. By that time his parents had decided to emigrate to America and he accompanied them, realizing that he had little chance for self advancement in his native land but that the United States offered abundant opportunities to the industrious and deserving. After his arrival in this country he worked on his parents' farm and also at times in the woods in the vicinity of Grand Rapids. In 1873 he married Hannah P. CLINKER, a native of Denmark like himself and daughter of Mr. and Mrs. Hans CLINKER, who had remained in their native land. In 1884, two years after his father's death, Mr. HANSEN came to Merrill, Wis., and was employed in railroad construction work under Tim O'CONNELL until Mr. O'CONNELL had completed his contract. He then took up his residence in Rhinelander, being joined by his family whom he had left behind in Michigan, and for six years he worked there as a common laborer, finding plenty to do, as it was in the early days of that city, when it was building up rapidly owing to the development of the lumber industry there. At the end of that period he came to Tomahawk, and began to advance a little in position, as he was a fireman and engineer in mills for three years and subsequently worked seven years as electrician in the employ of W. H. BRADLEY. By this time he had realized that if he remained a mere wage earner he could never do much more than make a bare living, and that in order to really prosper he must work for himself. The only way to do this was to get on the land, and so in 1898 he homesteaded 160 acres in the town of King, and set to work in an effort to wrest fortune from the soil. Those who have tried it know that this is no easy task, particularly when you have to begin at the beginning, as Mr. HANSEN had to do. There were no improvements on the place, the land being all covered with timber, and he began accordingly by making a small clearing and building a log but or house, in which he and his family took up their quarters. His subsequent experience was much like that of all pioneers who have to fight the battle with nature. Progress was slow but fairly steady and each year found him with a little more land cleared and in a better position than the one before, but the first years were hard ones and there was no luxury and none too much comfort in the Hansen home. But things have changed since then. When the right time came Mr. HANSEN bought 80 acres more, adjoining his original tract, and he has since cleared a part of that. He has now 95 acres cleared and under cultivation. When prosperity began to dawn upon him he replaced his original log house with a good frame one and built a substantial barn and other useful or necessary buildings, he and his family personally doing all the work. The farm is now operated by himself and his son Theodore under the firm name of Hansen & Son. They are engaged in general farming and dairying, have a herd of 25 registered and grade Holstein cattle and are milking on an average 15 cows. They made specialties of dairying and raising potatoes, and are well supplied with all necessary machinery, including a grain separator and a Fordson tractor. It has taken a good many years to develop this fine place into its present condition, but the labor has been well spent and the Hansen farm is now numbered among the best in the county for its size. Mr. and Mrs. HANSEN have three children, two sons and one daughter, namely: Clifford C., who is a farmer in the town of Lincoln; Dadmar Victoria, widow of John WOODCOCK and a resident of New York City, and Theordore H. The last mentioned was born in Michigan in 1883, was educated in the schools of Tomahawk, Wis., and has always remained at home helping his parents to improve the farm. The elder son,

Clifford, in July, 1918, entered the United State service, becoming a member of the Engineer Corps of the "Cactus Division," and being stationed in Texas until after the armistice was signed.

Macomber, Charles E. organizer and president of the Bank of Tomahawk, was born on a farm near New Lisbon, Wis., Aug. 13, 1858, son of Stephen D. and Elizabeth (MEAD) MACOMBER. Both parents were Native Americans, the father having been born in Pennsylvania in January, 1832, and the mother in Ohio. Both died on the farm above mentioned on which the subject of this sketch was born. Charles E. MACOMBER was educated in rural and city schools, also in the Oshkosh Normal School at Oshkosh, Wis., and subsequently taught a few terms of rural school. But however elevated may be the calling of a teacher, it is not usually very remunerative and in 1882 Mr. MACOMBER purchased the mercantile business of E. B. NICHOLS at New Lisbon, subsequently conducting the store until the spring of 1888. In the meantime, in the fall of 1887, he established a drug store in Tomahawk, so that for some five or six months he was conducting two store in different places, but in the spring of 1888 he sold the New Lisbon business and took up his residence in Tomahawk with his family. Here he carried on his drug store, giving his exclusive attention to it until 1895, in which year he established a private bank which in 1904 was incorporated under the laws of the state as the Bank of Tomahawk. He was the first president of the bank and is still serving in that capacity. He is also interested in the drug business, which is now incorporated and is under the management of E. W. SMITH. Politically Mr. MACOMBER is an old-time Republican and has always stuck close to his party, though he has taken no active part in politics beyond casting his vote. He was married in May, 1881, to Gertrude M. CARR, daughter of Willard P. and Carrie CARR of New Lisbon. On this union one child was born, Winnefred C., July 13, 1886, who married E. C. PERRY. She died in February 1920, leaving an only child, Gertrude K., and the latter with her father now reside with Mr. and Mrs. MACOMBER in their comfortable home at No. 110 S. Second Street. Mr. PERRY is a traveling bond salesman, selling to banks only. The religious training of Mr. and Mrs. MACOMBER was in accordance with the creed of the Baptist Church, but there being no Baptist congregation in Tomahawk, they affiliated with the Congregational Church. He is a member of the Masonic Blue Lodge of this city.

Macfarlane D.D.S., William I. head of the Macfarlane Dental Clinic, of Tomahawk, and secretary and treasurer of the Service Drug Co. of the same city, was born at Perry, Dane County, Wis., Dec. 25, 1880, son of William M. and Sarah M. (IVEY) MACFARLANE. The father, who was a physician, was born on a farm in Guernsey, Ohio, in 1846 and died in Dane County, Wisconsin, on Aug. 18, 1885. His wife Sarah was a native of Wisconsin, born at Moscow, Iowa County, May 18, 1855. After his death she married Peter HOUNS of Blanchardville, Wis. She died at the home of her daughter, Mrs. Herbert YOUNG, of Milwaukee, on April 5, 1922. By her first husband, Dr. MACFARLANE, she had two children: William I., subject of this sketch; Mae, wife of Thomas J. DARROW, a farmer living near Blanchardsville, Lafayette County, Wis. The children by her second husband, Mr. HOUNS, were: A. R. HOUNS, D. D. S., of Tomahawk, who is associated professionally with the subject of this sketch; Dorothy, wife of John FARMER of Blanchardville, and Nadine, wife of Hobart YOUNG of Milwaukee. William I. MACFARLANE for two years in his youth attended the Blanchardville High School. In the fall of 1902 he entered the Chicago College of Dental Surgery, from which he was graduated in 1905, beginning the practice of his profession at McConnell, Stevenson County, Illinois. It was in the following year, 1906, that he came to Tomahawk and opened an office, and in the 17 years that have since elapsed he has built up a large practice here and became widely and favorably known. In 1920 he organized the Macfarlane Dental Clinic, with Dr. A. R. HOUNS as assistant operator and Miss Gladys VAN GALDER in charge of the dental hygiene department. Two other young lady assistants are also employed, Evelyn DRAEGER and Gladys BAME. The establishment of this clinic has proved a happy thought, as it has been remarkably successful and draws patronage from a wife section of central Wisconsin. A fine suite of rooms in the Gesell Block are occupied and the scientific equipment is complete and thoroughly up to date. With Dr. L. M. PEARSON and O. A. PETERSON of Tomahawk, Dr. MACFARLANE organized the Service Drug Company, which was incorporated in 1923, and of which he is secretary and treasurer, with Dr. PEARSON president and O. A. PETERSON vice president, which also has proved a successful undertaking. The concern occupies a substantial one-story brick building at No. 207 Wisconsin Avenue, with provisions for another story which was built by Drs. PEARSON and MACFARLANE. Dr. MACFARLANE occupies a prominent place in his profession, of which he long since proved himself a master. For five years he served as secretary and treasurer of the Central Wisconsin Central Society, and was subsequently its president for five years, retiring from that position in June, 1922. In 1920 he was vice president of the State Dental Association, and in 1921 became a member of the Dental Legislative Committee, being re-elected to that position in 1922, and he is now a member of the executive committee of the society. In 1920 he was a member of the committee on dental ethics. During the participation of the United States in the World War his brother entered the dental corps, leaving the doctor to attend to the entire practice of both and as he could not leave the practice, he did the next best thing and took an earnest part in some of the most important home activities, serving as chairman of the Tomahawk division of the Red Cross, and as chairman of the Y.M.C.A. drives in the district. He has also from time to time taken a useful part in civic affairs. He is fraternally affiliated with the Masonic Lodge in Tomahawk and the Royal Arch Chapter in Merrill; also with the Knight Templar Lodge in Wausau. Dr. MACFARLANE was married June 16, 1909, to Jennie B. JOHNSON, daughter of Henry A. and Sarah (FLETCHER) JOHNSON of Tomahawk, and he and his wife reside with her parents. They had one child a son, William J., who died in infancy. Mrs. MACFARLANE is prominent in the church, social and musical work of the city, while the Doctor takes a equally active part in the Tomahawk Civic and Business Men's Club. Both are members of the First Congregational Church of Tomahawk.

W. I. MacFARLANE, D. D. S.

Major, Henry T. now engaged in the meat business in Tomahawk, and formerly a county official, was born in Canada, Oct. 15, 1885, son of Louis and Ann MAJOR. The parents were natives of Canada and when a young man Louis MAJOR was a dock laborer there. After his marriage he and his wife came to the United States, locating first at Manistee,

Mich., and later at Ishpeming, and in 1887 they came to Parrish, Lincoln County, where he worked for a year in the mill. From there he went to Harrison, where he worked in the mill and also in the woods. On May 10, 1889, he and his wife arrived in Tomahawk and here he worked in mills until 1905, after which he and his wife engaged in the hotel business, conducted the Farm Home until May 26, 1921, when he died. She conducted it subsequently until July that year, in which month she sold it to her son Henry T. and Archie BARNEY. She subsequently married August MORAN. The children of Louis and Anna MAJOR were Henry T., Fred, Albert, Louise, Excina and Anna. Louise is the wife of Wilbur MORIN, a merchant; Excina, the wife of Art BARNEY, a head sawyer and hotel proprietor; and Anna, the wife of Phil LENNERT, a railroad man. Henry T. MAJOR was four years old when he accompanied his parents to Tomahawk. Here he was reared and attended common school, after which he began industrial life working on the river boom, keeping tally on the logs. His next job was as a member of the police force, at which he remained for a year and a half. Then for four years he was agent for the Miller Brewing Co. and subsequently engaged in the garage and auto livery business. This he sold to Ed SUTLIFF and opened a soft drink parlor, conducting that and the hotel until Oct. 7, 1922, on which date he opened his present butcher shop with Frank WIERCINSKI under the firm name of Major & WIERCINSKI. They carry on a regular meat market business, doing some killing of local stock. The store is equipped with new modern fixtures and with the carbonic cooling system. Mr. MAJOR is a member of several fraternal societies, including the Eagles, Catholic Foresters, Woodmen of the World and Elks, of which last mentioned lodge he is a life member. For 14 years he served as deputy sheriff under Sheriff KRAFT. On Sept. 9, 1907, Mr. MAJOR was married in Tomahawk to Cecelia ALLARD, daughter of Peter Fred and Josephine ALLARD, early settlers in this locality who are living retired. Mr. and Mrs. MAJOR have three daughters and one son, namely: Stella, Marion, Helen and Henry T., Jr., all born in Tomahawk.

    Martz, Leo who for a number of years has been successfully engaged in the plumbing business in Tomahawk, and is also chief of the city fire department, was born in Germany in 1875, son of Mr. and Mrs. Rudolph MARTZ, the father being a farmer by occupation. In 1881 they came to the United States, locating at Fort Wayne, Ind., where the mother died. Rudolph MARTZ then moved to Big Rapids, Wis., near which place he followed farming. He also married for his second wife a Mrs. LULL, a widow, and they are both still living. Of his first marriage there were four children born, namely, Adolph, Rudolph, Leo and Martha, of whom the last mentioned, is deceased. The children of his second marriage are Ernest, Harvey, Lillie and Ruth. Leo MARTZ attended school at Big Rapids until 16 years old. He then came to Tomahawk, where he worked in the mills for a while, and also at several other jobs, being box tender for the McBride concern. After that he entered the employ of R. F. KOTH to learn the plumber's trade, remaining with him until 1906, and from that year to 1910 was with the Northern Hardware Co. He next engaged in the plumbing business on his own account, with William KEELING as a partner, this association lasting till 1919, in which year he bought Mr. KEELING'S interest in the business and since then he has conducted it alone. He is a skilled and practical sheet metal worker, supplies hot air and hot water heating apparatus, and does general plumbing, carrying a full line of plumbing and heating supplies and furnaces. He is favorably known both for the quality of his work and for his fair dealing. On June 7, 1907, Mr. MARTZ was appointed by Louis THIELMAN chief of the city fire department and has since continued to serve in that office. The department is voluntary, with a yearly salary for the chief of $125 and for the other men $90. The fire equipment consists of a Republic hose truck carrying 1,000 feet of hose and a chemical truck of 42 gallons. In May, 1917, Mr. MARTZ showed his patriotism by enlisting in the Home Guards, formed for riot protection, and served until the close of the war. He was married in 1904 to Louise KEELING, daughter of Mr. and Mrs. Henry KEELING. Mrs. MARTZ died may 5, 1906, leaving no children.

McCarthy, James L. an active business man of Tomahawk, Lincoln County, was born in the logging camp on Wolf River, Waupaca County, May 9, 1880, son of Jerry and Anna (DORIN) MCCARTHY. The father was a native of New York State who, when young, accompanied his parents to Wisconsin, the family settling in Brown County. There after reaching manhood he married and in 1887 he came with his wife and children to Tomahawk, where he worked in the mills and drove a team for the W. H. Bradley Company. In 1906 he opened a hotel, which he conducted for a time until he retired from active work. His death took place in May, 1921. His wife Anna, who was born in Canada, is now living with her daughter Ethel in California. Mr. and Mrs. Jerry MCCARTHY had seven children, five sons and two daughters, namely: Thomas H., William S., James L., Margaret, Richard, Robert and Ethel. Margaret is the wife of Charles SIEVERSON and lives in the state of Washington, and Ethel is now Mrs. Charles SCULLEN of Sacramento, Calif. James L. MCCARTHY was seven years old when he came to Tomahawk with his parents. After attending school he learned the barber's trade, which he followed for 20 years in this city, for 12 years of that time conducting the Mitchell Hotel shop. He then bought a soft drink parlor, to which he added four bowling alleys. He keeps all kinds of soft drinks, candy and cigars and is doing a good business. As a progressive citizen he has identified himself with the Commercial Club, while his fraternal affiliations are with the Knights of Columbus, the Elks, Eagles and Modern Brotherhood of America. Mr. MCCARTHY was married in Tomahawk, June 15, 1904, to Mary ST. PETER, daughter of

Peter and Margaret (BODEN) ST. PETER. Her father, a native of Canada, came to the United States when young, locating at Eau Claire, Wis., where he and his wife were married, and where for some time they conducted a hotel. Later they moved to Eagle River, Vilas County, and opened a confectionery store. In 1898 they came to Tomahawk, and here Mr. ST. PETER was for some time engineer at the city pumping station, but is now retired. Of the children in the St. Peter family, five died in infancy, but three are now living, George Peter, Jr., and Mary. Mr. and Mrs. MCCARTHY have had three children: Francis W. and Beatrice H., who are living, and Roland, who died.

McCormick M.D., William Charles of Tomahawk, Lincoln County, a well known member of the medical profession of this county, who saw active service in the World War, was born in Tomahawk, Wis., July 16, 1893, son of Charles and Sarah (MCCUTCHEON) MCCORMICK. The parents were both natives of Canada, the father having been born in Ottawa and the mother in Toronto. Both came to the United States when young and single, and after their marriage in Michigan, they settled in Tomahawk, Wis. This was in 1889 and as the village has been started but two years before, they were not far behind the original pioneers. Charles MCCORMICK was a veterinary surgeon, and as the horse was more in evidence in those days than it is now, he found sufficient employment and followed that occupation until he died in 1906. His wife Sarah is still living, being now 63 years old. They had three children who grew to maturity: Irwin, wife of I. S. BALLARD of Akron, O.; Charlotte, formerly a teacher but now attending the University of Wisconsin, and William C., of Tomahawk. William C. MCCORMICK as a youth attended the grade and high schools of Tomahawk, being graduated from the latter in 1911. He spent a year in preparatory medical work in the university at Valparaiso, Ind., and the following year in the George Washington University at Washington, D.C.

He then entered the Chicago College of Medicine and Surgery, from which he received his degree of M.D. in 1916. Returning to Tomahawk he began the practice of his profession here as partner with Dr. George BAKER, under the firm name of Baker & McCormick, and the association has since remained unbroken, the two physicians enjoying a large and lucrative practice. Through his membership in the Lincoln County Medical Society, the Wisconsin State Medical Society and the American Medical Association, and in other ways, Dr. MCCORMICK keeps in close touch with the progress of his profession. He belongs to several other societies, including the Eagles and Phi Chi Medical Fraternity, and also to the American Legion. His war service began in April, 1917, when he enlisted in the Medical Corps, being subsequently commissioned lieutenant. Before receiving his commission, however, he was connected with the 16th Machine Gun Battalion, going out as a private. With the 6th Division he trained at Camp Wadsworth, was transferred to the 78th Division, and spent one year in France as Battalion surgeon. He was at Chateau Thierry and in the Argonne and was twice gassed. He received his discharge from the army on June 1, 1919. Dr. MCCORMICK was married at Gary, Ind., Nov. 1, 1919, to Laura JOHNSON, daughter of Amandus and Mary JOHNSON. Her parents, early settlers in Lincoln County, are now living on a farm hear Spirit Falls. The Doctor's wedding was part of a big celebration, his sister Irwin, a practicing attorney, being married at the same time. Dr. and Mrs. MCCORMICK are the parents of two children, Dorothy M. and Evelyn R.

WILLIAM C. McCORMICK, M. D.

McHenry, James W. president of the Tomahawk Shoe Company, of Tomahawk, Lincoln County, was born in St. Louis, Mo., Oct. 15, 1886, son of Alfred and Emma (WOERNER) MCHENRY. The father, a printer by trade, was a native of England and the son of a shoemaker. His wife was born in St. Louis. They had seven children, of whom the three now living are Edwin T., William H. and James W. James W. MCHENRY acquired his education in St. Louis and began industrial life as office boy for the Robert Johnson Shoe Co. Through close attending to his duties, with efforts at self improvement, he rose from one position to another until he became office manager under Superintendent H. L. NUNN. His next promotion was to the position of assistant superintendent, and while in the employ of that company he acquired a thorough knowledge of the business, both the art of manufacture and methods of distribution. When he left that concern he became traveling salesman for a shoe machine company, and afterwards sold shoes for Harsh & Edmonds of Milwaukee. Later he was with the Nunn & Bush Shoe Co. of Milwaukee. In 1914 he became connected with the Tomahawk Shoe Co. and took up his residence in this city. Up to June, 1921, he was vice president and treasurer of the company and since that time has been president. An account of the founding and development of this concern may be found in the chapter on the history of the city of Tomahawk. Mr. MCHENRY was married in Milwaukee, Wis., Dec. 26, 1914, to Florence O'ROURKE, of Dubuque, Iowa. Mr. and Mrs. MCHENRY are the parents of four children, Webster, Robert, Edwin and Jane.

Morin, Wilbur A. who is numbered among the thriving merchants of Tomahawk, Lincoln County, was born at Grandfather Falls, this county, May 23, 1882, son of Octave and Emma MORIN. The parents were natives of Canada, and Octave MORIN when a young man came to Wisconsin, locating at Wausau, where he found employment at logging. After a while he moved to Merrill, then known as Jennie, where he became foreman of the logging camp for P. B. CHAMPINE, and later logged for himself. In 1878 he took up his residence at Grandfather Falls, where he opened a hotel and saloon, both of which he conducted for 15 years, or until 1906, when he sold out to John O'DAY and retired, coming to Tomahawk to spend his remaining years. Both he and his wife have passed away. They had three children: Stella, now the wife of Alexander ROBARGE of Tomahawk; Wilbur A., subject of this sketch; and Nettie, who is now deceased. Wilbur A. MORIN was reared at Grandfather Falls, where he attended school. He worked for some time in his father's hotel, and also at farming and logging. Having accompanied his parents to Tomahawk in 1906, he found employment working in the woods of this vicinity, also at time in the local mills and in the roundhouse of the Chicago, Milwaukee & St.

Paul Railway, and so continued until Feb. 26, 1923, when he engaged in his present business, buying the grocery store of Joseph DANE. In addition to a full line of groceries, he deals in fresh and smoked meats and is enjoying a good trade. A Catholic in religion, he belongs to the order of Catholic Foresters. Mr. MORIN was married in 1906, in Tomahawk, to Louise MAJOR, daughter of Louis and Anna MAJOR. He and his wife are the parents of two children, Lawrence and Alberta, the former of whom is assisting his father in the store.

Myre, Elzeor a prosperous business man of Tomahawk, and a property owner, was born in Philomeny, Province of Quebec, Canada, Jan. 29, 1864, son of John and Adeline (SCHAINCK) MYRE, who also were natives of that province. There were seven children in the family of John and Adeline MYRE, Lorenzo of Montreal and Elzeor, subject of this sketch, being the only ones now living. The mother died when the latter was only four years old, or in 1868, and John MYRE subsequently remarried. The children of this second marriage now living are: Melvina, wife of Edward BOLU of Montreal; Nellie of Montreal; Blanche, who is a sister in a convent in Montreal; and Wilfred, who for 25 years has been chief of the Montreal fire department. Elzeor MYRE resided with his parents until arriving at the age of 13 years, at which time he came to the States, finding employment at Woonsocket, Mass. In nine months he had saved enough money to bring him west, which was the part of the country he wished to try his fortunes in, and so he came to Wisconsin, locating at Chippewa Falls, where he had an uncle on his father's side. With that uncle he lived for a short time and then took a separate residence, remaining in Chippewa Falls, however, for ten years, during which time he was engaged in various occupations. It was about the end of that period that he married and in the following year, 1888, came with his wife to Tomahawk, which place was then in the early stages of its existence. Mr. MYRE put up a building at the corner of Tomahawk and Spirit avenues and opened a saloon. Later he erected a boarding-house connected with the saloon on the south (on Tomahawk Avenue), and this place he conducted for 14 years. In 1904 Mr. MYRE erected a sub-brick veneered block at the corner of Tomahawk and Spirit avenues, directly north of his former place. This block is a two-story building with a 25-foot front on Tomahawk Avenue and a depth of 142 feet on Spirit Avenue. Mr. MYRE has his restaurant on the first floor, which he rents, and family residence above. He also owns a garage 22x140 feet adjoining on the north, which he rents to Frank BURTON as a sales and repair shop. Politically he is a Democrat in principle, but notes for the candidate of his preference irrespective of party. He was one of Tomahawk's first aldermen, serving four years, and was subsequently re-elected but declined to qualify. It was on Oct. 11, 1887, that Mr. MYRE was united in marriage with Adeline, daughter of Charles and Emeline (WARNER) GOULD. She was born at Chippewa Falls, Wis., Oct. 26, 1856. Her father, who fought for the Union in the Civil War until its close, for a number years operated a dray line in Chippewa Falls, in which city he died about 1901. His wife, who survived him, passed away in 1914. Their family consisted of nine children, of whom those now living are: Harriet, wife of Gregoire LE CLAIRE of Tomahawk; Adeline (Mrs. Elzeor MYRE); Henry, of Spokane, Wash.; Emeline, now Mrs. Frank WOLFRON of Canyon Creek, Mont.; and Thomas of Chippewa Falls. To Mr. and Mrs. MYRE have been born seven children, Maude M., Mary Myrtle, Nellie, Lee, Ray, Leona and Viletta. Two of these, Mary and Nellie, died in infancy. The individual records are briefly as follows: Maude M., born at Chippewa Falls, Sept. 2, 1888, became the wife of Maynard O'CONNELL and died at Tomahawk on Jan. 19, 1922. Mary Myrtle, born Oct. 29, 1889, died Sept. 6, 1890. Nellie, born Dec. 20, 1892, died Nov. 6, 1894. Lee, born Oct. 12, 1895, is married and resides in Tomahawk. Ray, born May 9, 1897, is as yet unmarried and resides in Tomahawk. After the United States entered the World War he was inducted into the service and was stationed in a training camp but was not called into action otherwise on account of the war ending. Leona, born may 10, 1906, was graduated from the Merrill Business College in 1923. Viletta, born Oct. 10, 1908 has passed the eighth grade in school. The family are members of St. Mary's Catholic Congregation.

Nelson, Frank A. representative and manager in Tomahawk for the Inter-State Oil Co. of La Crosse, and a citizen who is widely known and respected, was born in Ljunsby, Sweden, June 20, 1882, son of Carl J. and Mary C. (ANDERSON) NELSON. The father was born in Sweden, Feb. 10, 1846, and the mother April 1, 1855. They were married in their native land and came to America in 1883, settling in Muskegon, Mich., where they resided some 12 or 13 years, Carl J. NELSON being employed as a lumber grader in the mills. He then moved with his family to Tomahawk, where he worked in the same capacity for the Bradley Lumber Co., remaining with that concern until they closed down their mill. Having been a hard worker for many years he then retired and built a comfortable home at 12 East Prospect Street, where he died May 22, 1922, and where his widow still resides. The children of Mr. and Mrs. Carl J. NELSON were are follows: Gustaf, born in Sweden Aug. 22, 1880; Frank A., subject of this sketch; Sarah M., born at Muskegon, Mich., June 10, 1885, and now living with her mother in Tomahawk; Jennie E., born at Muskegon Sept. 23, 1886, now Mrs. S. Y. CURVAN of Milwaukee; Edith W., born at Muskegon, Aug. 12, 1888, unmarried and residing in Milwaukee; Albert J., born at Muskegon, March 26, 1896, now residing in Tomahawk; and three younger children who died in infancy. All the surviving children were given the opportunity of a good public school education, two of them, Edith and Albert, being graduated from the high school, and the others might have done so too had they so desired. Both parents and children were affiliated with the Swedish Mission Congregation, and politically Carl J. NELSON was a Republican. Frank A. NELSON came to Tomahawk before the other members of the family. He was a mechanic and became a locomotive engineer. From 1889 to 1909 he followed railroading, working as a railroad mechanic, and traveling through nearly every state west of the Missouri River. It was in 1914 that he settled in Tomahawk and having formed a partnership with J. A. FITZGERALD as senior member of the firm they engaged in business as local agents for the Ford Company. In 1918 this partnership was dissolved, owning to the failure of Mr. NELSON'S health, and he then bought a 200-acre farm in the town of Bradley, a mile and a half south of Tomahawk, which was a good farm with an improved set of buildings, and here he engaged in general farming and dairying. The outdoor labor brought back his health and he continued to do active work on it until March 14, 1923, at which time he hired a man to look after the place and moved into the city of Tomahawk. He directs the operations of the farm, however, has good buildings, and is developing a good Jersey Herd of cattle, gradually discarding his former Holsteins. On Dec. 27, 1922, he entered into his present employment in town as representative and manager for the Inter-State Oil Co. of La Crosse, which has an established trade here, having bought the interests of the Star Oil Co. of Sutcliffe. The territory covers a radius of 20 miles from the town. Mr. NELSON is a Republican, but not a strong party man, voting as his reason and conscience dictate. He is affiliated religiously with the Swedish Mission Congregation and belongs to the Masonic Blue Lodge in Tomahawk. He was married May 3, 1918 to Cora E. WHITNEY, who was born Dec. 6, 1897 near Merrill, on the farm of her parents, William and Emma (KLUBENAU) WHITNEY. Mrs. NELSON is a graduate of the Lincoln County Training School and taught for some time in the rural schools of that county. She is a Baptist in religious belief. Mr. and

Mrs. NELSON have one son, John Whitney NELSON, who was born Feb. 5, 1919.

Nerli, Anton proprietor of the Tomahawk Creamery was born in Norway, Feb. 9, 1886, son of Ole E. and Anna NERLI. The parents came to the United States in 1889, settling on a farm at Iola, Waupaca County, Wis., where they are still residing and engaged in general farming. They have four children living, Henry, Ingebrit, Gena and Anton. Anton NERLI was reared on his parents' farm in Waupaca County, attending district school, and when he was old enough, assisting his father. In 1910 he began to learn the art of butter making in the Iola Creamery from C. L. PASSMORE, one of the best butter makers in the state. In 1912 he went to Big Falls to manage the Farmers' Creamery there. From there he went to Amherst to take charge of the Farmers' Co-operative Creamery, subsequently spent two years in Peru and then came to Tomahawk, where on March 1, 1922, he purchased the Tomahawk Creamery from Art SEARL. This he has built up into a first class plant, in the midst of the season having about 150 patrons. His summer output of butter in 1922 was from 5000 to 6000 pounds per week, while the winter output is about 2000 pounds. In 1923 he added the manufacture of ice cream to his other activities, hiring an expert making, and in this line also he is doing a good business. (See chapter on history of Tomahawk). Mr. NERLI was married in 1912 at Big Falls, Wis., to Agnes C. KILLIN, daughter of Mr. and Mrs. Pat KILLIN, the parents being natives of Ireland. Mr. KILLIN is now living on his farm at Big Falls, where prior to the death of his wife he conducted a hotel. Mr. and Mrs. NERLI have three children: Vernon, born in 1914; Bernard, born in 1918; and Harlan, born in 1920.

Nick, Sr., Jacob head of the firm of Jacob Nick & Sons, engaged in the furniture and undertaking business in Tomahawk, was born in Germany, on the Rhine, in 1860, son of John and Katherine NICK. The father was a baker by trade, and after conducting a bakery for some time in Germany, he emigrated with his wife and family to the United States, locating in Marshfield, Wis., where he died many years later at the age of 73 and his wife at the age of 86. Their son Jacob, the subject of this sketch, as a boy attended school in his native place and subsequently learned the cabinet and burial casket maker's trade, which for a time he followed there. It was in 1882 that he came to the United States, settling in Milwaukee, and he there followed his trade until 1889. He then came to Tomahawk and with his brother Matt opened a furniture store and undertaking business, adopting the business style of Nick Bros. The business prospered and at the end of eight years Jacob bought out his brother Matt and carried on with the assistance of his two sons, the firm becoming Jacob Nick & Sons. Their location is at 102-106 West Wisconsin Avenue. They manufacture burial caskets for the trade, making 14 complete caskets a day, which are sole in the states of Michigan, Wisconsin and Minnesota. For this they employ 14 workers and their business is increasing so fast that they expect to double their output in the near future. Mr. NICK also manufactures tables and carries on a general furniture business. In 1903 he built a sawmill, a shingle mill and excelsior mill at Spirit Falls, which he operated subsequently for six years, at the end of which time he turned them over to his brother Matt. He is a member of the Catholic Church, Knights of Columbus, Foresters, Maccabees and Equitable Fraternal Union. Jacob NICK, Sr., was married in Milwaukee in 1887 to Katherine HERTE, whose parents, Mr. and Mrs. Jacob HERTE, were long residents of that city, Mr. HERTE, indeed, was born there; he served with a Wisconsin regiment in the Civil War. Both he and his wife have passed away. Mr. and Mrs. Jacob NICK, Sr., have five children, namely, Jacob J., William M., Isabelle M., Benjamin L. and George M. All the sons are associated with their father in business. William and Benjamin were in the United States' service in the World War, Benjamin serving eight months in France in the Aviation department, while George entered the navy and was stationed at Great Lakes.

Oelhafen, John generally known as the "Father of Tomahawk," whose lumbering and mercantile interests have been for many years among the leading activities of the place, was born in Germany, Jan. 22, 1836, son of Alexander and Elizabeth (BECK) OELHAFEN. He was nine years old when he came with his parents to America, the father buying a quarter section of wild government land in Washington County, in what was then the territory of Wisconsin, and engaging in agricultural operations. The whole territory was then but thinly settled, the upper portion being entirely wild. After a number of years Andrew OELHAFEN sold his farm and moved to Milwaukee, then but a small place, where he subsequently died, his wife Elizabeth having previously passed away on the farm. It makes one pause to reflect on this wife and mother coming from a thickly settled portion of the Old World where every comfort and luxury of the day was obtainable by those of fair means, and where one was surrounded by scores of friends and acquaintances, saying goodbye to them all, knowing that she would probably never see them again, and following her husband to a little known wilderness, to a life of hard work, bearing and rearing children, attending to the many household duties, and perhaps helping her husband in the fields, and at last after many years of exile and patient toil quietly yielding up her life; and to think also of her husband, worn out by the long struggle with nature, and broken by the loss of his beloved partner, giving up the place which they both had started together to develop into a new and permanent home, and seeking the nearest settlement to pass away his few remaining years. But such was the history of many a pioneer family of this and other states. The son John, who is the more direct subject of this memoir, grew to manhood on the

Washington County farm, on which he learned the valuable lesson of industry, though a book knowledge he had little, having no opportunity to acquire more than the rudiments of an education. In 1863 he married Sophia MILLER, a native of Germany, and while still a young man moved to Milwaukee and established a grocery store, which he conducted until 1871 or 1872. He then moved to Wausau and entered into a similar business there, being very successful and his trade extending over a large territory. That place was then and for many years afterwards a noted headquarters of the lumbering industry, in which many made their fortunes, and it was not long, therefore, before Mr. OELHAFEN became interested in the land and timber business, engaging in it personally and becoming a practical worker, besides knowing it throughout in all its details. Before the advent of railroads he ran great quantities of logs down the Wisconsin River. When Tomahawk was started in 1887, he saw an opportunity to "get in on the ground floor," and coming here started a store which was the first on the site of the village, and continued to be the first, or among the first, in importance for many years, almost indeed, to the present time. He also engaged in the logging and lumber industry here, the members of his family becoming his associates in the concern, which was one of the most active and noted in this section. Besides improving and extending his own business, he was among the leaders in promoting the growth of the city and the interests of the county generally. He had large personal interests in land and timber and also owned a large farm of 800 acres, three miles west of Tomahawk, which he developed into a high condition, erecting a fine set of buildings, stocking it with cattle, hogs and other farm animals, and equipping it with everything necessary to the most modern agricultural processes. He operated from four to six logging camps every winter, owned a delightful summer home, and also had large land holdings in South Dakota. Indeed, he was esteemed a millionaire, yet he had started in life with the capital of the average farmer's boy. His fortune came from industrious and frugal habits, a quick eye for opportunities and straightforward dealings with all those with whom he came into contact in a business way. In 1914 he retired from active work and went to Wausau to pass his remaining years, where he lived until his death on Aug. 9, 1923, but he will be remembered as one of the notable pioneers of Tomahawk so long as this city endures. He was a director in the Bradley State Bank and a prominent and helpful member of the German Lutheran Church. His marriage to Sophia MILLER has been already mentioned. To them were born six children: Elizabeth, wife of August ZASTROW of Tomahawk; Andrew, residing in Tomahawk, a prominent representative of the lumber industry; John W., now one of the leading merchants of the city who is elsewhere given separate mention; Mary, wife of George PFUFFER of Wausau; Annie, wife of Ed SEIN of Wausau; and William, who has taken over his father's mercantile business and is continuing it at the original stand, 117 W. Tomahawk Street.

Oelhafen, John W. proprietor of the Oelhafen Daylight Corner Department Store in Tomahawk, Lincoln County, and a prominent and successful business man of the city, was born in Milwaukee, Wis., May 11, 1866, son of John and Annie Sophia OELHAFEN. In 1872 he accompanied his parents to Wausau, this state, where he attended the grade school, and later assisted his father, who kept a store there. In 1887 the family moved to Tomahawk, then a small settlement not long started, as the store that he opened here was the first in the place. John W. worked in that also and with other members of the family acquired an interest in it, the business being conducted under the style of "John Oelhafen Co.," and incorporated as such in 1914. He was connected with the concern for the long period of 37 years, working in the store until Jan. 1, 1922, and during the next 12 months being engaged in settling up the lumber interests of the company. In August, 1922, he began the erection of the business block he is now occupying, a handsome two-story brick and tile structure on the corner of Wisconsin Avenue and E. Second Street, having a frontage of 50 feet on Wisconsin Avenue and a depth of 142 feet on E. Second Street. On the lower or ground floor he is conducting a first class, modern department store with suitable surroundings and fine equipment. The interior is finished in walnut and the cases and counters are among the finest products of their kind to be obtained in Grand Rapids. In a spacious balcony extending over the rear part of the store is the office of the concern, an elegantly furnished ladies' rest room and a fire-proof vault for the firm's books. The cement-floor basement under the entire building is occupied by the vapor-heating plant and is also used for surplus stock, while the upper story contains office rooms occupied mostly by logging, land and lumber firms. The building in fact, in view of its purpose, is one of the largest and best fitted out of its kind to be found anywhere outside of the large cities, and the store itself is stocked with the most up to date goods of various kinds, retailed in various departments, such as groceries, ladies' ready-to-wear, men's furnishings, dry goods, trunks and valises, etc. The practical experience of a life time in the person of the proprietor, Mr. OELHAFEN, is plainly visible in the result obtained, and is proving a potent factor in making the enterprise successful. He also has the capable assistance of his two sons, Fred M. and Edward G., who, like their father, have grown up in the mercantile business. Mr. OELHAFEN was married June 23, 1888, to Catherine ZANDER of Milwaukee, who was born in that city Jan. 21, 1867. To him and his wife have been born seven children, Fred M., Adelia, Edward G., Alma, Norma, Katherine and John W., Jr. Fred M. was born in Tomahawk, Dec. 2, 1890, and was educated in the public schools of this city and in the Spencerian Business College in Milwaukee, being graduated from the latter in 1898. He was married Dec. 28, 1914, to Glada J., daughter of A. E. and

Jane SUTLEFF of Tomahawk, and they have two children, Marjorie Jane, born oct. 27, 1915, and Wayne Robert, born Oct. 21, 1919. Fred M. is a member of the Elks Lodge in Merrill. Edward G. OELHAFEN was born in Tomahawk Nov. 27, 1892, and was educated like his brother Fred, being graduated from the business college in Milwaukee in1909. He was married July 21, 1915, to Helen A., daughter of William and Jennie (RUDD) FOOTE of Oshkosh, Wis., she having been born in that city Nov. 8, 1890. Mr. and Mrs. Edward G. OELHAFEN have one child, Helen Sherry, who was born Aug. 1, 1917. The family are members of St. Mary's Catholic Church, Edward G., being also a Knight of Columbus. John W. OELHAFEN is a member of the Cohassett Lodge, No. 11, K.O.T.M., of Tomahawk.

Olson, Albert E. a former resident of Tomahawk, for many years engaged in railroad construction work, was born in Trondjhem, Norway, Dec. 17, 1848, son of Mr. and Mrs. Ole ALBERTSON, the parents being farmers by occupation who spent their lives in their native land. Albert E. had but a limited schooling. He remained at home until reaching his majority and then, in 1869, came to the United States, locating in Sioux City, Iowa, where he lived for two years employed in railroad construction work. He then went to Texas to engage in the same kind of work, and from there came to Wisconsin the year before the Wisconsin Valley Railway was built from Tomah to Wausau. During the building of that road he occupied the position of grade foreman, when the "Valley Road," (now the C. M. & St. P.) was extended north from Tomahawk to Star Lake, he worked during the summer as grading boss and during the winters as section boss on the line south of Tomahawk. It was in 1887 that he moved with his family to Tomahawk. Mr. OLSON continued in the harness until a week before his death. The last call was sudden and unexpected; while at the C. M. & St. P. depot in Tomahawk he was stricken with paralysis, from which attack there was no recovery, and thus another good and worthy citizen passed to his reward. Mr. OLSON married Elizabeth M. PHILLIPS, who was born in the township of Arthur, Ontario, May 8, 1858, daughter of John and Margaret (FINUCANE) PHILLIPS. The parents were natives of Ireland who had settled in that township on emigrating to America and who later moved with their children to Grand Rapids, (now Wisconsin Rapids), Wis. To Mr. and Mrs. Albert E. OLSON were born five children: Margaret, Feb. 20, 1878, at Grand Rapids; Albert E., Jr., Nov. 29, 1881; Otto G., April 29, 1884; Herbert L., March 15, 1890, and Ruth E., Nov. 15, 1895. Margaret is now Mrs. Hiram R. RAYMOND of Antigo, Wis., and has two children; Cecelia B., born Feb. 22, 1880, and Frances Rae, born Dec. 12, 1880. Albert E., Jr., died in Tomahawk Sept. 14, 1905. He was in the grocery business here and had been married Sept. 12, 1904 to Mary BOURCIER of Tomahawk, who subsequently remarried. Otto G. married Ruth TREAT of Tomah, in which place they reside, he being a conductor on the C. M. & St. P. Railway and also proprietor of a posting service at Tomahawk, called the Olson Posting Service. Herbert L. was in the United States' service from April, 1917, to May, 1919, and in the World War was a member of the Rainbow Division, in the 166th Infantry. He enlisted at Toledo, Ohio, was first assigned to guard duty at the bridge at Bowerstown, Ohio. There he was transferred to the 42d Division and was sent to Camp Perry, Ohio, and in September to Hoboken, N. J., whence he sailed for France, being landed at Brest Oct. 17, 1917. He was with the first American troops to go into action under General Pershing, was gassed twice and was wounded by shrapnel, two fingers on his left hand being disabled. He returned to his country in May, 1919, and is now living in Chicago. Ruth E. OLSON was married Feb. 4, 1920 to Lloyd F. KOTH of Tomahawk. She is a graduate of the Tomahawk High School class of 1913, subsequently took a commercial course in Ashland, Wis., and was there for two years in the employ of the Tomahawk Shoe Co. as stenographer. After that she was employed for three and a half years in the office of the Bradley Company. She and her husband are the parents of two children, Lloyd, Jr., born Nov. 7, 1920, and Robert A., born Sept. 26, 1922. The Koths live with Mrs. KOTH'S mother at No. 118 Lincoln Avenue, Tomahawk. The Olson family are members of St. Mary's Catholic congregation. Mr. OLSON, the subject of this sketch, was, however, reared a Lutheran. He was for 46 years a faithful and valued employee of the C. M. & St. P. Railway, and when he passed away he left his widow the comfortable home which she now inhabits.

Olson, Anton J. one of the pioneer merchants of the city of Tomahawk, Lincoln County, was born in Mauston, Wis., in 1858, son of Ole T. and Sarah OLSON. The parents, natives of Christiania, Norway, came to the United States about 1850, settling first at Muskego, or Muskego Center, Waukesha County, Wis., whence they later moved to Mauston, where Ole T. OLSON followed the shoemaker's trade, which he had learned in Norway, continuing thus employed to the end of his life. He died in 1921 at the venerable old age of 96 years, having survived his wife, who had passed away in 1894 at the age of 75. They had in all a family of seven children, Mark, Sam, Mariah, Ever, Anton J., Christina and Edward O. Of these, Mariah died young; Ever is a physician in Osseo, Wis.; Christina is the wife of James H. CAMPBELL of Mauston; and Edward O. died in 1874. Mrs. Sarah OLSON, the mother, was twice married, first to a Mr. EVERSON, who died in Norway, leaving one son, Peter A., who came to the United States with his mother, and in 1961 enlisted in a Mauston Company and Wisconsin regiment, serving through the Civil War. Anton J. OLSON, after attending common school in Mauston, in 1875 took a course in a commercial college in La Crosse. He then worked eight years as a bookkeeper in Mauston, part of the time being employed in a bank and the rest in the post office. At the end of that time he went to Wonewoc, Juneau County, to become bookkeeper for the Case Wagon Co. Subsequently he went from there to Cumberland, in Barron County, where he spent eight years in the lumber business, being also chief of the fire department and first city clerk. His next move was to Sioux Falls, S. D., where he engaged in the lumber business. In 1889 Mr. OLSON came to Tomahawk, built a frame store building and opened a hardware store, which he conducted subsequently for 33 years. He was the first clerk of the city of Tomahawk, has been a member of the council, and is now secretary of the board of education. He was the first master of the Masonic Blue Lodge in Tomahawk and is a member not only of that lodge, but is also a Royal Arch Mason and Knight Templar. Thus he has enjoyed an active and varied existence and has seen the city grow from a rude backwoods hamlet to the populous and high civilized community it is today, and in that notable growth he has, himself, been an active factor. Mr. OLSON was married at New Lisbon, Wis., May 11, 1879, to Carrie Bell SOUTHWORTH, of which union there were three children born: Alta, now Mrs. F. P. WERNER of Tomahawk; Norman T., a civil engineer in the employ of the government of Wyoming, and living in Thermopolis, that state; and May, who died in 1909. Mrs. Carrie B. OLSON, who died Oct. 10, 1917, was a member of the local chapter of the Eastern Star, the Women's Literary Club, the Red Cross, and the Ladies' Aid Society of her church. In June, 1919, Mr. OLSON married Mrs. Harriet M. SMITH. He has in his possession a pine made of a foreign coin the size of a half dollar, which Peter A. EVERSON, his half brother, had made for their mother while serving in the army. It is engraved with the initials "P. A. E."

Osborne, L. M. one of the owners of the Tomahawk Leader, was born in Brodhead, Wis., May 3, 1893. He acquired a public school education and subsequently learned the printer's trade in the shop of the Independent Register a Brodhead. In 1917 he purchased an interest in the Tomahawk

Leader. On May 15, 1918, he entered military service but was discharged two months later on account of physical disability. He is a member of Bronstad Post, No. 93, A. L., and also belongs to the local lodges of Masons and Knights of Pythias. On Feb. 12, 1920 he was united in marriage with Elda THIELMAN and he and his wife are the parents of one child, Helen, age two years.

Osborne, L. W. editor of the Tomahawk Leader, was born at Beloit, Wis., March 5, 1890. His boyhood was spent at Brodhead, Wis., and he was graduated from the Brodhead High School with the Class of 1908. He began to learn printing in 1906 while attending school and after his graduation he became a member of the trade and employed in newspaper work. He was foreman on the Beloit Daily Free Press from 1912 to 1915 and foreman on the Ironwood (Mich.) Times from 1915 to 1917, and it was in the latter year that he purchased the Tomahawk Leader. In June 1918, he entered into World War service and after remaining in the army until December, that year, was discharged at Camp Grant, Ill., with the rank of regimental sergeant-major. He is a member of Bronsted Post. A. L., of which he was adjutant for three years. As a member of the library board he has rendered useful service, and he is fraternally affiliated with the Masons and Knights of Pythias. Mr. OSBORNE was married July 14, 1921, to Lutie PARKER. He is a member of the Methodist Episcopal Church, and Mrs. OSBORNE is a member of the Christian Science Society of which she serves as clerk.

Ostrander, Clayton now living retired in Tomahawk after a long career in the building trade and other mechanical employments was born at Mayfield, Fulton County, N. Y., Sept 26, 1854, son of Alva and Phoebe Ann (TURNER) OSTRANDER. The parents were natives of New York State, where they lived for many years both before and after their marriage. Later they moved to Michigan, where Alva

OSTRANDER died in 1857. After that event Clayton went to live with his grandparents, Mr. and Mrs. Daniel R. TURNER and his mother taught school. The grandparents came to Wisconsin soon after-in the same year in fact-settling first at Blue Mounds, Dane County, and later in Vienna Center in the same county, where they homesteaded land. After residing with them until 12 years old Clayton began to contribute to his own support, working on farms in summer and doing chores in winter for his board and the opportunity to attend school, which he did until he was 20 years old. In 1867 he attended the Poynette High School and at the same time began to learn the carpenter's trade, which he later followed there, also working in the lumber yard of Jamison Bros., and subsequently he managed a farm of 400 acres owned by Scott & Wilson. In 1890 he came to Tomahawk, which place had been started three or four years previously and was being rapidly built up. Here he helped to build the Mitchell Hotel, after which he returned to Columbia County and for two years was a resident of Lodi. In 1892 he moved his family to Tomahawk where he helped to build the Tomahawk Bank and many residences and store buildings, besides a number of rural schoolhouses. He also operated a wood-working shop for making extra-sized doors, screen frames, etc. In 1920 he sold his business to his son Ervine and has since lived retired. His mother, after the death of her first husband, Alva OSTRANDER, married W. S. KNAPPEN, by whom she had one son. She was later married to a third husband, Asa CLOSE, but is now deceased. Clayton OSTRANDER was married at Poynette, Columbia County, Wis., July 3, 1878, to Martha KERSHAW, daughter of Isaac and Mary KERSHAW, her parents being farmers of English descent, who were early settlers of Poynette. Both are now deceased. Mr. and Mrs. OSTRANDER have five children living: Ervine C., William W., May Belle, Jennie and Martha. May Belle married A. C. ANDERSON of Tomahawk; Jennie is the wife of John BOGIE of Medford, Wis., and Martha is the wife of Ward FULCHER, a paper maker with the Pride Paper Co. Mr. OSTRANDER has a good public record, having several times served as alderman from the First Ward, as county supervisor and as assessor for the city of Tomahawk. He is a man of many friends and his wife and children are equally esteemed.

Ostrander, Ervine C. proprietor of an up-do-date wood-working shop in Tomahawk, Lincoln County, was born at Poynette, Columbia County, Wis., March 14, 1879, son of Clayton and Martha (HERSHAW) OSTRANDER. The parents were both born in New York State, and from there Clayton OSTRANDER came west to Wisconsin when 12 years old, settling in Columbia County, where during the summers he worked on farms and in the winters attended school. Later he became employed in the lumber industry, rafting lumber down the Wisconsin River and through the Dells to the Mississippi and down to St. Louis. After his marriage at Poynette to Martha HERSHAW he engaged in farming and also worked in the lumber yard of Jamison Bros., later taking up carpenter work. About the year 1890 he came to Tomahawk and helped to build the Mitchell Hotel, after that following carpenter work as a contractor. He is now retired and is residing with his wife in this city. They have had seven children, those now living being Ervine C., Wallace, Maybelle, Jennie and Martha. The other two were Carl and one who died in infancy. Maybelle married B. A. ANDERSON and resides in Tomahawk. Jennie is the wife of John BOGIE, engineer in a sawmill at New Medford, Wis., who formerly served as alderman and assessor in Tomahawk. Martha is the wife of Ward FULCHER of Tomahawk. Ervine C. OSTRANDER as a boy attended school in Poynette and in 1892, at the age of 13, accompanied his parents to Tomahawk, where he finished his schooling. He then worked as clerk, bookkeeper and driver of a delivery wagon for E. W. WHITSON, and afterwards as clerk for Mr. JEFFRIES, remaining with the latter for one year. At the end of that time he went to Menoken, N.D., where he worked on a ranch for three years, after that going on to Oregon in which state he learned butter making. For two years he worked in a creamery and then for three years conducted one of his own. At the end of that time he returned to Tomahawk, Wis., and bought his father's woodworking shop, which he is now conducting, making frames, doors, screen-doors and carrying on a general woodworking business. He uses electric-motor power to drive his machinery. Fraternally he is affiliated with the Odd Fellows and Rebekahs. Mr. OSTRANDER was married at Coquielle, Oregon, June 15, 1917, to Myrtle RYCKMAN, daughter of Albert and Harriet RYCKMAN of Tomahawk. Mrs. OSTRANDER'S father is deceased but her mother is still residing here.

Parker, Ira John engineer for the Tomahawk Pulp & Paper Co., at Tomahawk, Lincoln County, was born on a farm in Waushara County, Wisconsin, Dec. 14, 1861, son of A. R. and Sarah E. PARKER. The father, a native of Vermont, was the son of Ira PARKER, a miller who operated a grist mill in that state and who came to Wisconsin in the early 40's, settling at Oshkosh, or close to the site of that city, where he engaged in farming. At that time A. R. PARKER, father of the subject of this sketch, was a young man. Subsequently the family moved to Waushara County, where Ira PARKER took a government homestead which he farmed until his death in 1864. A. R. PARKER, who accompanied his parents to Waushara County, remained with them on the farm there and after his father's death bought the interests of the other heirs, conducting it himself until about 1893, when he and his wife moved to Berlin, Wis., where they now reside. He is a Civil war veteran, having enlisted in the Wisconsin regiment in 1863 and served until the close of the war, taking part in numerous engagements and skirmishes. His wife Sarah was born in New York State. They have had three children: Jane, who married George JENNINGS and is now a widow residing with her parents; Ira J. of Tomahawk; and Edward of Spring Lake, Wis. Ira John PARKER attended school in Waushara and worked on his parents farm until 1885, when he gave up agricultural pursuits and took up stationary engineering, which he has since followed. In 1891 he came to Tomahawk and ran an engine in the Bradley sawmill. He also operated the engine of the Bradley tug boat on the Wisconsin River and the Bradley famous boat train. Afterwards he was with the Crane Lumber Co. as engineer and from there went to the Tomahawk Pulp & Paper Co. for C. B. PRIDE as engineer, and he has now been with that concern for 18 years. He was also for one year formerly engineer in the city waterworks of Tomahawk. He belongs to the fraternal order of Woodmen of the World. Mr. PARKER was married in Waushara County, Wis., in 1886 to Mary L. SHELDON, daughter of Palmer and Lucy (CORSE) SHELDON, her parents being natives of New York State who settled and farmed in Waushara County, but are now both deceased, the mother having died Jan. 31, 1922, at Wautoma, Wis. The father, who died Dec. 3, at Wautoma, Wis., was a Civil War veteran, having served in the 52d Wisconsin Regiment. Mr. and Mrs. PARKER are the parents of three children, Ira Sheldon, Lutie Jane and Robert Albro, of whom the following is a further record. Ira Sheldon PARKER was born at Cadott, Chippewa County, Wis., on June 20, 1887. He moved with his parents to Tomahawk, Wis., when three years old, subsequently attended the graded school there and was graduated from the high school in 1904. For two years he worked in the Bradley Bank of Tomahawk. He then attended Ripon College at Ripon, Wis., was graduated there in 1910, and for a year and a half subsequently was engaged in teaching history and economics. He was then appointed first income assessor of Lincoln, Oneida and Vilas counties and held that office for five years. In 1916-17 he attended law school at the University of Wisconsin, and in 1918 he was appointed income assessor of Marathon County, a position that he held for three years. Then he accepted a position with the Great Northern Inc. Company of Wausau, Wis., which in January, 1922, sold out to a Chicago Company, though still retaining the name of the Great Northern Inc. Company. He went with it to Chicago and is now its assistance secretary. Lutie Jane PARKER, born in Tomahawk, Aug. 27, 1895, attended the grade and high schools of the city, being graduated from the latter in 1912. In 1917 she was graduated from Ripon College; during the two following years she taught history and English in the high school at Wausaukee, Wis., and in 1920 and 1921 in the high school at Tomahawk. She was married July 14, 1921, to Willis OSBORNE, editor of the Tomahawk Leader. Robert Albro PARKER was born in Tomahawk, Wis., July 16, 1897. He attended the graded and high schools of Tomahawk and was graduated from the high school in 1916. In 1917 and 1918 he was a student at Ripon College, but in October of the latter year he enlisted in the United States service and was sent to Camp Shelby, Mississippi, where he had training in a replacement camp. He was all ready to go overseas when the armistice was signed, and he was honorably discharged Dec. 30, 1918. During the years 1920 and 1921 he attended River Falls Normal School at River Falls, Wis., where he was graduated June 8, 1921. He is now teaching at Seneca, Wis., where he has been principal for two years.

Pfalzgraff, William H. a prominent farmer and member of the side board in the town of Tomahawk, Lincoln County, was born in Le Sueur County, Minnesota, July 28, 1886, son of William and Rachel (QUEST) PFALZGRAFF. The father was a native of Germany who came to America with his parents when four years old, the family settling in Le Sueur County, Minn., before the Civil War. Like other immigrants who arrived at that period, they found work scarce and living conditions hard, so that the father of the family (grandfather of the subject of this sketch) in order to get money for living expenses, risked his life by entering the army as a soldier and going out to fight for the American Union. He was in the army four years and sent home his pay as he received it, except such small amounts as he personally needed. William PFALZGRAFF grew up in that country and remained for a number of years in Le Sueur County, where he married Rachel QUEST. After her death which occurred in 1890, he married again, and is now operating a farm in Crow Wing County, Minnesota. William H. PFALZGRAFF was reared in Le Sueur County, Minn., where he attended the district schools. He remained with his parents until attaining his majority, and then in 1907 went to eastern Colorado, taking a homestead in Cheyenne County, on which he subsequently proved up, also cultivating 84 acres of it and building up a farm. This work took him nine years, at the end of which time he sold his farm, containing 328 acres, and, coming to Lincoln County, Wis., purchased 160 acres of mostly wild timber land in Section 3, Township 34 north of Range 4 east, where he is now building up another farm. When he bought this property there were no buildings on the land and only 31 acres had been cleared. He has now 45 acres cleared, 25 of which are under the plow. He has built an addition to the house and has built a good barn 36x60 feet. Since coming to Lincoln County, Mr. PFALZGRAFF has done logging every winter. This brief sketch of his career marks him out an an energetic, enterprising man who makes the most of his opportunities and is pretty sure to fall on his feet whatever changes may occur in the progress of events. His fellow citizens have recognized his ability and usefulness and in the spring of 1923 he was elected side supervisor of the town of Tomahawk. On July 20, 1907, Mr. PFALZGRAFF was married at Knox Mills, Price County, Wis., to Enna EITTRIEM, and he and his wife are the parents of four children, David, Wilbert, Gladys and Eveline, all of whom are attending school.

Pingel, George J. proprietor of a successful plumbing business in Tomahawk, Lincoln County, was born in

Stockbridge, Calumet County, Wis., Dec. 14, 1881, son of Frederick and Christina PINGEL. The parents were natives of Germany who came to the United States in 1854, locating first in Chicago, where they remained two years, and removing to Calumet County, Wisconsin, in 1856. There Frederick PINGEL bought timber land from the Fox River Valley Improvement Co., which he cleared and on which he followed farming until well on into the Civil war period, when he was drafted and assigned to the 18th Wisconsin Infantry. Having received a wound at Goldsboro, N. C., owing to which he lost one of his legs, he was discharged from the army and returned home. But he was too badly handicapped physically for the active and strenuous work of a farmer, and accordingly sold his farm and built a hotel at Stockbridge, later known as the old Stockbridge House, which he conducted until 1879. He then sold out and bought a small dwelling-house in which he and his wife made their home for the rest of their lives (he died in 1909 and she in 1916). They had nine children, those in addition to the subject of this sketch being: Bertha, wife of J. H. SEARCHER of Barron, Wis.; Ernest of Stockbridge; Ida, widow of Phillip HEIN, who was a shoemaker engaged by the U. S. Government to teach shoemaking to the Indians on the Menomonie reservation; Will, John and Tena of Stockbridge; Fred, a blacksmith in the employ of the Langlade Lumber Co.; and Henry, a foreman in the Bergstrom Paper Co.'s plant at Neenah, Wis. George J. PINGEL was educated in his native town of Stockbridge, attending both grade and high school. He worked more or less at farming until he was 17, after which he learned the plumbers' trade and worked at it for 11 years in Oregon and California. He then returned to Wisconsin, settling in Lincoln County, in 1916, and following farming for four years, at the end of which time he opened his present plumbing shop. He keeps a full line of plumbing materials, does sheet metal work and installs heating apparatus. Mr. PINGEL was married at Klamath Falls, Ore., in October, 1913, to Florence ELDRIDGE, daughter of Henry and Mary (SNIDER) ELDRIDGE, early settlers in Calumet County, Wis., but who are now deceased.

Poutre, Joseph business man and farmer, and a pioneer of Tomahawk, Lincoln County, was born at St. John, province of Quebec, Canada, Dec. 4, 1864, son of Napoleon and Julia POURTE. The parents were of French-Canadian birth and ancestry and the father, Napoleon POUTRE, was a farmer who had inherited his farm from his father, Petre POUTRE, who was the original progenitor of the family in Canada, having come to that country from France. In later life Mr. and Mrs. Napoleon POUTRE retired from farming and took up their residence in the city of St. John, where both died, the former in 1900 and the latter in 1914. They had a family of 13 children, Napoleon, Raphael, Azinda, Charles H., Aurore, Joseph E., Joseph, Malvina, Josephine, Eugene, Delema, Calixt, and Hyppolite, the three last mentioned being now deceased. Joseph E. is now a physician in Manistee, Mich. Joseph POUTRE, the direct subject of this sketch, was reared in Canada, where he attended school, and subsequently worked on the home farm. In April, 1887, he crossed the border into the United States and went to Muskegon, Mich., where for four months he was employed in sawmills. From there he went to Minneapolis, where he also worked in mills, and during the following winter of 1887-88 in the woods at logging. In the fall of 1888 he came to Tomahawk, where the lumber and logging industry was in full swing, and he was in the woods during the ensuing winter. In the summer of 1889 he returned to Minneapolis. In the fall of that year he worked for Ross & Brooks at Harrison, Wis. Then in the spring of 1890 Mr. POUTRE opened a saloon in Tomahawk which he has conducted ever since, for the last few years as a soft drink emporium. He is also engaged in farming a tract of 80 acres of partly improved land. He is a stockholder in the Bank of Tomahawk and from 1905 to 1910 was connected with a cigar factory in this city. He is a member of the fraternal order of Eagles, and is well known and popular. He has never married.

Powell, William R. a successful merchant of Tomahawk, in which city he has resided for 18 years, and is therefore one of its well known citizens, was born in Ontario, Canada, Sept. 14, 1863, son of David and Calista (WRIGHT) POWELL, who were also natives of that province and farmers by occupation. The father died years ago, but the mother is still living and resides in Manitoba. Their ancestors were English and one or more of them took part in the Revolutionary War. William R. POWELL acquired his education in rural schools, which he attended until he arrives at the age of 18 years. For the next three years he was employed as clerk in a general store, and in the meanwhile, from the age of 21 until he was 33 he was engaged in school teaching. In 1891 he came to the States, locating at Medford, Taylor County, Wis., where he taught for several years, after which he spent four years in the U.S. mail service there. It was in 1905 that he came to Tomahawk, where he secured employment as a manager of a livery business and was also agent for the Atlantic & Pacific Tea Company. In 1911 he engaged in mercantile business in Tomahawk and has since built up a good business. In 1918 he erected a two-story building in South Tomahawk, 64x164 feet in dimensions, and consisting of a store and warehouse below and residence above. Politically Mr. POWELL is independent and he and his family are affiliated religiously with the Episcopal Church. Through an accident sustained while in Manitoba in 1887, Mr. POWELL had the misfortune to lose a leg. He was married Oct. 31, 1883, to Mary HAMILL, daughter of Thomas and Jane (MULLIGAN) HAMILL of Ontario, her parents being pioneers of the locality in which they settled. They were both natives of the north of Ireland, but were married in Ontario April 2, 1848, by Rev. John COMI, a Presbyterian minister. Mr. HAMILL died in 1894; Mrs. HAMILL was born in 1831 and died in 1863. They had 14 children, five of whom are still living, namely: Thomas, of Whitewood, Saskatchewan; Samuel of Marilla, Ont.; Hugh of Markham, Ont.; John of Marrila, Ont.; and Mary, now Mrs. William R. POWELL of Tomahawk, Wis. Mr. and Mrs. POWELL are the parents of four children: Genevieve, born Dec. 18, 1885; who resides in Manitoba; Garnett C., born June 29, 1890, now of Minneapolis, Minn.; Maxfred H., born Jan. 14, 1892, a resident of Chicago; and Hugh S., born Sept. 14, 1901, who lives at home and is assisting his father in the store. Hugh S. POWELL was in the United States Naval service during the recent great war, his record being as follows: Enlisted as second class seaman June 22, 1918, and trained at Great Lakes, Ill.; was transferred to Camp Logan, Ill., for marksmanship training on range, and was later transferred to the military academy at Annapolis, Md., for further training on range. From there he was transferred to Submarine Chaser No. 41 as a member of the U. S. Naval Reserve forces and was on coast service between Annapolis and Norfolk and on active duty for 14 months. On account of an injury was released from active duty Aug. 19, 1919, and was discharged at Great Lakes, Ill., Sept. 30, 1921. On his return home he entered the Milwaukee School of Engineering, April 4, 1921, but owing to ill health had to leave June 6, 1922 and again returned to Tomahawk, since which time he has been in the store with his father. He has been a member of every firing squad detailed from the local military company for salute work, and similar duty. Garnett C. POWELL saw army service in the Great War. He entered the service March 2, 1918, in the aviation development, being a resident of Cloquet, Minn., when he enlisted, and was at the time a married man, having previously married Anna LAWSON of Grove City, that state. He trained at Kelly's Field, Houston, Texas, and in July, 1918, sailed for overseas. In France he was detailed on field duty to pick up felled planes and never missed a day's service. He served in France until March 25, 1919, and was discharged at Camp Grant, Ill., April 5, 1919.

Of the two brothers having war records Hugh is a member of Bronsted Post No. 93, American Legion, Tomahawk.

Schrader, William who is profitably engaged in the livery and dray business in Tomahawk, in which city he settled only some four or five years after it was founded, was born in Catteraugus County, New York, Dec. 29, 1863, son of John and Louisa (RUTER) SCHRADER. The parents were of German origin and the father a mason by trade. They never came west and both are now deceased. The son William attended school until the age of 13, at which time be began earning his own living at common labor. In 1883, being then in his twentieth year, he came to Wisconsin, locating at Stevens Point, where he remained for two or three years, subsequently going to Knowlton, Wis., and coming to Tomahawk in 1891. Here he found work about the lumber years at teaming and soon entered the employ of the Bradley Lumber Company with who he remained until 1904. In that year he bought a four-dray livery business of Louis HILDEBRAND, which he operated for eight years in connection with a dray line. In 1920 he took Albert SCOTT into partnership and the firm name is now Schrader & Scott. It is to Mr. SCHRADER'S credit that although starting in life as a poor boy without capital he has been successful. He is the owner of one of the largest and finest gravel pits in this part of the state. He is a member of the Equitable Fraternal Union and in politics a Republican. On July 4, 1887, Mr. SCHRADER was married at Steven Point, Wis., to Ella May, daughter of John and Sarah PETRICK. The parents, American born, were of Scotch and New England origin, and the father, a machinist by trade, operated a machine shop in Stevens Point, where the daughter Ella May was born May 1, 1864. It was just after their marriage that Mr. and Mrs. SCHRADER moved to Knowlton, Marathon County, where they began home making. They have had two children, Jennie Louella, born at Knowlton, Feb. 9, 1889, and Delbert William, born at Stevens Point,

Aug. 14, 1896. Jennie Louella after passing through the grades attended high school two years in Tomahawk, and then entered the Allen Business College at Stevens Point for a commercial course, but while there she took sick and died, March 24, 1906, before she had completed her course. Delbert William attended the town and graded schools and then went to Milwaukee, where he learned the trade of automotive electrical engineer. On June 21, 1918, he entered the United States navy as electrical engineer, and after training one month at the Great Lakes was sent to New York, where he was assigned to the U. S. S. Mont Claire for service. On this vessel, which was engaged in carrying supplies to our soldiers in France young SCHRADER made three round trips and started on the fourth, but the ship had to turn back. On this trip he was taken sick and one reaching New York he was sent to the naval hospital at Norfolk, Va., where he remained for a while until his recovery. On July 29, 1919, he was discharged at Great Lakes and returned home on the following day. On one of his trips between this country and Europe the ship was at sea 34 days on account of stormy weather. At the time the armistice was signed it was in the port of St. Nazaire, France. In 1920 young SCHRADER entered the Milwaukee Motor School, from which he was graduated that fall. He then entered the Milwaukee School of Engineering taking a complete course, and is now doing practical work with the Automotive Electric Co., and pursuing his studies. He makes his home with his parents in Tomahawk. In 1917 the subject of this sketch built a neat and comfortable modern house, the outside of "pebbledash" finish, at 124 Railway Street, in which he and his family reside. They are members of the Episcopal Church, and Mrs. SCHRADER is affiliated with the local Royal Neighbors, the Maccabees, and the Equitable Fraternal Union.

Schultz, Reinhold E. a former citizen of Tomahawk, familiarly known as "Ryan," who was for many years in railway service, both here and elsewhere, was born in Germany, March 18, 1873, son of Carl and Charolotte (MATHEY) SCHULTZ. He was but three weeks old when he was brought by his parents to this country, the family settling at Portage, Wis., where they remained three years, subsequently moving to a farm in the town of Lewiston, Columbia County. There Reinhold attended common or district school. As his earliest occupation, aside from farm work, he chose telegraphy, which he learned under his brother Herman, having entered the employ of the C. M. & St. P. Railway Co. His first regular position was at Hazelhurst, Oneida County, as agent and operator, and from there he was transferred to Star Lake, and later to Merrill as cashier in the company's office. After remaining in Merrill two years, he came in 1890 to Tomahawk as operator, in which position he remained until his death on March 9, 1913, as the result of an automobile accident three months previous. At Portage, Wis., on June 14, 1889, Mr. SCHULTZ was united in marriage with Emma L., daughter of Carl and Amelia (ZESKE) SCHULTZ of that place, where she was born Aug. 13, 1877. Her parents were natives of Germany, the father born in September, 1850, and the mother May 5, 1852. The came to the United States at the ages of 18 and 16 respectively and were subsequently married at Portage, where Carl SCHULTZ died Feb. 23, 1909, and Mrs. Amelia SCHULTZ on July 23, 1922. Mr. and Mrs. R. E. SCHULTZ, the latter of whom as may be noticed, did not change her name on marriage, began domestic life together in Merrill. To them was born one child, Karl R., March 4, 1909, who was graduated from the grade school in Tomahawk. Mr. SCHULTZ was a member of the Masonic order, belonging to the local Blue Lodge and Eastern Star Chapter; also to the Modern Woodmen of America, the Maccabees and the Order of Railway Telegraphers. He was the owner with his brother Herman of 160 acres of cut-over land adjacent to the city of Tomahawk. The family home is at No. 203 Second Street.

Schultz, Herman F. a well known railway man of Tomahawk, who though now an invalid has not entirely given up work, was born in Germany, Jan. 1, 1869, son of Carl and Charlotte (MANTHEY) SCHULTZ. He was about four years old when he accompanied his parents to America and for three years subsequently he lived with them on their farm in Portage County, Wisconsin, the family later moving to a farm in Columbia County, where he spent a number of years. After that they moved to Tomahawk, where the mother died Feb. 18, 1903, and the father Nov. 24, 1906. They had been married in Germany, where for 20 years Carl SCHULTZ had been coachman for a millionaire. The children they brought to America with them were: Amelia, now Mrs. William BLANK of Sparta, Wis.; Herman F., subject of this sketch; and Reinhold E., of whom separate mention is made in this volume. Later they had two children born in Wisconsin: Emma, who is Mrs. John PETERSON of Adams, Wis., and Albert J. of Tomahawk. Herman F. SCHULTZ in his boyhood attended rural school, and also for one winter the public school in Portage. At the age of 15 he entered the employ of the C. M. & St. P. Railway Co. as section hand at Lewiston, and during the year he spent there he learned telegraphy at the Lewiston station, subsequently working at various points as supply. On July 22, 1884 he was placed at Arlington station as operator, and after two years' service there was made night operator at Tomahawk, Wis., where he remained until October 16, 1887. He was then transferred to Tomahawk as operator. In May, 1888, owing to the sickness of C. H. SANBORN, agent at Tomahawk he was placed in the latter's position, in which he served for two years. Mr. SANBORN dying in Colorado, Adelbert C. CARTER was made agent at Tomahawk and Mr. SCHULTZ returned to his former duties as operator, serving in that position under Mr. CARTER and also under Riley S. DICKENS, the latter's successor. In 1899 he was transferred to Babcock, where he remained for a time, but was subsequently returned to Tomahawk and made local agent, serving as such until 1913, when, owing to disability caused by illness he had to give up that position and resume the duties of operator. As such he worked steadily up to 1918 and still holds the right of position, being employed whenever able to work. His malady is locomotor ataxia, which so far has not affected his general health to any perceptible extent, and in summer he goes about in a wheel chair. For the last 26 years he has resided at the family home of his brother Reinhold. Mr. SCHULTZ belongs to the order of Railway Telegraphers and is affiliated religiously with the German Lutheran Congregation. He is part owner of 160 acres of cut-over land adjoining Tomahawk.

Searl, Art head of the firm of Art Searl & Co., operating a feed mill in Tomahawk, Lincoln County, and who for some years has taken a prominent part in civic affairs, was born in Merrill, this county, in 1888, son of C. E. and Emma SEARL. The father who was born in Wisconsin Rapids, and who became a jeweler, was at the time of his death on March 29, 1820, the oldest business man in Merrill. The mother is still living and is now a resident of Tomahawk. They had five children, Ethel, Earl, Nile, Art and Ed, of whom Ed is now deceased. Art SEARL was reared in his native town of Merrill, where he attended school. He then became a traveling salesman, working nine years for a grocery and fruit house in Minneapolis. It was in 1915 that he came to Tomahawk and engaged in farming on a 400-acre farm, which he owns and 140 acres of which is under cultivation. He also buys and sells potatoes and at one time owned five warehouses, at Rhinelander, Tomahawk, Merrill, Cassian and Bass Lake respectively, but in 1921 disposed of those at Rhinelander and Merrill. On Feb. 1, 1920, he established the feed mill he is now conducting and which has a capacity of ten tons daily. He grinds all kinds of feed for stock and poultry and is also conducting wholesale and retail flour, feed and hay business, employing five men altogether and having a three-ton truck for delivery service. On his farm he keeps a herd of high grade Holstein cattle, with a pure-bred sire, also Chester-White hogs and Rhode Island Red, Barred Rock and White Leghorn chickens. He also owns the only heavy pure-bred Percheron stallion in the northern part of Lincoln County. He was chairman of the town of King in 1919-20, and as such a member of the county board, and was elected alderman from the First Ward of Tomahawk in 1922. He is secretary of the Lincoln County Holstein Breeder's Association. Mr. SEARL was married in Merrill in 1915 to Nine DAVIS, daughter of Mr. and Mrs. O. D. DAVIS, who were early settlers in this part of Wisconsin. Mr. and Mrs. SEARL are the parents of two children, Davis and Arnine. In their home they have the first piano that was ever brought into Lincoln County.

Seidle, Charles A. a respected citizen of Lincoln County, who is active in several lines of industry, conducting his chief business in Tomahawk, was born in Germantown, Juneau County, Wis., Aug. 21, 1864, one of the four children of Charles and Hannah SEIDLE. the parents, who were born and married in Brestlau, Germany, came to America and to Wisconsin in the latter 60's. The father was a slater by trade and worked at it for several seasons in St. Louis, Mo. About 1867 he moved his family to Necedah, Juneau County, Wis., where his wife subsequently died. Later he remarried and moved with his second wife and his children to Mauston. Charles A. was then a boy of about nine years and he resided in Maustone until he was 21, receiving, however, but a limited schooling. He then went to New Lisbon, Wis., where he learned the art of photography under J. F. RAMSEY. In the spring of 1889 he came to Tomahawk and established a studio at No. 28 N. Fourth Street, also building a residence across the street from it. Until 1913 he conducted his photo business, his specialty being view making for the Bradley Company and others. He had in the meanwhile bought 120 acres of uncultivated land one mile north of town, there being only a little clearing and a small log building on it and in 1911 he took up his residence on the place and began its development. He has now from 50 to 60 acres under cultivation and has a large frame house there and other commodious buildings. He is engaged in general farming and dairying, his place being well stocked with high grade Holstein cattle. Though a mile north of the settled portion of Tomahawk, it is still within the city limits. Besides being an artistic photographer and a successful farmer, Mr. SEIDLE is a skilled taxidermist, having learned that business with John LAMBERT of Taylor, Wis., and practiced it up to the present time, and it forms no unimportant part of his work. His ability in these different lines of enterprise, coupled with a high standard of integrity, have made him well and favorably known and he is respected throughout Lincoln County. On Jan. 1, 1891, Mr. SEIDLE was married to Minnie CLARK, of Black River Falls, Wis., who was born near that place July 22, 1860, daughter of Mark and Caroline (SYVERSON) CLARK. The father was born near St. Thomas, Ont., and the mother in Bergen, Norway, the former coming to the United States and to Wisconsin as a boy, and the latter at the age of 11 settling with her parents at Coon Prairie (now Westby), Vernon County, Wis., but later moving with the family to Jackson County.

Seth, James Arthur now engaged in the real estate and insurance business in Tomahawk, in which city he is well known, being one of its original pioneers and for many years one of its public officials, was born in Delaware County, New York, Sept. 6, 1849, son of George and Janet (OWEN) SETH. The parents were natives of Scotland, where the father was born in 1812. It was in 1848 that they came to the United States, locating at Jersey Heights, New York City, where George SETH followed farming, until the money thus earned he bought a farm in Delaware County, N. Y., on which the family settled. It was only the first step in their westward journey, however, as in 1855 they left there and came to

Wisconsin, locating at Ripon, there the father engaged in general teaming and also followed farming, and where he died in 1881. His wife Janet died at Ripon in 1901, having survived him 20 years. They had seven children, of whom those now living are: Margaret, who married P. T. TUCKER and is now in Redwood, California; and James Arthur of Tomahawk, Wis. Those deceased are George, Elizabeth, John and Alison. James a. SETH was about six years old when his parents settled in Ripon, and his education was acquired in the common schools of that place. He then learned the trade the painter, paper-hanger and decorator, which he followed for a time, afterwards working four years in a flouring mill. He then returned to his former trade and also conducted a meat market. When Tomahawk was founded in 1887 he came to this place, setting out from Superior, where he then happened to be, and walking the latter part of the distance from Bradley, as there was no railroad here then. He crossed the river in a dugout and found two stores here, one conducted by John OELHAFEN and the other by Mr. ROBERTS. Stumps were everywhere in the streets and there were no sidewalks, as that it was a dirty, and rather dreary-looking place, and very muddy after a rain. But the elements of progress were there and he remained, taking up his trade of painting again and also carpenter work, for which there was a good demand. After being thus engaged for a few years, he entered into the real estate and insurance business which he has since followed. Having closely identified himself with local interests and proved his capacity and reliability, it was not long before his fellow citizens elected him to public office, and thus he served ten years as justice of the peace, was alderman from the Fourth Ward two terms, served one term as city clerk, was a member of the school board and poor commissioner, and served three terms as supervisor on the county board. He is fraternally affiliated with the Odd Fellows and Maccabees, and is one of the best know citizens of Tomahawk and highly respected. Mr. SETH was married at

Ripon, Wis., Oct. 28, 1875, to Sarah Albie WELCOME, daughter of Eben Decatur and Esther (HERRICK) WELCOME, the parents being natives of Maine, who on coming to Wisconsin had settled on a farm in Waushara County. In 1863 Mr. WELCOME was drafted into the Federal army for service in the Civil War, being assigned to the First Wisconsin Cavalry. While engaged in active service he was captured by the Confederates and confined to the notorious Andersonville prison, where he died in June, 1864. He and his wife Esther were the parents of five children, of whom four are now living, namely: Sarah A., now Mrs. James A. SETH; Francella, who married James PYNCH of Ripon; Elizabeth, wife of Phineas SHUTE of Winona, Minn.; and Decatur, who lives in California, where he is engaged in the real estate and investment business. The one deceased is Lois. After her husband's death in a war prison, Mrs. WELCOME married his uncle, John B. WELCOME, and having survived him, became the wife of Henry Clay WELCOME, who was her first husband's cousin, and who, like him, had served in the Civil War. On the day she married her third husband, her daughter Sarah became the wife of James A. SETH, the occasion being a double wedding. By this last husband she had a son, Harry Claude, who is now in Kansas City, Mo. She died in Tomahawk in 1916 at the advanced age of 84 years. Mr. and Mrs. James A. SETH have one child, Florence, now the wife of Herbert R. MILLER of Minneapolis, and who has three sons, Paul and Norman (twins) and Herbert Ray.

Smith, George W. who in association with his son-in-law, Roy A. CONANT, is engaged in agriculture at Bradley, Lincoln County, has in his day been a man of many activities and is still in the harness, able to do a fair day's work when it is necessary. He was born at Burnett, Dodge County, Wisconsin, May 7, 1850, son of John and Caroline (TAYLOR) SMITH. One or more of his earliest ancestors in this country were among the Mayflower's passengers in 1620, and a

Thomas SMITH in direct line came over in 1621. John SMITH, father of George W., was born in Duxbury, Mass., July 21, 1814, and was married to Caroline TAYLOR in Vermont, which was her native state, she having been born at Waterbury Feb. 14, 1816. In 1847 they came to Wisconsin, which was then under territorial government, settling in Dodge County, at a point seven miles from Beaver Dam and five miles from Horicon. There they were engaged in farming for 13 years, at the end of which time they moved to Outagamie County and later to Waupaca County, where Mrs. Caroline SMITH died in 1889. After her death, and in the same year, her husband accompanied his son George to Tomahawk and from there to Bradley, where he died in February, 1901. Mr. and Mrs. John SMITH had five sons and two daughters. The brothers of the subject of this sketch were Willis, Ira J., Edwin and Charles C., and the two sisters, Abigail and Minerva, all of whom are now deceased. George W. SMITH as a boy attended common school in Dodge County and subsequently, through a correspondence course, learned civil engineering, being qualified by the age of 20 years. He at once actively engaged in that profession and during many subsequent years followed it in various parts of the state. He was for some time county surveyor for Waupaca County and was county surveyor for Lincoln County for ten years after coming to the county in 1889 with his family. He also engaged in lumbering, and in mercantile business at Bradley, in association with E. L. TAYLOR and under the firm name of Smith & Taylor. After four years he sold his interest in the store to Mr. TAYLOR but retained his interest in the lumbering business for 15 years, or until 1918, when they creased active operations in that direction. It was in 1909 that Mr. SMITH took steps to establish himself as a farmer, selected 120 acres of cut-over land in Section 5 and 8, town 35-6, close to Bradley village. Of this tract he has since developed 70 acres and erected a fair set of buildings and is every year making further improvements. The farm is well stocked with pure-bred Jersey cattle, and in its management and ownership he is associated as already mentioned, with his son-in-law, Roy A. CONANT. Mr. SMITH'S other activities have been largely of a public nature. At a time when the town of Rock Falls comprised about one-quarter of the present area of the county, he served as it assessor. He also at another time for several years served the city of Tomahawk in the same capacity; he was for several years chairman of the town board of the town of Tomahawk, and for two years was clerk of the town of Bradley. A member of the Republican Party he was a delegate to the Republican convention at Madison when Robert M. LA FOLLETTE was serving his second term as governor. Such statements are quickly made and take up little space, but are full of meaning to those who can read between the lines, telling plainly of a large amount of work performed by Mr. SMITH for the public good and in addition to his own personal business. When the Odd Fellows' Lodge was formed in Iola, Waupaca County, Mr. SMITH became one of its charter members, and he still belongs to the order, being a member of the lodge in Tomahawk and the encampment in Merrill. George W. SMITH was married Dec. 24, 1882, to Jennie A. MCGUINNES, who was born in Newcastle, New Brunswick, March 6, 1864, daughter of Thomas and Sarah MCGUINNESS, the parents being of Scotch-Irish stock, and natives of the province of New Brunswick and the State of Maine, respectively. It was from Maine that they came to Wisconsin, locating in Waupaca County, and for some time in the village of Iola, where they were at the time of their daughter's marriage to Mr. SMITH. Subsequently they moved to Lincoln County, where Mr. MCGUINNES died Sept. 9, 1917; his wife, who survived him, is now living with her son-in-law, Mr. SMITH. She has not only survived her husband, but also her daughter, as Mrs. Jennie A. SMITH died in Tomahawk on Aug. 16, 1904. One child was born to Mr. and Mrs. SMITH, Bessie I., on Sept. 26, 1883, who is now Mrs. Roy A. CONANT of Bradley.

Stone, Patrick E. one of the early settlers in Tomahawk, Lincoln County, and still residing here, was born in the province of Quebec, Canada, in March, 1855, son of John and Ann STONE. The parents, who were both born in Ireland, immigrated to Canada when young, the usual emigrant vessels of that day sometimes taking 11 weeks to make the voyage. They were married in Canada, where they spent the rest of their lives. They had three sons: John, who resides at International Falls, Minn.; Patrick E., of Tomahawk; and one who died young. Patrick E. STONE as a boy attended school in Canada and did farm work there until he came to Tomahawk in 1889. At that time this section was covered with timber and there were but two stores and a very few dwellings on the site of the village, while sidewalks or other municipal improvements, while perhaps thought of, were not yet in evidence. Mr. STONE had learned the carpenter's trade in Canada, which he found useful in Tomahawk while the village was building up. In the winters he worked at logging and at various times in mills. In those occupations, including general lumbering, he was engaged until 1921, in which year he met with an injury and retired from active work. For about five years he served as city street commissioner. He was the owner of some city property, including several houses which he rents, and also has a cottage on Half Moon Lake, where he and his daughter Anna spend their summers. Mr. STONE was married in Canada in 1884 to Bridget CURLEY, daughter of Mr. and Mrs. Owen CURLEY, her parents being natives of Canada, where both spent their lives. She died in 1904, having been the mother of six children, namely: Anna, who keeps house for her father and is a member of the Helping Hand Society; John a master mechanic residing at Antigo, Wis.; Patrick T., who is the present city attorney of Wausau; Mary E., wife of Thomas KELLEY of Tomahawk; Bess E., now Mrs. Sherman WADE of Antigo; and Florence, who is in the employ of the United States Shipping Board and lives in

Washington, D.C. Patrick T. STONE enlisted in the navy during the recent great war, and trained at Great Lakes, but did not go across.

Sutliff, Albert E. a prominent citizen and business man of Tomahawk, Lincoln County, which city he has served in various public offices, including that of mayor, was born in Newaygo County, Michigan, March 18, 1861, son of Calvin A. and Emily (WOODWARD) SUTLIFF. He come of a long line of American ancestry, beginning with Abraham SUTCLIFF who emigrated from Plymouth England, to Plymouth, Mass, in 1623. This line of descent, with other information about the family may be found given in the biography of Solon D. SUTLIFF of Rhinelander, who is brother of the subject of this sketch. In this article it is only needful to mention that the parents of our subject, Mr. and Mrs. Calvin A. SUTLIFF, who were long residents of Newaygo County, Mich., where Mr. SUTLIFF was engaged in logging, buying and selling timber and farming, are both now deceased. They had in all 13 children, of whom eight are living and five deceased, the former being Solon D., Frank A., Milan R., Charles A., Albert E. Mattie E., Lottie G., and Helen M., and the latter Ella, Nettie, Libby E., Jessie E. and Flora E. Albert E. SUTLIFF was reared on his parents' farm in Newaygo County, Michigan, and when young attended district school. He continued agricultural work during the summers until he was 21 years old and then took a position as fireman on a logging railroad, being thus engaged for one summer. Then with his brother Solon he engaged in the livery business at Newaygo, Mich, Charles F. KEEFE, his brother-in-law, being associated with them. A year and a half later he gave up that business and renewed his connection with the lumbering business, logging in the woods and working on the rivers and on the boom till 1889, in which year he came to Tomahawk. It was about two years after the village had been started and there was plenty of building and manufacturing going on, the lumber business being the chief industry. Mr. SUTLIFF obtained a job as saw filer in the sawmill of the Tomahawk Lumber Co. and later in the mill of Crane Bros., being thus occupied altogether for ten years. He then engaged in the land and timber business in company with O. M. SMITH, the association being continued until Mr. SMITH died in 1909, after which Mr. SUTLIFF cut timber alone, which he turned into logs, subsequently selling the land. From 1920 to 1922 he was engaged in the oil and gasoline business, with his son, W. D. SUTLIFF. On Nov. 1, 1922 they sold out of the Interstate Oil Co. and went back to the logging and lumbering business, sawing logs in the woods with a portable mill. Mr. SUTLIFF had not been in Tomahawk many years before he had become widely known and had made many friends and by them he was persuaded to engage more or less in local politics. He was county supervisor from this city for two terms, served as alderman from the fourth and also from the third ward, and was a member and president of the school board. It is now 37 years since he assumed the responsibilities of domestic life, being united in marriage Sept. 1, 1886, at Newaygo, Mich., to Jennie PURCELL, daughter of Peter and Mary (BARDEN) PURCELL. The parents were natives of Canada, both of whom died on their farm near Newaygo. They had nine children, of whom seven are living, Edward, Robert, Louise, Lizzie, Effie, Geraldine, and Jennie. Joseph and Marie are dead. Mr. and Mrs. SUTLIFF have two children: Warren D. and Glada, the latter being the wife of Fred OELHAFEN of Tomahawk.

Theiler, Frank an active lumber operator of Lincoln County, now serving as mayor of the city of Tomahawk, was born Dec. 9, 1883, on a farm in Marathon County, Wisconsin, son of Martin and Catherine (WOLTFOGEL) THEILER. Frank was the second born of their 11 children. He had but little schooling, and when 12 years old his father took him into the woods to give him an insight into the logging business. That business he has followed practically ever since. In 1902 he went to the harvest fields of South Dakota, having $30 with him when he left Tomahawk. When he returned in the fall he has $240, with which he bought 40 acres of timberland near Tomahawk, and he immediately began logging on his own account. For several years during the summers he made trips through the west and into Canada to accumulate more capital through farm work, and with the land he bought kept busy logging in the winters, which industry still engages his attention. Active and enterprising, he has been successful and is well known and respected throughout Lincoln County. When quite a young man he was elected a member of the county board of supervisors, being the youngest member ever elected in that office; he served as alderman from four different wards of the city of Tomahawk, and in 1920 he was elected mayor, in which position he is still serving. He is connected with business interests of Tomahawk as a stockholder and is one of the city's most prominent business men. Mr. THEILER was married in May, 1912, to Jennie J. STRONG, daughter of James and Agnes (LONG) STRONG of Calumet County, Wis., she having been born in Chilton, that county, in 1888. Mr. and Mrs. THEILER have four children, Columbia, Helen F., Francis and Delphine.

Theiler, Harry an active factor in the logging and lumbering business of Lincoln County, and a widely known resident of Tomahawk, was born at Wausau, Wis., Aug. 19, 1886, son of Martin and Catherine (WOLTFOGEL) THEILER. He was but a year old when his parents moved from Wausau to Tomahawk, and it was in the latter place that he attended school. After completing his studies he entered the employ of C. M. & St. P. Railway, and after firing a locomotive for four years was promoted in 1908 to the position of engineer. In 1918 he left the road and engaged in the logging business, which he has since followed summer and winter. He has enjoyed success in this enterprise and owns a good home at No. 4, East Spirit Avenue. He belongs to the local lodges of

Elks and Knights of Columbus. Mr. THEILER was married June 5, 1912, to Alma P. CONANT, who was born in Wausau, Wis., March 27, 1890, daughter of Herbert and Abigail (WOODARD) CONANT, and who came with her parents to Tomahawk when she was five years old. To Mr. and Mrs. THEILER have been born five children: Marion E., March 8, 1913, Ruth A., March 11, 1915; Mildred L., Dec. 1, 1917; Jean H., Nov. 25, 1919, and Norma H., Sept. 24, 1921. Mrs. THEILER is a graduate of the Tomahawk High School, class of 1908. The family stands high in the community and are members of the St. Mary's Catholic Congregation.

Theiler, Martin a surviving pioneer of the city of Tomahawk, a man well known and widely respected, was born in Switzerland, July 4, 1859. He was there married in 1881 to Catherine WOLTFOGEL, who was born in that country Aug. 21, the same year, and immediately after their marriage they started for the United States, their journey to this country being therefore somewhat in the nature of a honeymoon. On their arrival here they settled in Wausau, Wis., where they resided for three years, except for a brief trip to Kentucky, subsequently moving to a farm in Marathon County, where also they resided three years. When the village of Tomahawk was laid out in 1887, Mr. and Mrs. THEILER came here among the first settlers, taking a house close to their present location at No. 12, Spirit Avenue. Strong and sturdy they have enjoyed good health, done a large among of useful work in the world, and have reared a family of ten sons and one daughter, namely, Lena, Frank, Harry, Louis, George, Carl, William, Joseph, Martin, Edgar and Robert. In regard to these children the following individual record is available. Lena, the only daughter, who was born May 24, 1883, is now Mrs. Charles LATTIMER of Wausau, Wis., and has two children, Edwin and Charles. Frank THEILER is a prominent business man of Tomahawk. Harry's record is contained in a separate article in this volume. Louis, who was born June 30, 1888, was educated in the Tomahawk schools and saw service in the World War. He was in France with the First Gas Company and served 10 months altogether. After receiving his discharge and returning home, he engaged in logging with his brother Frank, and he is now following the same occupation near Spirit Falls, in company with his brother George. George THEILER, born June 11, 1891, is a graduate of the McKillip Veterinary College of Chicago, class of 1918, and had just started to practice his profession in Tomahawk when he was called into the United States' service. He has enlisted while at college and attended officers' training camp at Camp Greene, Georgia. He was commissioned second lieutenant and discharged to Camp Greene Dec. 17, 1918. On his return home he resumed the practice of his profession, in which he has been successful, having many patrons scattered within a radius of 20 miles around Tomahawk. He has been active in promoting the best stock breeding and has done good work in helping to built up the dairy interests. He has also taken a leading part in the organizing and conducting of the county fair held annually at Tomahawk. He served as grand knight of K. C. Council No. 2066, and was vice commander one year and then commander one year of Bronsted Post, No. 93, A. L. Carl THEILER is a resident of Harrison, Lincoln County. William THEILER was born March 14, 1896, was educated in the Tomahawk schools and in his youth worked on his parents' farm. In 1916 he purchased 160 acres in the town of King and is there engaged in general farming and dairying. He has cleared 120 acres, erected some new buildings and improved others. The remaining children, Joseph, Martin, Edgar and Robert, all reside in Tomahawk and were educated in the local schools. Edgar is a student at Marquette College, Milwaukee, and is taking a course in economics. Robert, born Aug. 7, 1904, was graduated from the Tomahawk High School. He works for his father on a farm during the summer and in the woods in winter. Mrs. Martin THEILER before her marriage was a nurse, and after coming to the United States from Switzerland studied her profession in Milwaukee. As one of the pioneer women of Tomahawk, she was often called upon in early days to tend the sick and was glad to do so. At times she had some remarkable experiences, not only tending the women and children in their homes but also going out to lumber camps. She is a remarkable woman for her age; she has reared a family of 11 fine children and still does her own housework. The Theiler family have all pulled together, making possible the success of the father, Martin THEILER, who for years has been actively engaged in logging, and also owns a 160-acre farm within the city limits of Tomahawk.

MARTIN THEILER AND FAMILY

Theilman, Robert C. the veteran meat dealer of Tomahawk, who is one of the original pioneers of this city, was born in Watertown, Wis., Dec. 1, 1866, son of Gottfried and Julianna (BAUM) THEILMAN. Both parents were born in Germany, being worthy members of the middle class. They resided for a while in Oconomowoc, Wis., and moved from there to Watertown, the father for a number of years following the trade of bridge builder in the employ of C. M. & St. P. Railway. He died in 1908, after which his wife took up her residence in Merrill. Robert C. THEILMAN acquired his elementary education in the public schools and was subsequently a student for two terms at Northwestern University, Watertown. It was in 1881 that he first saw the site of Tomahawk, which was before the village had been established. He was engaged in the meat business in a small way when the grade work for the railroad was being done, and in 1887, the summer of which the village was laid out, he came here to make his permanent home, having been previously associated in business with his brother Julius in Merrill. With this brother he opened the Theilman Bros.' meat market on Wisconsin Avenue, which they conducted together until R. C. purchased his brother's interest in the business which he has since carried on alone. This, however, has not been his only sphere of activity, as in 1890 he engaged in the land and timber business, in which he still continues, also dealing in farm lands. He owns a tract of many acres adjoining Tomahawk, a part of which he has platted and added to the city as Theilman's Addition. In 1914 he owned 300 acres within the city limits. In public life Mr. THEILMAN has been equally prominent and he is a leading member of the local Democracy. He was the first man outside the city of Merrill to serve as chairman of the county board, and he served 12 terms as mayor of Tomahawk, making a fine record in that office. He was president of the city's fire and police commission, president of the park board, and served on the county board many years in addition to the time that he acted as its chairman. As president of the Tomahawk Chamber of Commerce he performed valuable service and was active in various ways in promoting the growth and development of the city and conserving its best interests. As the result of all these activities he is one of the best known citizens in Lincoln County and has always enjoyed a life of popularity. He is a member of the Elks Lodge of Merrill and the Maccabees' of Tomahawk, and also belongs to the Hoohoos, which is a social organization of lumbermen with a membership extending all over the country. Mr. THEILMAN was married in January, 1888, to Mary EIDEN of Stevens Point, Wis. Her parents, John and Margaret EIDEN, settled in this state while it was yet a territory. In 1849 they both joined in the rush of gold hunters to California and were absent in the far west for 11 years. They then returned to Wisconsin and for 30 years subsequently, or until 1890 made their home in Stevens Point, moving then to Tomahawk. Mr. and Mrs. THEILMAN are the parents of three children; Ada, Vena and Elda.

Thielman, Louis G. for 36 years a resident of Lincoln County, who for a number of years has been engaged in mercantile business at Harrison, in addition to being the owner of farm and resort lands, was born at Watertown, Wis., in November, 1871, son of Gottfried and Julia (BAUM) THIELMAN. The parents were born and married in Prussia, Germany, whence they came to the United States in 1852, settling at Watertown, Wis., and the father worked 25 years as contractor for the C. M. & St. P. Railway. In 1888 the father moved to Merrill, where both parents died. A list of their children may be found in the biography of Julius THIELMAN. Louis G. THIELMAN was reared at Watertown, where he attended school until he was 14 years old. In 1887 he came to Merrill, Lincoln County and entered the employ of his brother Emil as delivery boy. In 1891 he came to Tomahawk and for 17 years thereafter was employed in the meat market of his brother Robert. It was at the end of that time that he took up his residence in Harrison, the place being a logging camp, and opened a general store. Later the post office was located in the store with Mrs. THIELMAN as post mistress. Mr. THIELMAN is still conducting this business and is also active in other ways. In 1922 he bought 40 acres of land near Lakes Butteau, Fish and Long, and also owns 80 acres of water frontage on Lake Butteau. All these lakes are well stocked with pike and big-mouthed bass. Mr. THIELMAN'S farm is cleared, and while his wife and son attend to the store and post office he is doing general farming, his cattle being high grade Holsteins. In the present year (1923) he is building an addition to his barn, making it 36 by 80 feet in size, with a full basement and modern equipment. When Mr. THIELMAN came to Tomahawk the location was covered with dense timber and he has seen the settlement grow from two or three primitive buildings in the midst of the pine forest to the thriving city of nearly 3,000 people that it is today. While residing there he was a member of the fire department up to 1907, one year serving as chief. Thus he has been one of the active factors in the development of the county and as such is well known within its limits. Mr. THIELMAN was married at Wausau, Wis., in 1895 to Elizabeth GOETZ, daughter of Mr. and Mrs. William GOETZ of Marshfield, Wis., and who was born in the city of Milwaukee in October, 1873. Her father, a native of Germany, is still living being now 82 years of age. He is a widower, his wife having passed away in 1922. Mr. and Mrs. THIELMAN are the parents of five children: Esther, residing in Milwaukee; Archie, associated in business with his father; Viola, clerk in her father's store; Alvera, at home; and Robert, working for his father.

Tweedy, Robert B. one of the leading business men of Tomahawk, was born in Milwaukee, Sept. 27, 1864, son of John H. and Anna M. (FISHER) TWEEDY. The father was a native of Connecticut and the mother of Boston, Mass. It was

SHOW UP YOUR CITY

IS EACH CITIZEN OF TOMAHAWK DOING his best in pointing out the beauties and advantages of our city to the strangers within our gates? There are many things which we know so well, and with which we are so familiar, that we are apt to take it for granted that they are the same to every one else, or we do not think of them at all. Each citizen owes a duty to the place of his residence. Whatever is for the benefit of the city, is of benefit to each one personally. Think of all the things that make Tomahawk a desirable place of residence, and point these things out to strangers, as you have opportunity. You will be doing them a favor by indicating things of interest. This will add to the pleasure of their stay in town. It may prove greatly to their advantage in a business way. It will make our city favorably known throughout the land as it ought to be known. Do not take things too much as a matter of course. Be interested yourself, and interest others.

The Tomahawk – 1902

in 1836 that they settled in Milwaukee, then quite a small place, and it required no effort for Mr. TWEEDY, a man of liberal education and a lawyer by profession, to take a prominent place in the community. He grew up with the place and in a few years his reputation extended so far beyond its limits that he was elected one of the representatives to organize the territory of Wisconsin into a state and settle the vexed boundary question, for which purpose conventions were held, one in 1846 and another--the final one-- in 1847-48. He was on a later occasion a candidate for the office of governor. Robert B. TWEEDY was reared in Milwaukee and acquired his education partly there and partly in Boston, Mass. He subsequently followed railroading in the employ of the Wisconsin Central Railway, being thus occupied until 1901, and after the death of Mr. BRADLEY in 1903 he had charge of the Bradley holdings and later as president, which position he still retains. At Milwaukee in 1891 Mr. TWEEDY was united in marriage with Edna BRADLEY, daughter of Mr. and Mrs. Edward BRADLEY, her father being a brother of William H. BRADLEY above referred to, who was for many years one of Lincoln County's foremost citizens.

Wallis, Charles H. one of the leading merchants of Tomahawk, Lincoln County, proprietor of an up to date jewelry store and watch repairing business, was born in the town of Rubicon, Dodge County, Wis., June 12, 1863, son of Charles and Sarah (RAMSEY) WALLIS. The father, who was the Scotch antecedents, was born in England in 1827; while the mother was of English descent and was born in Pennsylvania, this country, in 1834. The former followed chiefly the occupation of a farmer, but after he family moved to Neosho, Dodge County, Wis., which happened in or about the year of 1869, he operated a stage line for some years between Oconomowoc and Woodland. He died Jan. 4, 1911, being survived by his wife, who is now residing at Hartford, Wis. Charles H. WALLIS was six years old when he accompanied his parents to Neosho, a small village having now about 300 inhabitants. He attended public school there up to the age of 16 and then went to Milwaukee, where he learned the watchmaker's and jeweler's trade, and in 1884 he established himself in business in Plymouth, Wis., where he remained six years. In 1890 he moved to Ironwood, Mich., where he conducted a similar business for three years. For two years after that he was a traveling salesman. Then in 1895 he again engaged in business for himself, choosing Brillion, Calumet County, as his location. The place was small, but he remained there five years, at the end of which time, in 1900, he came to Tomahawk, Lincoln County, which opened up a wider field for his activities, and opened up a business here, which has since expanded to its present proportions. Politically he belongs to the Progressive wing of the Republican party, but has never held office here, though in Plymouth he served as alderman of his ward. He is a member of the Masonic order and served Tomahawk Lodge, No. 243, as Master for two years, and he formerly belonged to the order of Knights of Pythias. Mr. WALLIS was married Jan. 1, 1886, to Bessie BOWERS, daughter of Benjamin and Augusta BOWERS of Plymouth, Wis., where she was born May 31, 1867. Two children are the fruit of this union: Richard, born Jan. 17, 1887, and Christine, born Oct. 30, 1893. Richard, who is associated with the Tomahawk Lake Co., is married and has two children, Benjamin and Richard, Jr. Christine, now Mrs. P. M. SMITH of Tomahawk, has also two children, Wallace and Edward. Mrs. C. H. WALLIS and her children are members of the Episcopal Church, in which Mr. WALLIS was baptized, though he now affiliates with the Congregational Church. The home of the family, a good modern residence, is at No. 109 Wisconsin Ave.

Wetzel, George proprietor of the Wetzel Art Studio at No. 28 N. Fourth Street, Tomahawk, Lincoln County, was born at Hayton, Calumet County, Dec. 31, 1882, son of

Joseph and Minnie (MODELIN) WETZEL, who were farmers by occupation. The father was a native of Baden, Germany, and the mother, who was of Scotch ancestry, was born near Hayton, Wis., and it was in the latter place that her marriage to Mr. WETZEL occurred in the early 70's. Both she and her husband have passed away, the former dying in 1894 and the latter some years later. They had eight children: Henry, now of Powers, Ore.; Joseph E., deceased; Sarah, who is Mrs. Frank LYNCH of Kimberley, Wis.; Frank of Buffalo, N.Y.; Anna M., wife of Emil PAUTZ of Clintonville, Wis.; Jennie, now Mrs. Henry CLAUSEN of Grand Haven, Mich.; George, of Tomahawk, Wis.; and Susan, who lives in West Somerville, Mass., a suburb of Boston. George WETZEL has but limited educational opportunities. For about two years-from the age of 16 to that of 18-he worked as a farm hand. Then in the summer of 1900 he began learning photography with Ulrich MOECKLI of Sheboygan, Wis., with who he remained for three years. He then went with A. S. RALPH of Oshkosh, Wis., and later with Harry LYMAN of that city. On leaving Mr. LYMAN he became an organizer for the Modern Woodmen of America in the Oshkosh and Sheboygan districts and remained in that territory until Jan. 1, 1920, having for the last ten years of that time operated a studio in Sheboygan. He then sold out and until Nov. 1, 1920, was a salesman of Ford cars for a Mr. THEIMAN of Sheboygan, on the date last mentioned taking possession of his present studio in Tomahawk. This had been started in 1888 by Charles A. SEIDEL, who in 1913 sold it to a Mr. DOWNIE, from whom Mr. WETZEL purchased it about a month before he took possession. The studio is well equipped with all the necessary cameras, lenses and accessories for both portrait and commercial work and he has a good trade in both the principal branches of his profession. Above the studio is a flat which he occupies as a residence. Mr. WETZEL was married June 17, 1905, to Frances M. GERTH, who was born in Plymouth, Sheboygan County, Wis., Sept. 14, 1882, daughter of William and Amelia (KUEPER) GERTH, who were later residents of Sheboygan. The father was a native of Saxony, Germany, who came to America and to Wisconsin in 1848, during the revolutionary times in Germany. The mother was born at Stockbridge, Wis. Mr. and Mrs. George WETZEL are members of the Congregational church, and also of several societies, Mr. WETZEL belonging to the local Masonic lodge and Eastern Star Chapter, also to the camps of Modern Woodmen of America and Royal Neighbors of Sheboygan, Wis., and to the Tomahawk Commerical Club, while Mrs. WETZEL is a member of the Eastern Star Chapter and the Royal Neighbors.

Zastrow, August a well known pioneer of Tomahawk still residing in this city, was born in Germany, Dec. 26, 1856. As a baby of two years he was brought to America by his parents, who settled in Marathon County, Wisconsin. There he grew up, but had little schooling, and when 16 years of age he became connected with the lumber industry, cribbing logs down the Wisconsin and Mississippi rivers from Wausau to St. Louis. He worked for John OELAFEN when the latter logged Reb Hill adjacent to Wausau, and he continued in his employ for about 15 years. It was in 1887 that he came to Tomahawk, which was the year in which the village was platted, and for some time he followed the carpenter's trade, finding plenty to do during the influx of settlers. He then engaged in a business for himself in which he continued up to 1917, since which time he has been practically retired. He now makes his home with his daughter, Mr. Herman G. FOSTER. He was reared in the German Lutheran faith. Mr. ZASTROW was married Oct. 3, 1880, to Elizabeth A., daughter of Mr. and Mrs. John OELHAFEN of Wausau, and he and his wife began domestic life together in that city. They had four children: Carl, now a resident of Tomahawk; Emma, also of Tomahawk, who is now a widow, her husband, Gerbert G. FULLER, formerly city treasurer, having died Nov. 10, 1915; Anna, who is now Mrs. Thomas NASH of Tomahawk, and Lillian, born Sept. 22, 1888, who is the widow of Herman G. FOSTER and lives in Tomahawk.

Parshall, M. Le Roy who is engaged in farming and dairying in Section 35, town of King, Lincoln County, was born in Michigan in 1873, son of Reuben and Frances PARSHALL. The parents, who were natives of the states of New York and Pennsylvania respectively, settled on a farm in Michigan in 1854. The father died about 1884 and the mother in 1923. They had three children who grew to maturity, Otis, M. Le Roy and Reuben. Mr. Le Roy PARSHALL was reared on the home farm, attending district school in boyhood, and helping his father in the farm work until he was 20 years old. Then in 1893 he came to Tomahawk and for three years subsequently was employed in the woods and mills of this place and the vicinity. He then bought an 80-acre farm in the town of Bradley, which he subsequently sold. The next few years were spent as a traveling salesman, selling text books for the D. C. Heath Co. In all he made Tomahawk his home for eight years. In 1919 Mr. PARSHALL bought his present place, then consisting of 40 acres of wild land, which he at one started to improve, his first task being to clear a space for a house and barn, which he proceeded to erect. He has since kept up the work of land clearing, keeps a herd of grade Holstein and Guernsey cattle and raises purebred Duroc-Jersey hogs. For a number of years he has taken a more or less prominent part in public affairs. He was formerly chairman of the town of Bradley and served for a while as treasurer of the city of Tomahawk. In the years 1919, 1920, 1921 and 1922 he was chairman of the town of King, and therefore as such a member of the county board, and he is now a member of the highway committee and of his local school board, his election of these various offices of responsibility and trust proving that his fellow citizens recognize him as a man of ability and integrity, one in whom they can have confidence. Mr. PARSHALL has been twice married: first at Tomahawk in 1895 to Julia EMERY, daughter of Mr. and Mrs. George EMERY, who came to Tomahawk from Pennsylvania in 1890, and are both now deceased. Mrs. Julia PARSHALL died after eight years of married life, in 1903, leaving three children, Otis, Wavie and Wallace. In 1904 Mr. PARSHALL was married secondly to Emma ROBARGE, daughter of Thomas and Virginia ROBARGE. Her father, who was a native of Canada, has passed away, while her mother, who was born in Wisconsin, is living. Of the second marriage of our subject three children have been born, two of who are living, Grace and James, both at home. The mother died in 1916 and the daughter Grace is now keeping house for her father.

Conant, Roy A. an enterprising citizen of Bradley, Lincoln County, engaged both in agriculture and mercantile business, and who has also at different times rendered efficient public service, was born at Tunnel City, Monroe County, Wis.; March 14, 1884, son of Herbert L. and Abigail C. (WOODARD) CONANT. His school education was completed in the high school at Tomahawk, where he was graduated in 1903. He resided in that city from 1895 to 1903. It was in the latter year that he came to Bradley and began work as clerk in the general store of Smith & Taylor, remaining with them in that capacity until 1906. Then with George W. SMITH, who had in the meanwhile become his father-in-law, he entered into the manufacture of lath and shingles here. In 1909 he was appointed rural mail carrier, attached to the Bradley post office, and was the first to be thus appointed. Then in the following year, 1910, he became interested with George W. SMITH in the development of 120 acres of cut-over land adjoining Bradley village, and they began farming under the name of Smith & Conant. They have erected a substantial set of buildings, have about 70 acres under the plow, and are successfully engaged in general farming and dairying. In 1920, with his brother Lloyd, Mr. CONANT purchased the Johnson Bros.' store and stock in general merchandise at Bradley, and they are still carrying on the business, which is well established. The post office is located in the store, and in September, 1920, Lloyd CONANT was commissioned postmaster, with Roy as assistant. From 1913 to 1916 Roy A. CONANT was chairman of the Bradley town board, and as such had a seat on the county board of supervisors. For some time he served as town clerk and for about seven years as clerk of his school district, being one of the prominent men of his town who was expected, when need arises, to lend a helping hand in the affairs of local government, and in whose ability and integrity the mass of the people can confide. Politically he is a Republican with independent tendencies on Election Day. Mr. CONANT was married Nov. 7, 1905, to Bessie I. SMITH, daughter of George W. and Jennie A. (MCGUINNESS) SMITH of Bradley, and formerly of Waupaca County, Wis., where she was born Sept. 26, 1883. Mr. and Mrs. CONANT are the parents of four children, who were born as follows: George S., Oct. 30, 1906; Dorothy J., Oct. 16, 1908; Herbert G., Oct. 24, 1913; and Evelyn, April 29, 1919. Mr. CONANT was reared a Methodist but affiliates with the Congregational Church, of which his wife is a member. He belongs to Beaver Colony No. 70 at Tomahawk.

Raymond, Mitchel H. a prominent business man of Rhinelander, cashier of the Merchants State Band, was born in Plover, Portage County, Wis., Oct 18, 1861, son of James O. and Mary E. (HARRIS) RAYMOND. James O. RAYMOND, the father, was born at McDonough, Chenango County, N. Y. May 30, 1831. He was educated in the public schools and in an academy at Owego, N. Y., after which he taught four terms of school. At the age of 22 he began the study of law at Owego, continued it there for two years and then came west to Fond du Lac., Wis., entering the office of Edward S. BRAGG. In the fall of 1855 he removed to Plover, Wis., where he taught school one term, and on May 26, 1856, he was admitted to the bar and immediately after began practice. In 1866 he was admitted to practice before the Supreme Court and in 1873 before the United States courts. From the fall of 1855 to 1873 Mr. RAYMOND resided at Plover, removing to Stevens Point in July of the latter year, and in the latter place he resided until his death April 14, 1897. He had long survived his first wife Mary, who passed away in October, 1864. Mr. RAYMOND was district attorney in Portage County three terms, being elected in 1856, 1858 and 1866 and in 1865, after returning from the war, he was elected to the assembly. In 1881 he was appointed postmaster at Stevens Point by President GARFIELD, serving four years. On Feb. 1, 1861, he enlisted in Company C. 52d Wis. Vol. Inf., and was appointed first sergeant. He saw service at St. Louis, Pilot Knob, Mo., and at Fort Leavenworth, Kans., and at the expiration of his term of service, in September, 1865, he was brevetted second lieutenant. On Oct. 25, 1857, Mr. RAYMOND was married to Mary Eliza HARRIS of Canton, Onio, and of the three children born to them only one reached maturity, Mitchel H. On April 16, 1867, he was married to Mrs. Lucinda HANCHETT. Besides his wife and son Mr. RAYMOND left a step-daughter and step-son--Mrs. A. W. BROWN and James a. HANCHETT--both of Rhinelander, with the former of whom Mrs. Lucinda RAYMOND resided after her husband's death. Mitchel A. RAYMOND acquired his early education in the common school at Plover. He then attended Stevens Point High School and was a student for two years in the Lake Forest University at Lake Forest, Ill. In January, 1883, he returned to Stevens Point and was assistant postmaster there until 1885. On May 19, that year, he came to Rhinelander, finding employment in the office of the Brown Bros.' Lumber Company, and later he was clerk in their store, where he remained until they sold to Spafford & Cole. In 1888 he entered the Merchants State Bank as assistant cashier, and after serving as such until Jan. 4, 1894, was appointed cashier, which position he still holds. As a man who comes into close contact with a large section of the public, he is well known and is widely popular for his helpful service and unfailing courtesy, and he is always ready to aid in any reasonable project for the public welfare, having a good civic record. He has been treasurer of the Rhinelander Telephone Company since its organization, and also treasurer of the Rhinelander Refrigerator Company and for eight years was a member of the board of education. He belongs to the local lodge of Free Masons and in politics is a Republican. Fond of outdoor sports, such as fishing, hunting and automobiling, he was also for several years formerly a member of the Rhinelander base ball team. On Nov. 2, 1895, Mitchel H. RAYMOND was married at Beatrice, Nebr., to Sybil HALLIDAY, daughter of John H. and Sybil (ALBAN) HALLIDAY; her parents are now deceased. Mr. and Mrs. RAYMOND have one child, Ruth, who was born Aug. 29, 1898 and is now Mrs. H. C. SMITH of Rhinelander.

Bennett, Ellis George a well known representative of the agricultural interest of Lincoln County, who is operating and developing a good farm in Sections 25 and 36, town of Bradley, was born on a farm near Mayville, Dodge County, Wis., April 3, 1861, son of George and Sarah (MARTIN) BENNETT. The father was a native of England who came to the United States in 1842, locating in Ohio. Thence in 1846 he came to Wisconsin and settled on a farm near Mayville, which he cultivated besides following the trade of a millwright. His wife Sarah was born in the state of New York and came to Wisconsin with a family by the name of MAY, after whom the town of Mayville was named. It was there they were married and spent the remainder of their lives, which were prolonged to old age, Mr. BENNETT passing away at the age of 88 years and Mrs. BENNETT at that of 80. They had six children, four of whom are living, namely: Charles, Clarence, Ida and Ellis G. Ida married Howard BLANCHARD and lives at Ladysmith, Wis. The two who died were Frank and Marie. Ellis George BENNETT was reared on his parents' farm near Mayville, where he attended school. He worked on the farm until 18 years old and then with an enterprise beyond his years went to Nebraska, where he bought 160 acres of railroad land, costing $3.00 an acre, a bonus of $40 being allowed if 20 acres were broken the first year. After remaining on that place from 1879 to 1882, young Bennett went to Dakota and took a claim in Clark County, which he proved up, breaking 20 acres. He then sold it and returned to Nebraska, sold his land there, and came back to Mayville, Wis., where he farmed until 1917. In that year he came to Lincoln County, making Tomahawk his objective point, and here bought 520 acres of land in Sections 35 and 36, town of Bradley, 80 acres of it being within the limits of the city of Tomahawk. The place had been improved to some extent, but Mr. BENNETT has cleared more land and now as 150 acres under cultivation. He also has 60 acres of virgin pine timber. His buildings include a good modern barn of 36 by 100 feet with two silos; one frame house of two stories and basement, 34 x 38 feet, and a frame tenement house of six rooms. Both houses are supplied with running water and furnace heat and are electrically lighted from Mr. BENNETT'S own Delco light plant, as his other farm buildings are also. He does general farming and dairying, keeps a herd of 43 pure bred Holstein cattle and operates a milk route in Tomahawk. His industry and business sagacity have placed him high in the rank of Lincoln County farmers, and his farm is one of the largest in the county, with good prospects for future development. Mr. BENNETT was married at Mayville, Wis., in 1885, to Hattie HANSON, daughter of David and Emily HANSON, the parents being natives of New York State and early settlers of Mayville; both are now deceased Mr. and Mrs. BENNETT have had seven children, namely, Olive, Ervin, Morton, Wesley, Elton, Emily and Merrill. Olive married Lester PETTERSON of Sheldon, Wis. Emily married, Reinhold THIESON of Juneau. Merrill is deceased. Wesley was inducted in the United States' service in 1917 and served in an infantry division in France, having the rank of sergeant in his regiment. He was in the Argonne and at Chateau Thierry, and returned to the United States and was discharged in 1919.

Erickson, J. Adolph was born in the town of Farmington, Waupaca County, Wis., July 1, 1889, son of Hans O. and Hilda (PETERSON) ERICKSON. The father was a native of that county, born in 1862, while the mother was born in Sweden. The paternal grand-parents had also come from Sweden and were among the first settlers in Waupaca County, locating originally right in the midst of the Indians. Hans O. ERICKSON was reared on the farm which he helped to clear and improve. The he bought 120 acres in Waupaca County, and farmed there on his own account until he came to Lincoln County in 1895. Here he bought 160 acres in Section 25-26, town of Bradley, 80 acres lying within the limits of the city of Tomahawk. The land was unimproved and Mr. ERICKSON showed his energy by building at once a house and log barns and clearing that summer 11 acres. With the help of his sons he cleared 125 acres, which are all under cultivation. The house, a good one, is a frame structure, and in 1910 he building a basement under his barn and put up a silo of 14 by 29 feet. In 1922 his son Adolph building another silo, 10 by 34 1/2 feet, and Mr. ERICKSON was actively conducting his farm and planning further improvements when he was called away by death on March 11, 1917. His wife, who survived him is still living. Of their 12 children, ten are living, namely: Helma, wife of Pete PETERSON of Tomahawk; Clarence, who is a farmer in the town of King; Adolph, who has succeeded his father as owner of the home farm; Oscar, who is a farmer in the town of King; Emil, who is working for his brother Adolph; Elmer of Tomahawk; Alice, wife of Charles GLISNER of Rhinelander; August, a farmer in the town of King; Edith, widow of Robert

KRAIG, and who makes her home with August; and Cora, wife of W. S. SQUIRES of St. Paul. Laura and Minnie are deceased. In 1919 J. Adolph ERICKSON bought the farm from his mother, giving his 80 acre farm in the town of King, where he lived, in part payment. He has since improved the place, having added a Delco electric-light system which lights all the buildings, also pumping the running water on the place, and installed hot and cold water in the house. He is carrying on general farming and dairying, having a herd of 28 high grade Holstein cattle, with a pure-bred sire at the head, and is milking 19 cows. He was four years supervisor of the town of King, for three years being chairman, and as such a member of the county board; he was also school treasurer of King for three years and served as health officer, in all of which branches of public service he showed energy and ability, which have given him a high rank among his fellow citizens. J. Adolph ERICKSON was married in Merrill, Wis., Feb. 22, 1909, to Jennie JOHNSON, daughter of Iver and Hilda JOHNSON, old residents of Merrill, where the father is still living, the mother having passed away. Mr. and Mrs. ERICKSON have two children: Ella, born Feb. 7, 1911, who is attending school in Tomahawk, and Gordon, born March 7, 1919.

Morse, Andrew H. of Section 25, town of Bradley, who is a prominent representative of the agricultural interests of Lincoln County, was born in the town of New Haven, near Big Spring, Adams County, Wis., Aug. 13, 1853. His parents were Uri and Miranda (MOREY) MORSE, natives of new York State, who came to Adams County, Wisconsin, when young; he is 1849 came to Indian land, where he bought 320 acres of wild government land, covered with hardwood timber, and was one of the first three settlers in that part of the country. He cleared the land, erected buildings and spent the rest of his life farming there, dying Oct. 25, 1913, and his wife Oct. 6, 1910. They had five children, all of whom are now living: Lyman, Andrew H.,

Estella, Tina, and Chauncey. Lyman is now a resident of Kilbourn City, Wis. Estella is the wife of H. A. ATCHERSON of Tomahawk. Tina is the wife of Barton PERRY of Washington, D.C., a retired army chaplain and major. Chauncey still lives on the home farm. Andrew H. MORSE was reared on the home farm in Adams County and attended school at Big Springs. At the age of 21 he left home and took a rented farm, then bought 80 acres at Big Springs, adjoining the home farm, which he carried on until 1893. He then rented out the place and went to Milwaukee, where he was engaged in teaming until the panic came on, at which time he gave up that work and instead bought standing hay from two farms, and cut and hauled it to market at Milwaukee. In 1905 Mr. MORSE went to Chicago, in which city he engaged in teaming and contract work, the latter including excavating and grading, and he remained there for 11 years. Then in 1906 he came on a sort of prospecting trip to Tomahawk, and being satisfied with agricultural prospects in Lincoln County, he bought 120 acres of wild land in Section 25, town of Bradley. Since then he has erected buildings, dug a well, and cleared land until he now has 65 acres under cultivation, and is making good progress in general farming and dairying. His farm is well equipped with modern machinery, including a tractor. He is chairman of the Lincoln County Agricultural Society and president of the Tomahawk Potato Growers' Association, served one year as chairman of the Bradley town board, and hence as a member of the county board, and for a number of years was a member of the school auditing board, all of which shows that he is a man of action and has ability that is recognized by his fellow citizens. Mr. MORSE was married at Big Springs, in the town of New Haven, Adams County, Wis., in 1875 to Ida May BROOKS, daughter of Dr. Changler E. and Helen (SPERBECK) BROOKS, her parents, natives of New York State, having been early settlers of Adams County, Wis., but both being now deceased. Mr. and Mrs. MORSE have three children living: Frank A., a farmer in the town of King; Byron H., on the home farm; and Bertha M., who is the wife of William ROSCHE of the town of Bradley.

Nibler, Frank a well-known pioneer of Lincoln County, whose farm, carved from the wilderness, is in Section 13, town of Bradley, was born in Bavaria, May 19, 1861, son of Frank and Ida NIBLER. The parents were natives of that country, where both lived and died, having been occupied in farming during their active career. Of their four children, three are now living, Josephine, Henry and Frank, the one deceased being Leopold. Frank NIBLER was reared in Bavaria, where he attended school. Later, as every German youth must, he served several years in the German army. In 1884 he came to the United States, locating first in Milwaukee, where he lived for three years. Then he came to Lincoln County and buying 40 acres of land covered with hardwood timber near Gleason, began to develop it into an agricultural property. He was among the first settlers here and had to deal with primitive conditions, his work during the early years being constant and strenuous. His first task was to make a clearing and build a log house and barn. There were no roads but over an old trail through the woods he hauled shingles on a hand sled for his house and barn, and also groceries from Bloomville, a distance of 11 miles. At one time the family ran out of matches and were obliged to keep fire burning two weeks until he could get to town again. They had no well and had to get their water from a water-hole with a cup and pail. At another time Mr. NIBLER walked to Merrill and back, a distance of 52 miles in one day, in some places wading knee keep in mud, to get a pair of boots, and in place of wagons he had to use crotched poles for hauling purposes. He was the first man to hire a mule team and wagon to haul with, which was a wonderful and unaccustomed sight to his neighbors' children, not one of the neighbors having a wagon and some of the children never having seen one. In spite of hardships endured, however, he and his family kept health and needed no doctors. In clearing his land Mr. NIBLER burned the logs of maple and yellow birch to get them out of his way, though in these days he would be able to get a good price for it. The brush was piled up around the house and the deer used to come and feed on it. After living on his farm for 20 years Mr. NIBLER made a trip to Germany to revisit his native land and see such of his old Friends and relations as yet remained alive, and no doubt the story of his experiences found ready and eager listeners. After his return to the United States he spent a winter in North Dakota and then went to the Land of Dreams in Oklahoma, where he remained a year. From there he went to Colorado and in 1906 came back to Lincoln County and bought 160 acres in Section 13, town of Bradley, the place on which he is now living. In some respects it was also like beginning over again, as there were only 10 acres clear and the house on the place was a mere log shanty; but he was now a man of some means and could make faster progress. He soon built a nice frame house of nine rooms, together with barns and other buildings. Up to date he has cleared 50 acres of this farm and has 60 acres under cultivation. He is doing general farming and dairying, keeping a herd of Jersey and Holstein cattle. He also has a fine lake on his place well stocked with fish which furnish many a good meal for his table. For one term he served as clerk of the town of Bradley. Mr. NIBLER was married in Milwaukee in 1885 to Katherine FISHER, daughter of Carl and Anna (BOELER) FISHER. Her parents were natives of Bavaria, Germany, where the father died, Katherine subsequently accompanying her mother to this country, and it was at the home of Mr. and Mrs. NIBLER, her daughter and son-in-law, that Mrs. FISHER died. There were five children in the Fisher family, of whom those now living are Mrs. NIBLER and a stepbrother, Jacob SCHMIDTBAUER, son of Mrs. FISHER by her second husband, Anton SCHMIDTBAUER. Mr. and Mrs. NIBLER have had eight children, one of whom, Josephine, is deceased. The living are Margaret, Frances, Rose, Ida, Henry,

Benjamin, and Antonia. Margaret is the wife of Jacob SCHMIDTBAUER, Frances the wife of Fred SHORES, and Rose the wife of George COLLINS. The family are members of the Lutheran Church.

INDEX TO BIOGRAPHIES
(P) = Photo

Atcherson, Herbert A.	170
Baker M.D., George Rowe	172; (P)174
Ball, Mrs. Joseph A.	185
Ball, William H.	174
Bauer, J. August	175
Bauman, William G.	176
Baumgartner, William C.	177
Bennett, Ellis George	282
Bradley, William H.	179; (P)181
Bronsted, Henry E. and Martinson, Fred	181
Bronsted, John	182
Brooks, Hal L.	184
Conant, Herbert L.	194
Conant, Roy A.	279
Ernest B. Cronkite	134
Cutter M.D., John D.	196; (P)197
Danielson, Daniel	198
Draeger, William J.	199
Drever, William	200; (P)202
Eklund, John	188
Emerich, Erwin R.	189
Erickson, J. Adolph	284
Foss, Charles E.	190
Foster, Elmer D.	191
Foster, George H.	192
Foster, Herman G.	193
Gahan, Benjamin J.	202
Gillett, Harry Grant	205
Gillie, Robert J.	206; (P)207
Greggorie, George	208
Griffith, John S.	209
Hansen, Hans P.	213

Hildebrand, Henry L.	209
Houlahan, Edward	211
Jacks, Henry D.	169
Johnson, Charles M.	141
Johnson, Julius	144
Johnson, Henry A.	145
Jones, David C.	140
Kelley, John W.	142
Kilroe, Thomas H.	148
Klade, Fred C.	160
Koth, Reinhold F.	158; (P)160
Kuehling, Herman H.	162
Kuehling, William F.	163
Kummer, Peter J.	146
Labbe, Victor E.	164
Lambert, George	156
Lambert, John B.	155
Lambert, Leo L.	157
Larson, Albert C.	138
Larson, Bennett	137
Lee, John P.	168
Lewerenz, William	150
Londo, Orville	166
Macfarlane D.D.S., William I.	217; (P)219
Macomber, Charles E.	216
Major, Henry T.	219
Martz, Leo	221
McCarthy, James L.	222
McCormick M.D., William Charles	223; (P)225
McHenry, James W.	225
Morin, Wilbur A.	226
Morse, Andrew H.	285
Myre, Elzeor	227
Nelson, Frank A.	229
Nerli, Anton	231

Nibler, Frank	287
Nick, Sr., Jacob	231
Oelhafen, John	233
Oelhafen, John W.	235
Olson, Albert E.	237
Olson, Anton, J.	239
Osborne, L. M.	240
Osborne, L. W.	241
Ostrander, Clayton	241
Ostrander, Ervine C.	243
Parker, Ira John	244
Parshall, M. LeRoy	278
Pfalzsgraff, William H.	246
Philleo, Paul R.	153
Pingel, George J.	247
Poutre, Joseph	249
Powell, William R.	250
Raymond, Mitchel H.	280
Schrader, William	252
Schulz, Herman F.	255
Schulz, Reinhold E.	253
Searl, Art	256
Seidle, Charles A.	257
Seth, James Arthur	258
Smith, George W.	260
Stone, Patrick E.	263
Sutliff, Albert E.	264
Theiler, Frank	265
Theiler, Harry	266
Theiler, Martin	267; (P)270
Theilman, Louis G.	272
Theilman, Robert C.	271
Tweedy, Robert B.	273
Wallis, Charles H.	274
Wetzel, George	275
Zastrow, August	277

www.ingramcontent.com/pod-product-compliance
Lightning Source LLC
Chambersburg PA
CBHW080456110426
42742CB00017B/2906